THE GREAT BOOK OF
COMBAT
AIRCRAFT

PAOLO MATRICARDI

vmb
PUBLISHERS

VMB Publishers©
An imprint of White Star S.p.A., Italy
© **2006, 2007 White Star S.p.A.**
Via Candido Sassone, 22/24
13100 Vercelli, Italia
www.whitestar.it

PROJECT EDITOR
Ervin S.r.l., Roma

GRAPHIC DESIGN
Franco De Vecchis

COLOR SEPARATION BY
Tipocrom S.r.l., Guidonia (Roma)

PHOTOGRAPHIC EDITOR
Giorgio Apostolo

DRAWINGS
Carlo Castellani
Marco Giardina
Pierluigi Pinto

TRANSLATION
Simon Tanner edit by
Studio Traduzioni Vecchia

TRANSLATION EDITOR
Sam Merrel

ISBN: 978-88-540-0550-1

Reprints:
1 2 3 4 5 6   11 10 09 08 07

PRINTED IN CHINA

1 General Dynamics F-16.

2-3 Rockwell International B-1.

4-5 A McDonnell-Douglas F-15
Eagle during in-flight refuelling.

6-7 Grumman F-14A Tomcats on
the deck of an American aircraft
carrier.

8 McDonnell F-4 Phantom II.

10-11 A line up of Fiat C.R.20
Asso aircraft.

S ince its birth over a century ago, aviation has changed the world. It has triggered a revolution in transport and communications, has made important scientific discoveries possible, and has fostered progress, by bringing peoples and nations closer together. But that's not all. This exciting technological innovation was soon transformed into an instrument of military supremacy, radically changing the rules of war, the structure and organization of armies, tactics, and strategy, often to the point of making the difference between victory and defeat. It is no coincidence that the airplane's most rapid and significant developments have been fuelled by conflicts, or that it is has played a major role in modern history, for better or worse.

This book aims to look back over this long journey not merely by listing facts, or recounting challenges and adventures, but by showing the development of military aviation in pictures.

This is the story of a hundred years of military aviation, a story that begins with the faded photos of pilots and airplanes of bygone days posing in front of the camera. It includes the dramatic testimonies of past and recent battles fought in the skies and ends looking to the future with modern fighting aircraft, which represent an extreme combination of highly sophisticated technology and weaponry, placing in the hands of a single man, the devastating power of an entire army in the past.

12 bottom Captain Piazza's Blériot XI monoplane on its first combat mission to Libya in October 1911.

13 bottom The German-built Etrich Taube aircraft used by Lieutenant Giulio Gavotti in the first bombing mission of the Italo-Turkish War.

The origins of military aviation

Monday, October 23, 1911 was the first time an airplane was used in a military operation, which took place in Tripoli, Libya during the Italo-Turkish War. The airplane was a Blériot XI monoplane, the same aircraft that Louis Blériot had flown across the English Channel two years earlier. This time, the pilot was Captain Carlo Piazza. The flight, which lasted 61 minutes, was a reconnaissance mission to find out how well artillery fire could be observed from the air. A few days later, on November 1, Lieutenant Giulio Gavotti made the first aerial bombing raid in history. From his Etrich Taube monoplane he launched four hand-held bombs: one on the enemy camps at Ain Zara; and three on those stationed at the oasis of Tagiura. The raid did not cause much damage, but had an enormous psychological effect. A new weapon had been born, as well as a new threat, one that was more devastating than the aerostats and balloons of the time, which were limited in their movements and made easy targets. A whole new range of possible uses opened up for the

14 top Gennaro Ruggerone
Maurice Farman in the biplane
at the Aerodrome in Milan in
1910: he was the first Italian
to win the Milan contests.

machine that was "heavier than air." The driving force behind this new weapon was no longer the enthusiasm and the excitement of flying pioneers, but cold military logic, which not even the poet Gabriele D'Annunzio managed to soften in the lines of his Song of the Diana, celebrating the event in the *Corriere della Sera* newspaper on November 23, 1911:

> "... in the air can be heard a whistling sling.
> In the sky a pale vulture flies over.
> Giulio Gavotti bears bombs on the wing."

However, these flights by Piazza and Gavotti were a mere beginning to the use in combat of the airplane, whose potential had been untapped, due to the widespread and deep-rooted suspicion aroused by this radically new and little-tested means of transport. The first, tentative attempts to provide armies with the machine that was "heavier than air" became concrete only after the general acceptance of motorized flight.

14 bottom Glenn Curtiss won
the trophy donated by
the magazine Scientific
American in his June Bug,
with a flight of over 1 mile in
July 1904 in the United States.

15 bottom Wilbur Wright with
his biplane on the airfield at
Centocelle in April 1908. The
airplane that Wright brought to
Italy—the model A—was very
different from the one he had
flown in the United States
in December 1903.

The turning-point came in 1908, with the trip to Europe of Wilbur Wright and his latest airplane, the Flyer A. From August to December on the fields of Le Mans, the American pioneer's demonstrations not only fired the enthusiasm of overseas enthusiasts, but led to shared experiences that would turn out to be decisive in the development of the airplane.

It was during those years that Orville Wright, who had remained in the United States, continued with the difficult task of convincing the American military authorities that the US Army needed his airplane. He had realized the potential at the time of the Flyer's maiden flight, but his plans had suffered from the indifference of public opinion. It is worth looking at the steps in this journey, which finally led to the birth of the Signal Corps Airplane N° 1, the world's first military airplane, on August 2, 1909.

After the historic flight of December 17,1903 at Kitty Hawk, and in the face of the general scepticism that had accompanied the Flyer's maiden flight, the Wright brothers had retired to their workshop in Dayton, determined to improve their airplane in secret.

15 top Gabriel Voisin's
biplane competing at
the Reims Aerodrome
in 1909.

18 top A Blériot XI and a Maurice Farman biplane on Reims airfield in August 1909, on the occasion of the world's first great flying show.

18 bottom left Changing a wheel on the Blériot XI.

18 bottom right The first test flights of Glenn Curtiss's Hydroplane in San Diego in 1911.

19 top The first biplane built by Gianni Caproni, the Ca.1.

19 bottom The Breguet III seaplane at the Monaco aerodrome in March 1912.

The great day finally arrived. On December 23, 1907 the first specification for a military aircraft, no. 486, was issued. The parameters were not easily satisfied: the airplane had to fly at a speed of 40 mph (around 65 km/h), have a range of two hours, seat two people, and carry enough fuel to cover 125 miles (200 km). In addition to these purely technical aspects there was another, more unusual requirement: it had to be possible to dismantle the airplane, transport it on carriages pulled by horses, and reassemble it before flight. The entire operation, moreover, had to take no more than one hour. The severe penalties for failure to respect these requirements (for example, 10 percent would be subtracted from the base price of $25,000 for every mile per hour below the agreed speed) did not frighten Orville and Wilbur Wright, who worked feverishly to build and develop the new airplane, together with their mechanics Charlie Taylor and Charlie Furnas.

On August 20, 1908 Orville arrived in Fort Myer, Virginia, the base chosen for the test flights, where

the Flyer had already been transported; tests began on September 3. The maiden flight was short, and left the large crowd unimpressed. But six days later Orville had already exceeded the specifications required, staying in the air for over an hour and setting new records with every flight. These successes, however, were marred by a serious accident. On September 17, during a test flight with Lieutenant Thomas E. Selfridge on board, a propeller broke and the airplane crashed into the airfield. Orville was seriously injured in the accident, and Selfridge died on impact, the first victim in the history of aviation.

This could have been the end of the great adventure, but the tragedy did not influence the military authorities' interest, which had now become considerable. Tests were suspended, but the original contract was extended, and once Orville had recovered from the injuries sustained in the accident, he returned to work on the new airplane. This was larger and heavier than the previous model, and flew for the first time on June 24, 1909. But only five

20 top A replica of a Curtiss A.1, the United States Navy's first seaplane. The aircraft was based on the Golden Flyer, which had witnessed the first deck landing on a warship.

20 bottom and 21 Wright, Farman and Voisin biplanes at the first Air Show in Reims in August 1909.

days later, despite pressure from the American Senate, which had asked for a demonstration, Orville gave a public display. His earlier disappointment had been immense, and he did not want to take off until he had fully checked the airplane and was certain that everything was in order. After a series of minor problems, the flights finally took place on July 27 and 30. In the first, Orville set records for time in the air with a passenger on board, staying up for one hour 12 minutes. In the second, he managed to achieve the more important goal, that of exceeding the minimum speed limits laid down by the official specifications: the Flyer flew at 42.583 miles per hour, setting yet another record.

The Signal Corps paid the Wright brothers $30,000, and the airplane was used to train the first military pilots up until March 1911. And while the American example was followed in Europe by pioneers such as Blériot, Farman, Breguet, Etrich, and Fokker, it was once again the United States that introduced another innovation—naval aviation—confirming that a new direction had definitively been taken in the history of aviation. The first deck landing on board a warship (the battleship Pennsylvania anchored in San Francisco bay) was performed on June 18,1911 by Eugene Ely in a Curtiss Golden Flyer. It was this same biplane, modified into a hydroplane and named the Curtiss Hydro A.1, that became the first "heavier than air" craft to be used by the United States Navy.

22 top One of the first mass-produced rotary engines, the 80 hp Gnome-Rhône.

22 bottom The Austrian ace Godwin Brumowski (35 victories) on board the Hansa Brandenburg D.I. fighter.

23 bottom The Farman MF.11 biplanes served in reconnaissance units in France, Italy, Great Britain, and Belgium up until 1915.

The First World War

T he process that led the United States Army to recognize and accept the worth of aircraft was long and complex. The situation was different in Europe where, after the initial decisive boost provided by Wilbur Wright in 1908, the world of aviation took off, leading the "heavier-than-air" craft to its first, real period of maturity. The military authorities were among those most interested in its development. Two great events contributed to heightened interest. Firstly, the crossing of the Channel by Louis Blériot, on July 25, 1909, which provided the first direct measure of the airplane's abilities and the level of efficiency so far achieved. The second was the Aviators' Meeting in Reims (August 22–29, Grande Semaine d'Aviation de la Champagne). This impressive show was sponsored by the president of the French Republic himself, and saw heated chal-

THE FIRST WORLD WAR

ed for the first time in 1913. The competition continued until 1931, with prestigious results, and became a technological training ground in the field of structures and engines—especially in the interwar period—that would strongly influence the development of the airplane, and consequently the military airplanes deployed in the Second World War.

But the First World War was imminent in the happy years of the first records and flying competitions. And this new form of transport, supported by significant technological contributions and experience, had already been transformed into a fearful weapon which armies felt they could not do without. Let's examine briefly the military organizations which were set up by the major industrial powers in the period, their airplanes, and the major milestones in their development, to which the conflicts gave a further, albeit brutal boost.

26 top The small 3-cylinder 25 hp engine of the Italian Alessandro Anzani, with a wooden Chauvière propeller, was fitted on the Blériot XI which made the first flight across the English Channel in 1909.

26 bottom The Voisin scouts, built in their hundreds and also adopted by the Italian Army, were fitted with a 180 hp Salmson (Canton-Unné) radial engine.

27 The first biplane designed by Gianni Caproni before its test flights. In the hands of the inexperienced pilot Ugo Tabacchi, the aircraft crashed on landing.

ITALY

The first approach of the Regio Esercito (Italian Royal Army) to motorized flight was in 1909, during the European visit of Wilbur Wright. After France, Italy was the second nation to host the great American pioneer, and in that year Major Maurizio Moris of the Aeronautical section of the Brigata specialisti del Genio (Specialist Brigade of the Engineers), who was chairman of the aviators' club of Rome, went to France and purchased a Flyer for 25,000 Lire. The same figure was offered to Wilbur Wright as payment for his work as an instructor; he reached Rome on April 1, 1909 and didn't waste any time. Fifteen days later, on the airfield at Centocelle, in the presence of the King Vittorio Emanuele III and the Queen Mother Mar-gherita, there began the training flights of the first two Italian aviators: Sub-lieutenant Mario Calderara and Lieutenant Umberto Savoia of the Engineers. Calderara held pilot's licence N°1, which he was awarded "by public acclamation" on September 12, 1909 during the first international Air Circuit in

28 top The first Macchi Parasol monoplane scout delivered to the 5th Squadron of Busto Arsizio in 1914. Note the unusual experimental Neri scimitar propeller.

28 bottom The first operational unit of the Regio Esercito (Italian Royal Army) was equipped with two-seater Caproni Ca.18 observation planes.

Brescia. The initiatives multiplied, and the same year saw the test flights, albeit with little success, of the first Italian airplane, a triplane produced by an enthusiastic engineer from Turin, Aristide Faccioli. In April 1910 in Turin, the first great National Air Show was held. One month later, on May 27, was the not very successful debut of the first product of a great future constructor, Gianni Caproni. The airplane, the Ca.1, was damaged on landing due to the inexperience of the pilot, who was a mechanic.

Growth, however, in the new industry was rapid. 1910 was a decisive year for the fortunes of the new specialty and marked the first official recognition of the airplane's operational validity and, thus, the birth of military aviation. The first military flying school was set up at Centocelle. The new air forces were reorganized and developed with the establishment, under the command of Lieutenant Colonel Moris, of the Battaglione specialisti autonomo del Genio (Independent Battalion of Specialist Engineers), of which the new Aviation Section was part. The latter was based in Turin, and placed under the command of Lieutenant Colonel Vittorio Cordero di Montezemolo. The unit initially had eight pilots and the same number of airplanes: three Farmans and five Blériots. By way of further recognition, there was an act of Parliament, which approved funding of 10 million lire for the construction of new airships, the purchase of 10 airplanes, and the payment of special indemnities to all the people working in the sector.

29 top left Two pioneers of aeronautical construction in Italy, the brothers Gianni and Federico Caproni who started business in the moors around Gallarate in 1910.

29 top right A replica of the Nieuport Bébé.

29 bottom Cell construction in the Savoia Pomilio factory in Turin. This is the S.P. scout.

In reality, military flight—even with the "lighter than air" craft —had been discovered a long time previously, back in 1884 when, under the orders of Lieutenant Alessandro Pecori Giraldi, an Aeronautical Service was set up in Rome at the Forte Tiburtino, and then at the barracks at Castel Sant'Angelo. In January of the following year, this became the Sezione aerostatica (Aerostatic Unit) of the 30th Reggimento del Genio (Regiment of Engineers). They did not make a great start, since the new service had extremely modest means, with two balloons, the Africo and the Torricelli, a hydrogen generator, and a steam winch for manouvring the cable.

30 top The one-seater Ansaldo A.1 Balilla was without doubt the best fighter aircraft designed and built in Italy, but arrived too late to take an active role in the First World War.

30 bottom SAML S.2 scouts lined up on the airfield of Cividate Camumo near Bresca. The biplane had been designed by the Società Aeronautica Meccanica Lombarda, and was based on an Aviatik Austro-Hungarian reconnaissance aircraft. It was fitted with a 280 hp Fiat A.12 engine.

31 top The Italian SIA 7B.2 scout, produced by Società Italiana Aviazione, was an inconsistent performer. Of the over 3000 ordered, only a few hundred were built and actually delivered to the units.

Progress was slow but constant. In 1887, the unit became part of the Compagnia specialisti (Company of Specialists) and two years later became the Brigata mista del Genio (Mixed Engineers' Brigade), divided into a Compagnia treno (Train Company) for the transport of supplies and equipment, and a Compagnia specialisti (Company of Specialists). In addition to the many training flights, they also had experience in the field, and took part in the expedition of General Asinari di San Marzano to Italian territories on the Red Sea, where three captive aerostats—the Serrati, the Volta, and the Lana—were used for reconnaissance purposes. In November 1894, the Minister for War decided to combine all the aeronautical services into a single unit. The result was the Brigata specialisti (Brigade of Specialists) which in 1909 would become independent. It was this unit that experimented with the move to a new phase of flight, from captive balloon to airship.

The first Italian military airship, the semirigid "N.1", designed and built by Captain Gaetano Arturo Crocco and Captain Ottavio Ricaldoni, was tested in 1908 and proved its worth in many flights. On October 30 it traveled the route Vigna di Valle-Anguillara-Rome and back, a total of 48 miles (80 km), in an hour and 35 minutes.

The Italian Fighter Ace

Francesco Baracca adopted the "rampant horse" emblem on his airplanes in late 1916, but duels with Austrian planes dated back to the summer of 1915.

April 7, 1916 saw his first victory. Baracca, who was stationed with the 70th Squadron, engaged in combat with an Aviatik and forced it to land, then landed near his adversary.

As hostilities intensified, Baracca's victories kept pace: by the end of 1917 the number had risen to over 30, thanks to new well-armed Spad XIIIs, with which his unit, the 91st Squadron, had replaced the small Nieuport planes. Baracca chalked up 34 victories in all.

The last mission of the Italian ace was on June 19,1980, but the

circumstances of his fall have never been clarified.

31 bottom Francesco Baracca in front of his airplane, a Spad S.XIII of the 91st Squadron. Above: The sign of the "rampant horse".

In spring 1911, the Roman School at Centocelle was closed and the students and airplanes were transferred to two new schools at Aviano and Malpensa. It was in this period that the Libyan adventure of Piazza and Gavotti took place. They were part of a team of five pilots and six reserves with nine airplanes at their disposal: three Nieuports, two Blériots, two Etrich Taubes, and two Farmans.

A further step forward in the organization of the air force took place in 1912, with the establishment (June 27) of the Servizio Aeronautico (Aeronautical Service) and of the Sezione Idroplani della Marina (Navy Seaplane Division), in October. The same year saw the launch of a development program for the construction of ten airships and the creation of ten squadrons with 150 airplanes by spring 1913. A great boost to this expansion was given by an officer who would become part of the history of aviation as the first theorizer of the fundamental role of combat aircraft in battle, Major Giulio Dohuet. He was the first to perceive the enormous military potential of the airplane and its strategic role, a theory which he perfected in 1921 in a treatise entitled 'The domin-

ion of the air'. On January 7, 1915, with the war already in full swing, the Corpo Aeronautico Militare (Military Air Corps) was created. This would control the air force until the birth of the Regia Aeronautica (Italian Royal Air Force), on March 28, 1923. the new Corps was arranged into two Commands, four Battalions, an airplane construction plant, a Technical Office for Military Aviation and a Central Aeronautics Institute.

Despite all this fervour, when Italy entered the war on May 24, 1915, its force could not be considered on the same level as those of other nations, either in terms of quantity or quality. The dozen squadrons initially stationed at the front were equipped with a varied collection of French airplanes: 86 in all, of which there were 37 Blériots, 27 Nieuports, and 22 Farmans. On a strictly industrial level, the aeronautics sector had still not managed to produce competitive military airplanes, especially fighters. Exceptions were naval aircraft and bombers, fields in which Macchi and Caproni's excellent craft placed Italy firmly at the forefront. Things began to improve only in 1916, when overall production figures reached 1255, while the number of operational units had risen to 49 squadrons: 13 bomber squadrons, 22 reconnaissance, nine fighter and five for the defence of particularly important strategic areas. In 1917, 3861 airplanes were built, while the air force was restructured and reorganized. By the time of the Armistice there were 1683 front-line aircraft, while the overall number produced had reached the respectable figure of 11,986. In 1918 the first nationally produced fighters began to be delivered to the units, although their contribution to the course of the war proved to be relatively unimportant. The burden of the conflict had already been borne extensively by various types of French-produced fighters.

32 top The Macchi M.5 fighter seaplane equipped various units in the Tyrrhenian Sea and the Adriatic, performing numerous escort and protection missions for Italian ships.

32 bottom The single-engined Savoia Pomilio was an aircraft with various design faults, such as a double-tail boom, pusher propeller, and poor front weaponry.

33 bottom The prototype of the great Caproni Ca.4 triplane awaiting testing. Designed in 1915 to strike Vienna, it was used to a limited degree on the Italian front in 1917–18.

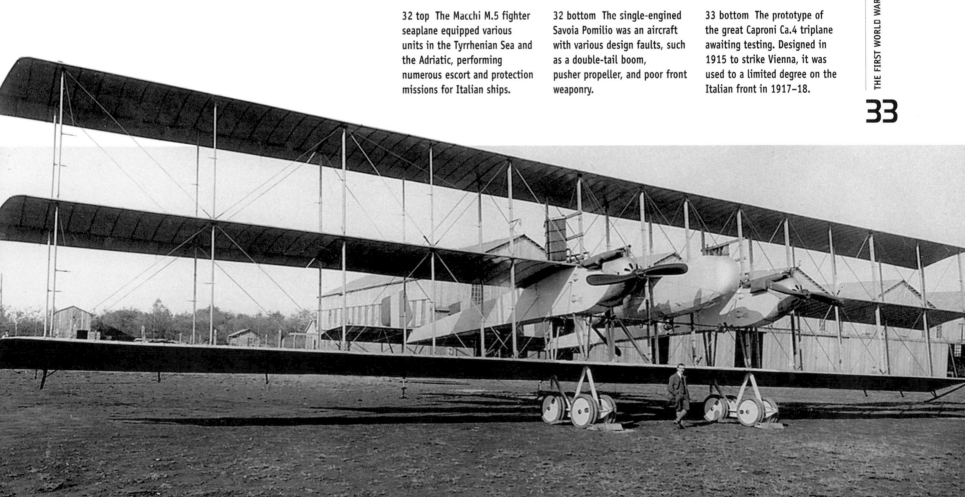

FRANCE

Cradle of European aviation, from many points of view, France represented the backbone of the Allied forces. Using the great resources of its aeronautics industry, which in 1914 was considered the most advanced in the world, it gave a vital contribution to the creation and support of the air power used to combat that of the Central Empires. It did so in the first years of the war by providing airplanes and engines, and later by deploying formidable aircraft which helped overturn the balance of power in the skies. The airplanes that equipped the units of the American Expeditionary Force and the Belgian air force were French, as were most of the aircraft used by the Russians. The fighters of the Italian front line, those that fought in the crucial phases of the long conflict, were also French. In the moments of most pressing need, even Great Britain, another country at the forefront in the field of aviation, equipped itself with aircraft designed by its rivals on the other side of the Channel.

34 top A replica of the Morane-Saulnier, one of the first fighters to use the system of machine-gun fire through the propeller disc, designed by Roland Garros.

34 bottom Two examples of Farman scout-bombers, the M.F.11 and the more advanced F.40.

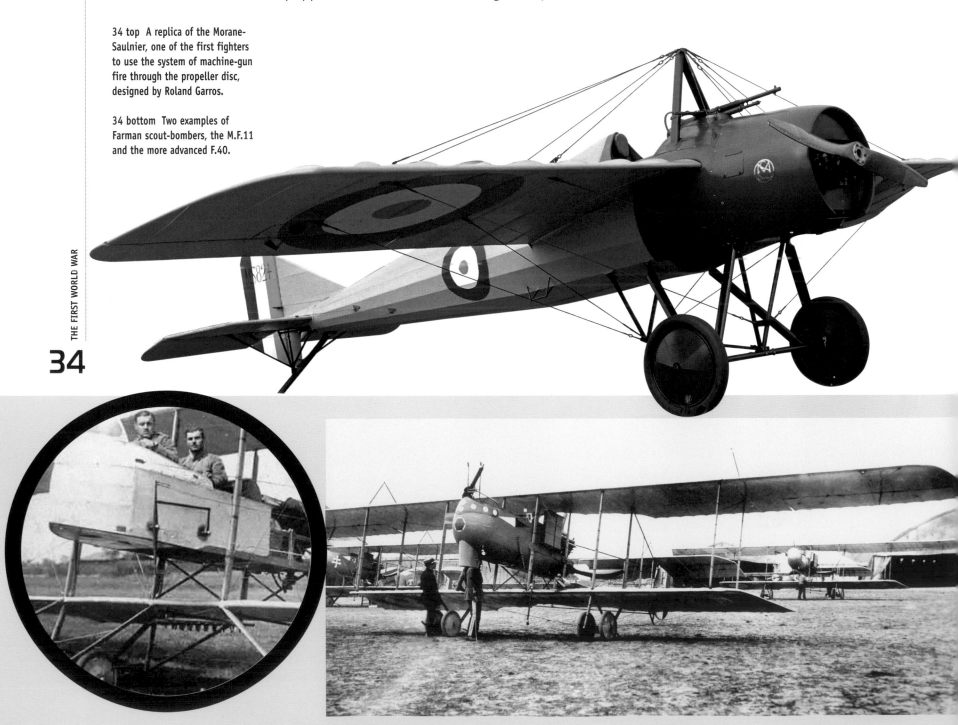

35 top The Nieuport 10 was the first fighter plane of the Italian Army air force. Originally a two-seater, it helped to create this new specialty.

35 bottom In the first year of the war, all the Allied countries widely used the single-rotor Caudron G.3 for bombing missions.

Nor should we forget the French military personnel who, from the early days of aviation in Europe, had actively participated in its development; in particular Captain Ferdinand Ferber, who in 1901 espoused the theories of the German pioneer Otto Lilienthal. Three years later he used his experience to design three years later a glider whose features would set the blueprint for all the future airplanes of European pioneers—a stable biplane with a fixed tail. Ferber had tested his airplane successfully, resolving all the problems of glider flight. Basically, he had gone through the same experiences as the Wright brothers before the Flyer was built. The only link missing in the chain was that of motorized fight, and it was to be Wilbur himself who provided Ferber with the link when he visited France in 1908 on his triumphal tour. "Without this man I would have been no one; without him my experiments would never have taken place," Ferber humbly declared.

But apart from the experiences of the pioneers and military researchers, the French government had also demonstrated singular farsightedness in recognizing the airplane's combat potential. On July 12, 1909, the Ministry of War had purchased a Wright biplane. Other aircraft were soon added and activity was significantly stepped up, with pioneering test flights aimed at assessing the possibilities that the new machines could offer the armed forces.

Nieuport 11

FRANCE

Designed in 1914 by Gustave Delage, the Nieuport 11 missed its scheduled appointment with the Gordon Bennett Cup, but became famous during the war instead, proving itself one of the most important Allied fighters.

Nicknamed "Bébé" due to its small size, this agile biplane was immediately ordered by the French and English and, after its introduction in summer 1915, proved itself able to effectively combat the threat of Fokker monoplanes.

During the Battle of Verdun (February 1916), Nieuport 11s flown by the leading French fighter pilots (Guynemer, De Rose, and Nungesser) inflicted such great losses on enemy squadrons that German commanders were forced to change their combat tactics.

In Italy, where 646 "Bébé" aircraft were built under licence by Macchi, the airplane remained the standard fighter until summer 1917.

The Nieuport 11 also served in the Belgian, Dutch, and Russian air forces and was used by the first American volunteers.

Nieuport 17

FRANCE

The model 17 is perhaps the most famous of Gustave Delage's designs. Developed from the "Bébé", it was the largest, strongest, and best armed. It was, without doubt, one of the most effective allied fighter planes until the arrival of the Spad S.VII. In March 1916, the Nieuport 17 reached the front, where it began to replace the fighters used until then by the French units. On May 2, it entered service with the 57th Squadron and, gradually, with another five units, including the famous 3rd Squadron, "Les Cigognes". The airplane was also adopted by the two British air forces, the

Royal Flying Corps and the Royal Naval Air Service, being issued to five units of the former and eight of the latter. Others entered service with the air forces of the Netherlands, Belgium, Russia, and Italy. In Italy, Macchi built 150 under licence, and the first aircraft were delivered to the units in October 1916.

The Nieuport 17 was one of the leading planes in Italian fighter units and was often used together with the "Bébé" in escort and interception missions. Use of the fighter spread so quickly among the allies that in August 1917 there were still 317 in service at the front.

Its characteristics made it a popular choice with the greatest aces of the period, such as the British pilots Albert Ball and Billy Bishop, and the French Nungesser, Guynemer, Fonck, and Navarre.

The Nieuport 17 proved its full worth during the hard-fought battles of the Somme and the Isonzo, impressively getting the better of the Fokker monoplanes and even the Albatros D.IIs.

Worried about the situation which threatened to overturn the balance of power to their disadvantage, the Germans decided to copy Delage's airplane, using as models some planes that had landed behind the lines and had been captured intact.

A faithful copy of the Nieuport 17 was produced by Siemens-Schuckert, but never became operational because the units had already started to receive the more powerful versions of the Albatros.

The three views show the Nieuport 17 of the Lafayette Squadron, whose emblem was a Seminole Indian chief's head.

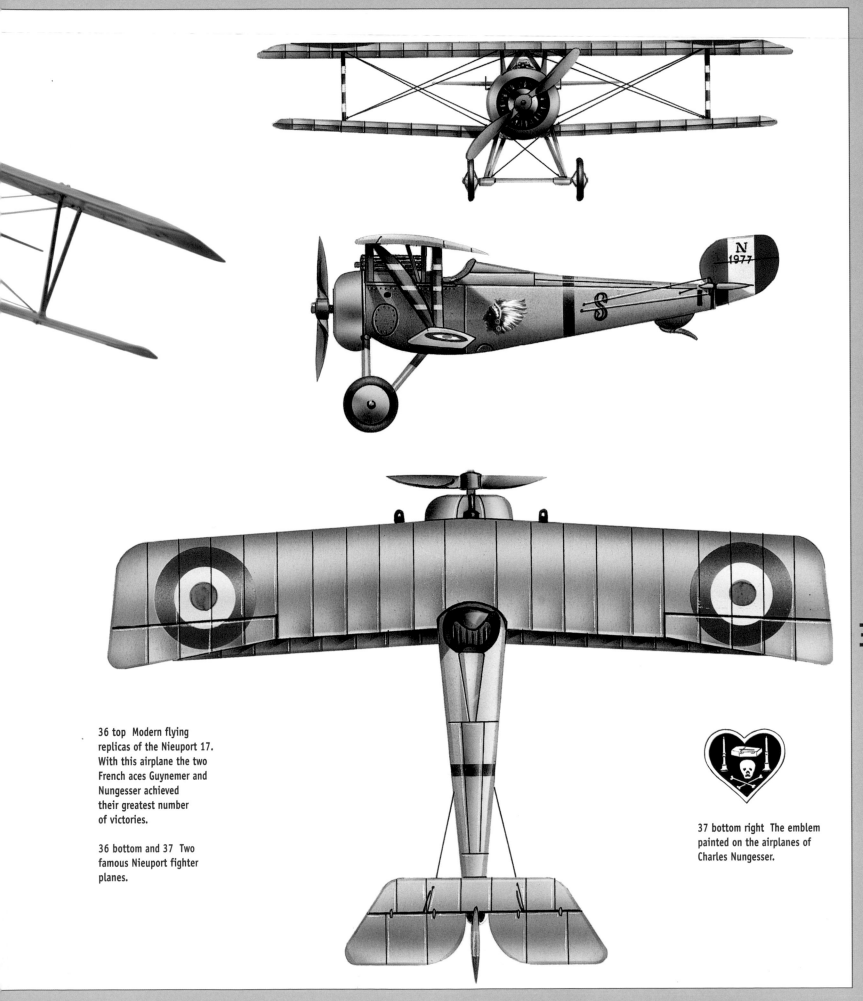

36 top Modern flying
replicas of the Nieuport 17.
With this airplane the two
French aces Guynemer and
Nungesser achieved
their greatest number
of victories.

36 bottom and 37 Two
famous Nieuport fighter
planes.

37 bottom right The emblem
painted on the airplanes of
Charles Nungesser.

Among the many experimental flights, we should mention one of the first long-distance fights, made on June 9, 1910 from the field of Châlons-sur-Marne in Vincennes by two officers, Albert Féquant and Charles Marconet, in a Farman biplane. There was not much space on board, and the navigator was forced to rest his maps on the shoulders of the pilot, and spoke to him by means of an ear trumpet, in order to be heard above the noise of the engine.

By October 1910, the armed forces owned 30 airplanes of various types, while another 61 aircraft had been ordered. In the same year, military pilots actively took part in numerous sporting competitions, fuelling the great French enthusiasm for aviation. And the military world soon provided another stimulus for industrial production, by arranging contests aimed at selecting aircraft suitable for use. The first in a long series was held in 1911, and had incredible success: 110 prototypes registered and 32 of them took part in the final competition. The specifications were strict: the airplanes had to be two-seaters, able to travel at least 180 miles (300 km) and transport a load of 69 lb (300 kg) at a speed of no less than 36 mph (60 km/h). There were three winners: Nieuport, Breguet, and Deperdussin and as a consequence orders for ten of the first, six of the second, and four of the third aircraft were placed.

The tradition of military air contests, subsequently taken up by other nations, gave an important boost to the new aeronautics industry, whose production soon reached impressive levels: 1350 airplanes were built in 1911, 1425 in 1912, and 1294 in 1913. Equally high were manufacturing rates in the engine sector: from 1400 units in 1911, the two following years saw the figure rise to 2217 and then 2440.

The approaching war thus saw the French air forces particularly well prepared. On August 28, 1912, the air forces were divided into three units, based

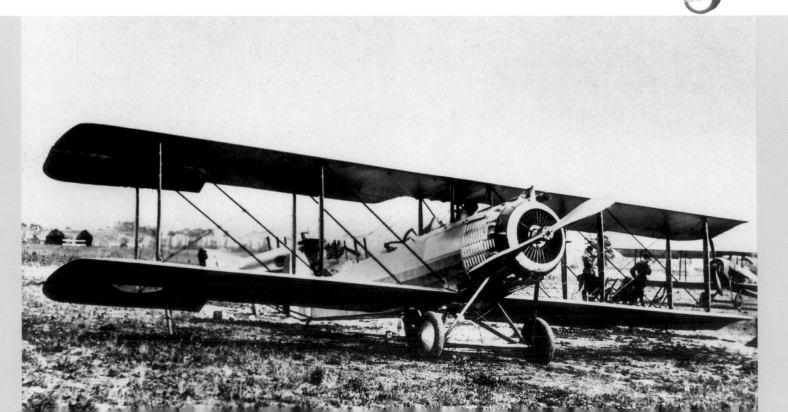

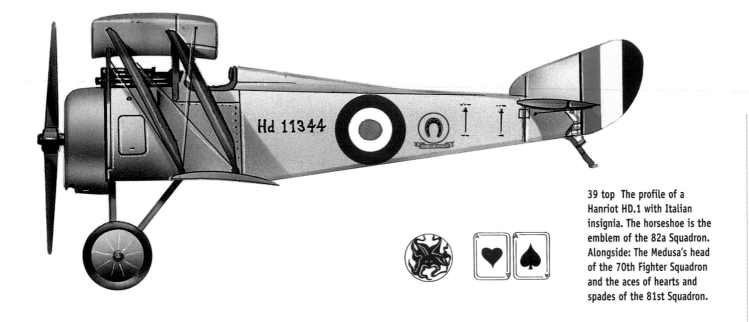

in Versailles, Reims, and Lyons. In February 1914, two distinct and independent services were created for airplanes and balloons. In August, on entering the war, there were 25 squadrons, of which 21 were each composed of six two-seaters and four three-seaters, for a total of 130 combat aircraft. It was a fairly varied force, composed of monoplanes and biplanes of various types, which was soon rationalized by classifying the aircraft on the basis of their operational roles: one-seater and two-seater fighters, daytime and night-time bombers, and long-haul airplanes.

The evolution of the war caused a formidable increase in the French military air force which, moreover, had the merit of deploying some of the best airplanes of the time: fighters like the Nieuport 11 and 17, the Spad S.VII and S.XIII, and the Hanriot HD.1 were the pride of the Allied forces and played their part in the exploits and legendary feats of their "aces". By Armistice day, the Aviation Militaire had 6000 front-line airplanes, 6417 pilots, and 1682 observers, out of a total of over 80,000 men. The naval air corps, meanwhile, had 1264 airplanes, of which 870 were front-line airplanes, plus 58 airships, 198 balloons, and 11,000 men. The overall number of aircraft produced now stood at 68,000. Of these, as many as 52,000—around 77 percent—were lost in battle, an unbelievable amount.

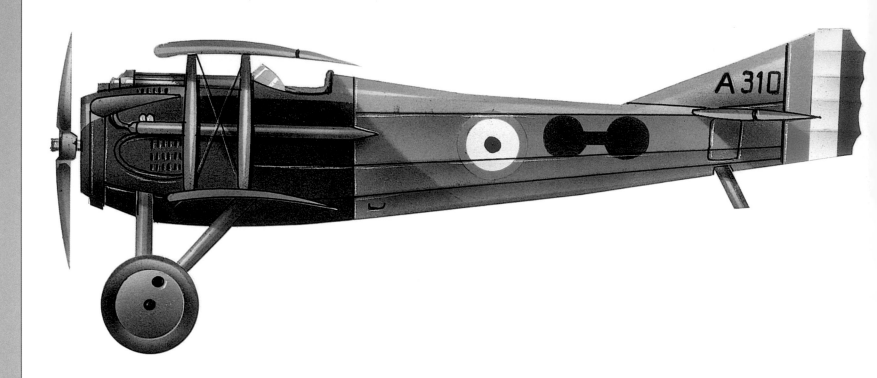

Spad S.VII and S.XIII

FRANCE

The Spad S.VIIs and S.XIIIs are considered the best fighter planes of the First World War. It was thanks to the potential of these aircraft that the great aces of the calibre of Baracca, Ruffo, Fonck, Guynemer, and Rickenbaker, achieved their most rousing victories. Designed by Louis Béchereau (the father of the Deperdussin monoplanes of 1912–13), the Spads were equipped with the new Hispano-Suiza engine, designed by the Swiss engineer Mark Birkigt. With its increased power and reliability, it marked the end of the rotary engine and the beginning of a new era in aircraft propulsion.

The prototype made its maiden flight in April 1916 at Villacoublay, and immediately impressed with its performance. Despite being fitted with a 140 hp engine that was not of the supercompression type, the airplane achieved speeds of up to 120 mph (196 km/h) at sea level and reached an altitude of 9840 ft (3000 meters) in 15 minutes. France immediately commissioned 268 S.VIIs (the picture shows a Spad S.VII of the 19th Squadron of the Royal Flying Corps). Deliveries began on September 2, and the airplane soon entered service in many fighter units of the Allied air forces. Great Britain, France, Italy, Belgium, Russia, and the United States built the aircraft under licence.

An enormous number of these aircraft were built, 5600 in France alone. The French squadrons supplied with the S.VII, including the famous "Les Cigognes", used the aircraft until mid-1917, when they decided to change over to the more powerful and better-armed S.XIII version.

In Italy, meanwhile, the Spad arrived in 1917, and remained in service after the arrival of the S.XIII. Some of the 214 planes received from France went to the 77th and the 91st Squadrons. Francesco Baracca, who served in the latter, soon exploited the airplane's potential, shooting down two Brandenburgs on May 13 and 21, 1917, and thus achieving his twelfth victory. The Italian ace continued to use the S.VII even after the arrival of its

40 and 41 top left The Spad S.VIIs and S.XIIIs illustrated on these pages represent the maximum development of French fighter aircraft during the war.

41 top right The S.VII was the favorite airplane both of French pilots and the Italian ace Francesco Baracca.

41 bottom The S.XIII of the famous Squadron "Les Cigognes".

more powerful successor. The 91st Squadron obtained significant results with the French fighter, and between October 25 and December 7, Baracca achieved his thirtieth victory.

The Spad S.XIII, the direct successor of the S.VII, was developed towards the end of 1916 to exploit the latest versions of the Hispano-Suiza engine, which could deliver 235 hp. While following the lines and general layout of its predecessor, the airplane was larger and offered significantly better performance. Its immediate success is demonstrated by production figures (8472 were built), and by the widespread use of the S.XIII in Allied units, which began to receive it in May 1917. The airplane equipped over 80 squadrons and made a fundamental contribution to maintaining the balance of power and subsequent Allied supremacy in the air. In Italy, the airplane arrived in mid-1918 and equipped eleven squadrons, although was not received with much enthusiasm.

Pilots, in fact, preferred the more agile Hanriot HD.1 to the heavy S.XIII: despite being an excellent shooting platform, exceptionally robust and powerful, the new plane was less easy to handle, and unreliable at low speeds.

GREAT BRITAIN

A similar process to that which took place in France was also seen in Great Britain, a nation which participated in the pioneering period of aviation with great enthusiasm. The first officially recognized flight was taken on October 16, 1908 at Farnborough by Samuel Franklin Cody, an American enthusiast who had built a Wright-style biplane for the Royal Engineers Balloon Factory.

With this airplane, named the British Army Airplane N° 1, Cody flew for 1356 ft (424 meters). Between 1908 and 1910, many of those who would become important builders, such as Alliot Verdon Roe, Robert Blackburn, and Geoffrey de Havilland, were also some of the best-known and most highly acclaimed aviators on the airfields. In those years the idea of the airplane as a military vehicle gained acceptance, and the most active drive was provided by three artillery officers: Lieutenant L.D.L. Gibbs, Captain J.D.B. Fulton, and Captain Bertram Dickson. With their active participation in experiments and test flights, these enthusiasts finally managed to overcome the doubts of the

42 top The Avro 504, one of the most famous and widely used British airplanes in the First World War: it served for fighter training, as a scout, and also as a bomber.

42 bottom The slow B.E.2c biplane from 1914 built by the Royal Aircraft Factory, used on the French front. Twelve squadrons of the Royal Flying Corps were equipped with this airplane.

military authorities. In 1910, Fulton set up the first flying school in Salisbury, where he was an instructor, and on September 24 Dickson performed the first aerial reconnaissance mission during the British Army's autumn manouvres. This news aroused great interest, and Winston Churchill himself, at the time Home Secretary, asked to be kept informed of the potential development of aerial reconnaissance in the event of war. One year later, on February 28, 1911, the Air Battalion of the Royal Engineers was formally set up, the first unit to be equipped with airplanes: in addition to a company equipped with balloons, it had another with five airplanes. The Air Battalion's main task was to perform reconnaissance duties.

In Britain, like France, the evolution was rapid. In 1912, in view of a hypothetical conflict, the Royal Flying Corps was set up as part of the Army. The Corps was arranged around a naval unit (Naval Wing), a land unit (Military Wing), and a flying school (the Central Flying School, based at Upavon). In Farnborough, the former balloon factory became the Royal Aircraft Factory and was transformed into a center for the

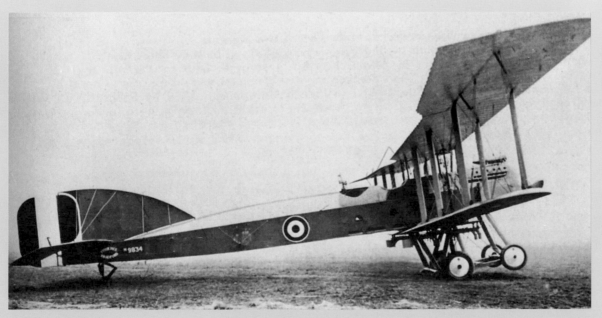

43 top The Airco D.H.2 biplane with pusher propeller. In 1916, it became the first one-seater fighter plane to be used by an English squadron in France.

43 bottom The bomber built by Short Brothers in 1915 was not widely used, and only entered service pending the arrival of the aircraft specifically designed by Handley Page.

tary airplanes. In the space of two years (June 23, 1914), the Royal Flying Corps was joined by a similar service in the Navy, the Royal Naval Air Service. At the outbreak of hostilities, the overall force was composed of about a hundred planes. These two structures bore the weight of the conflict, and only on August 17, 1917 did the War Cabinet begin to examine the proposal made by General Jan Christian Smuts of creating an independent air force. The harsh and bloody experiences on the Western front had revealed fully the tactical and strategic importance of aviation, and the decision was soon taken. After the act of Royal consent on November 29, the Royal Air Force was established April 1, 1918, bringing together the two existing services. This structural and organizational revolution laid the basis for the subsequent developments, which would make the RAF one of the most powerful military air forces in the world.

The influence of the British air forces in World War I was massive and covered all the fronts, from the Western and Italian fronts to Macedonia, the Aegean, and the Middle East. Experience of war led to a change in combat tactics: the initial solo flights or flights of pairs of reconnaissance aircraft in 1914–1915 was replaced by patrols in formation, which carried out a number of missions spread throughout the day. Moreover, the first homogeneous unit composed exclusively of fighters was British: the No. 11 Squadron RFC, equipped with the Vickers FB.5 began operations on July 25, 1915. During the course of the war, however, the British air force was not always up to the task of coping with the enemy's supremacy.

44 top The Bristol F.2A, which started life as a scout, served as the basis for the F.2B model, with structural changes and a more powerful engine of over 200 hp. It entered service in summer 1917 and over 3000 were built.

44 center A flying reproduction of the Bristol M.1C monoplane fighter.

44 bottom A flying replica of the Sopwith Triplane.

R.A.F. S.E.5 and S.E.5a

GREAT BRITAIN

More or less a contemporary of the Camel, the S.E.5 of the Royal Aircraft Factory shares with the Sopwith fighter the honor of being the best British fighting aircraft in the war.

Robust, fast, easy to handle, and well-armed, the S.E.5 showed itself to be superior to its better-equipped German rivals such as the Albatros D.III and D.V, the Pfalz D.III, and the Fokker Dr.I. This was the plane that brought fame to aces such as Mannock, Bishop,

and McCudden. From the maiden flight of the prototype, on November 22, 1916, to the end of the conflict, 5025 were built, equipping 24 British squadrons, in addition to two American and one Australian, and served on all fronts. The S.E.5 project was launched in summer 1916 by H.P. Folland, J. Kenworthy, and F.W. Goddard, who designed the airplane around the 150 hp Hispano-Suiza engine, which Great Britain had ordered in August 1915.

Test flights, in which

the prototype was set against two of the best fighters of the time, the French Nieuport 17 and Spad S.VII, confirmed its overall superiority. Its only weakness was the fact that it was more

difficult to handle than the Nieuport.

In production, however, after only 58 had been built, the initial version was replaced by the S.E.5a, which reached the units in June 1917. Due

to mechanical problems and the significant lack of supplies, the final version abandoned the 200 hp Hispano-Suiza engine in favour of a Wolseley W.4a of similar power.

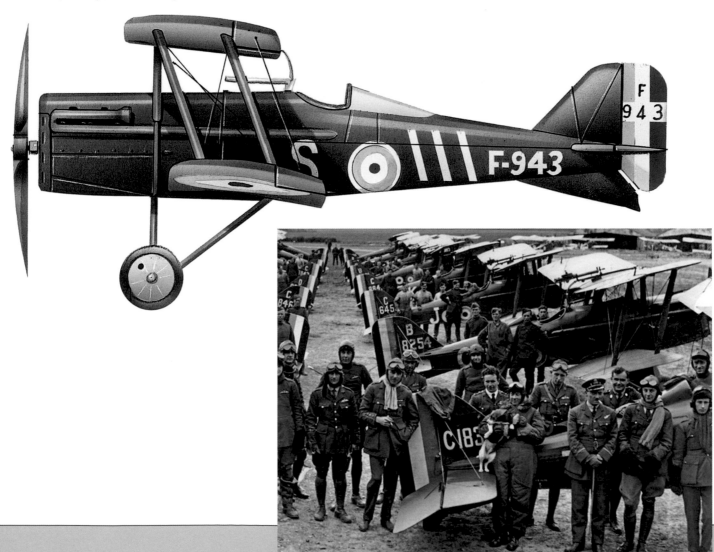

Sopwith F.1 Camel

Brilliant, nervous, and extremely agile, the Sopwith F.1 Camel revealed itself to be an exceptional fighting plane and one of the best British fighters of the war. During its intense career, it managed to shoot down an impressive 1294 enemy aircraft, and the 5490 aircraft built equipped not only the units of the Royal Flying Corps, but also those of the Royal Naval Air Service. The design was developed by Herbert Smith, of Sopwith Aviation, in late 1916.

The prototype flew on December 22 and immediately afterward construction was started on a small production run for test flights and trials with the various types of engines requested by the two air forces. For the first

time on a British aircraft, the weaponry was standardized, with two fixed front-mounted synchronized Vickers machine-guns, making it equivalent to contemporary German fighters. Deliveries to the units began in May 1917, and the Camels became operational in July.

The pilots' initial experience of the new aircraft, however, were far from encouraging. The fighter was extremely sensitive to the gyroscopic effect of the rotary engine, which caused sudden variations of attitude in turning, and pilots with little flying experience often found themselves unable to control the aircraft. Especially at the beginning, there were many accidents, and a two-seater version had to be produced for training purposes. However, in the hands of expert pilots, these same characteristics became the main source of the plane's superiority in air combat.

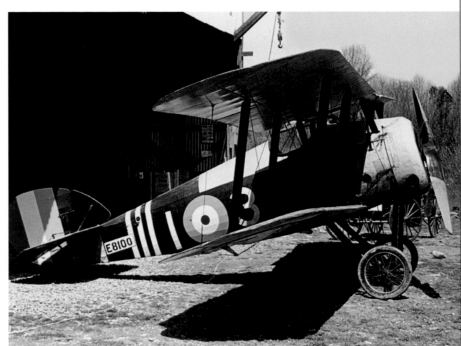

46 and 47 This fighter equipped many English units, both in the Royal Naval Air Service and the Royal Flying Corps

46 bottom right Major W.G. Barker flew it to gain many of his victories.

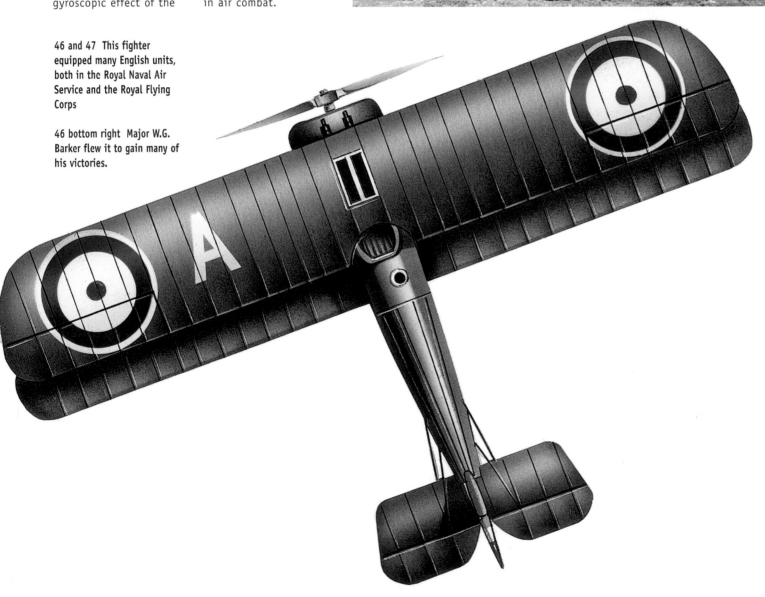

In some cases, the British were forced to equip themselves with foreign aircraft, in particular French, such as the Nieuport 11s and 17s at the height of German Fokker monoplane superiority, or the Spads, before the arrival of better home-produced fighters in the penultimate year of the war. These included the Sopwith Triplane and Camel, and the S.E.5s of the Royal Aircraft Factory. The last two, in particular, were considered the best British combat aircraft of the war.

But, apart from fighters, primary importance was given to the realization of strategic bombers. The Handley Page 0/100s and 0/400s of 1916–17 and the contemporary Short Bomber were the first in a long series of immortal giants of the air designed to spread terror and destruction among the enemy.

An idea of the great development in military aviation can be given by a few statistics: in October 1918, six months after being set up, the Royal Air Force could count on 291,784 men and 22,171 airplanes. Of these, 3300 were in service on the front line.

48 top The Sopwith Snipe fighter.

48 center and bottom The Vickers Vimy represented the last generation of heavy British bombers in the First World War, but only three reached the units. It became famous for performing the first non-stop flight over the Atlantic (June 1919) and the first flight from Great Britain to Australia (November 1919).

GERMANY

The evolution of military aviation in Germany was particularly rapid and extensive. Before the war, the successes of the Zeppelin airships from the end of the previous century had revolutionized the world of "lighter than air" craft. These airships had so fired the imagination of the German military authorities that initially the impressive debut of the airplane did not arouse much interest, and was actually viewed with great scepticism. But this attitude did not last for long. In 1910, a flying school was opened in Döberiz, west of Berlin, as a part of the new military manouvres. The following year another two similar centers were opened, the first in Merseburg, the second in Metz. In 1913, expansion was already consolidated and the air service had been organized into five battalions of balloons and airships, and four battalions of aviation staff and airplanes. On the field, these units were distributed to the army detachments in small groups (Feld-fliegerabteilungen), normally composed of six aircraft

to be used for reconnaissance duties, aerial photography, and artillery support. By August 1914, 34 of these units were available, employed by the high commands of the army, and initial operational needs led to the addition of another two airplanes performing escort duties.

49 top The German scout L.V.G. C.II

49 center A replica of the Rumpler C.I.

49 bottom One of the many biplanes of the Aviatik range used for the entire period of the war on the Western and Eastern Front. The C.II had a single two-seater cockpit with the observer in front and the pilot behind.

Fokker E

GERMANY

The turning point for the Fokker monoplane came on April 18, 1915, after the shooting down of the Morane-Saulnier L of Roland Garros and the creation of the first valid synchronization device for front-mounted machine-guns.

The first operational version of the airplane was the E.I, but it was rapidly followed by the other two main variants, the E.II and the E.III, differing in engine power and wing size. All three versions entered service in the fighter units. The basic weaponry was an LMG 08/15-type machine-gun, while some airplanes were equipped with two weapons, but to the detriment of overall performance. Max Immelmann even went so far as to mount three guns on a Fokker E.IV (a later, but little-used version) before going back to the double set-up he preferred.

The successes of these aircraft at the front led to the recognition of the first German aces: in addition to Immelmann (who was actually shot in a Fokker on June 8, 1916),Oswald Boelcke, and Kurt Wintgens.

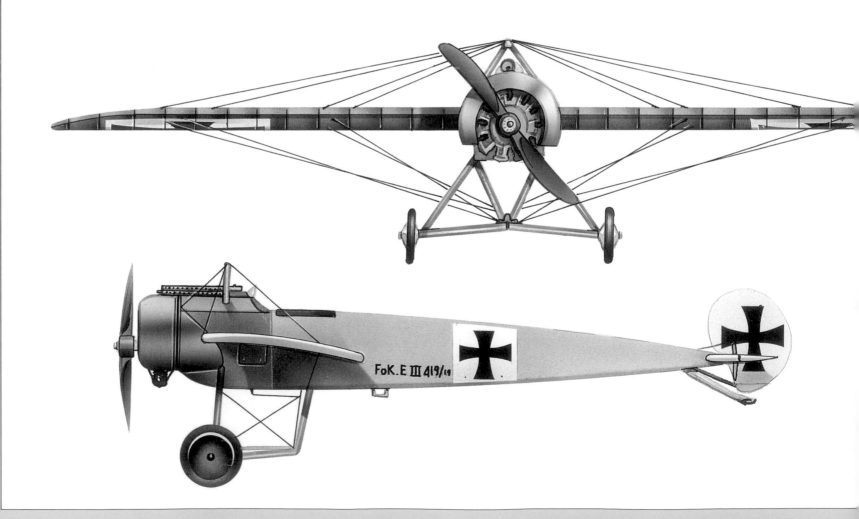

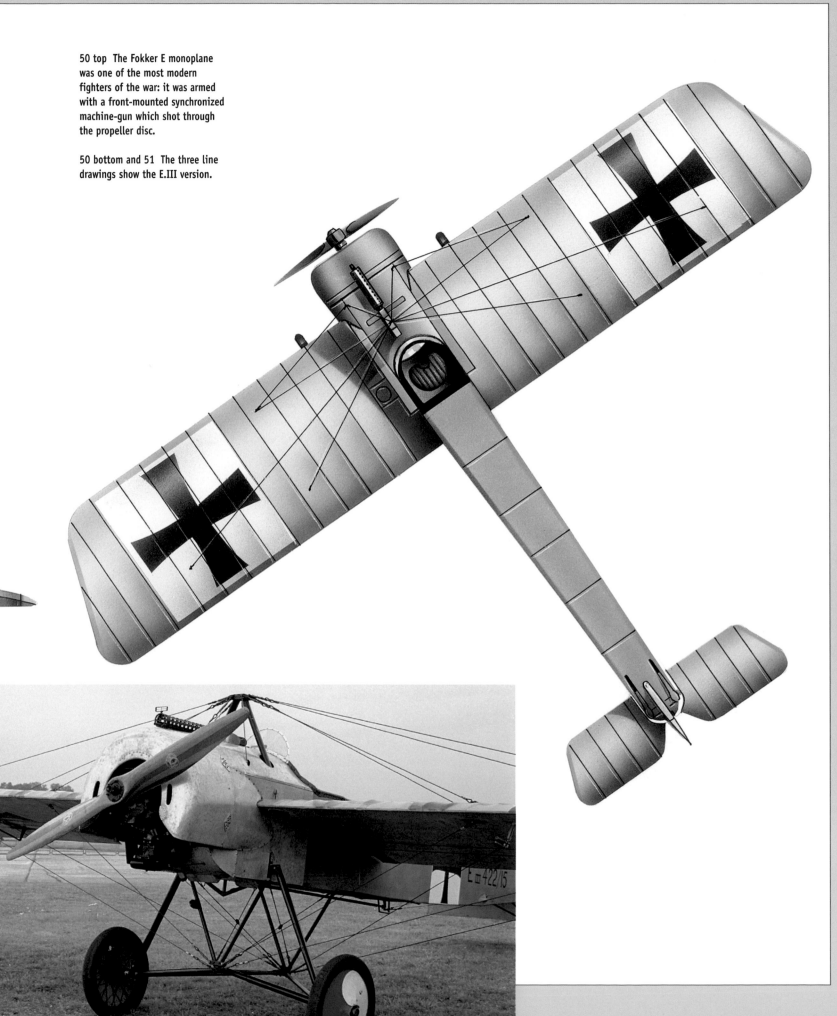

50 top The Fokker E monoplane was one of the most modern fighters of the war: it was armed with a front-mounted synchronized machine-gun which shot through the propeller disc.

50 bottom and 51 The three line drawings show the E.III version.

This initial organization was extended in 1915, when it became clear that there was a need for more specific roles, leading to the creation of units specializing in reconnaissance or fighter roles, known as Kampf und Feldfliegerabteilungen. Very soon, however, the air force developed into an independent service (November 1916), whose structure and organization underwent continuous development, dictated by combat experience. It was from these initial groups that the great fighter units were born, those that gave so many problems to the Allies in the crucial years of the war. The naval air service was created in a similar way and directly depended on the naval high command.

Aircraft production figures are particularly significant. From the 24 airplanes built in Germany in 1911, the number rose to 136 in 1912, and to 446 in 1913.

The aces

The evolution of the air war brought not only aircraft into the spotlight, but also the skill of the men who flew them. Particular fame was enjoyed by "fighter aces", initially due to propaganda aimed at exalting the exploits of the heroes of the air. The public needed its myths, and nothing could be more appropriate or better-suited to firing the popular imagination than the daring feats of these flying warriors.

The French government was the first to award the rank of ace to those "hunters" who had shot down at least five enemy aircraft, confirmed by an independent source.

The Germans followed suit, setting at eight (and later, 16) the number of aircraft which a pilot had to shoot down in order to be considered an ace and be nominated for the prestigious decoration Pour le Mérite.

A similar approach was adopted by the British, who awarded aces with the Distinguished Flying Cross after at least eight victories. In the crowded and bloody skies of the Western front, many planes were reportedly shot down, although reliable statistics are difficult to obtain. It was usual for pilots to boast of more victories than they had actually achieved, and in many units it was customary to assign relatively easy targets to the best aces, not only to increase their score, but also to encourage the younger pilots with their example. At the end of the war, both the victors and the defeated considered it a point of honor to list the number of victories achieved by the leading ace from each nation: 80 in Germany by Manfred von Richtofen; 75 in France by René Fonck; 72 in Canada by William Bishop; 61 in Britain by Edward Mannock; 35 in Austria by Godwin Brumowski; 37 in Belgium by Willy

53 top The best fighting plane
produced by Albatros was the
D.III, which entered service in
early 1917, re-equipping the

majority of German fighter
squadrons. It was a single-seater
aircraft armed with two machine
guns and had a top speed of 107

mph (174 km/h). It was the
airplane of choice for German
ace Manfred von Richtofen,
commander of the Jasta 11.

Coppens de
Houthulst; 34 in Italy
by Francesco Baracca;
26 in the United
States by Eddie
Rickenbaker; 17 in
Russia by Alexander
Kazakov.

Below are listed the
20 leading aces of
the war. The "Red
Baron" recorded most
victories, although
the French René
Fonck was the pilot
with most victories to
survive the war. In
many instances, the
fame of these men

was linked to that of
the aircraft in which
they performed their
most daring exploits.

Manfred von
Richtofen, for
example, despite
having fought in
various planes, was
associated with the
Fokker triplane, while
Willy Coppens de
Houthulst and
Francesco Baracca
became popular
legends in the
cockpits of the
Hanriot and the
Spad.

THE LEADING ACES NATION BY NATION

Germany:
Manfred von Richtofen 80
France:
René Fonck 75
Canada:
William Bishop 72
Britain:
Edward Mannock 61
South Africa:
A. Beauchamp-Proctor 47
Australia:
Robert Little 47
Ireland:
George McElroy 47

Belgium:
Willy Coppens de Houthulst 37
Austria-Hungary:
Godwin Brumowski 35
Italy:
Francesco Baracca 34
United States:
Eddie Rickenbaker 26
Russia:
Alexander Kazakov 17

53 bottom Manfred von
Richtofen

Fokker Dr.I

GERMANY

The Fokker triplane is eternally linked to the name of Germany's greatest ace Manfred von Richtofen, who met his death in his plane on April 21, 1918 in the Valley of the Somme. On a technical level, the boost to the development of this aircraft came in 1917, as Anthony Fokker responded to the appearance of the British Sopwith triplane, designed by Herbert Smith. Contrary to common belief at the time, the machine developed by Reinhold Platz was not a copy of its British rival, and in fact displayed significant differences.

The only things they had in common were the triplane layout and the type of engine, which was rotary. Four prototypes were produced, the last three fitted with two fixed Spandau front-mounted synchronized machine-guns supplied with 1000 rounds.

Combat testing was performed in two airplanes given to von Richtofen's Jagdgeschwader 1.

They met with immediate success: on August 30, 1917 Werner Voss shot down his first enemy, and in a little over three weeks of operations achieved a further 20 victories. Delivery of the first mass-produced Dr.Is, however, was delayed until November to allow a number of structural problems on the top wing to be resolved.

The triplane behaved admirably, especially in terms of handling. Many

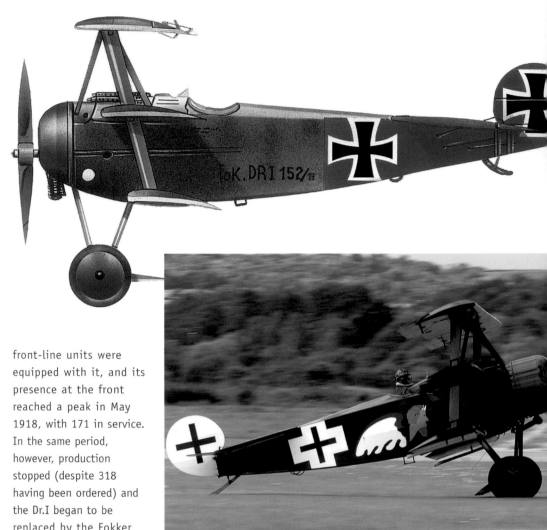

front-line units were equipped with it, and its presence at the front reached a peak in May 1918, with 171 in service. In the same period, however, production stopped (despite 318 having been ordered) and the Dr.I began to be replaced by the Fokker D.VII biplane.

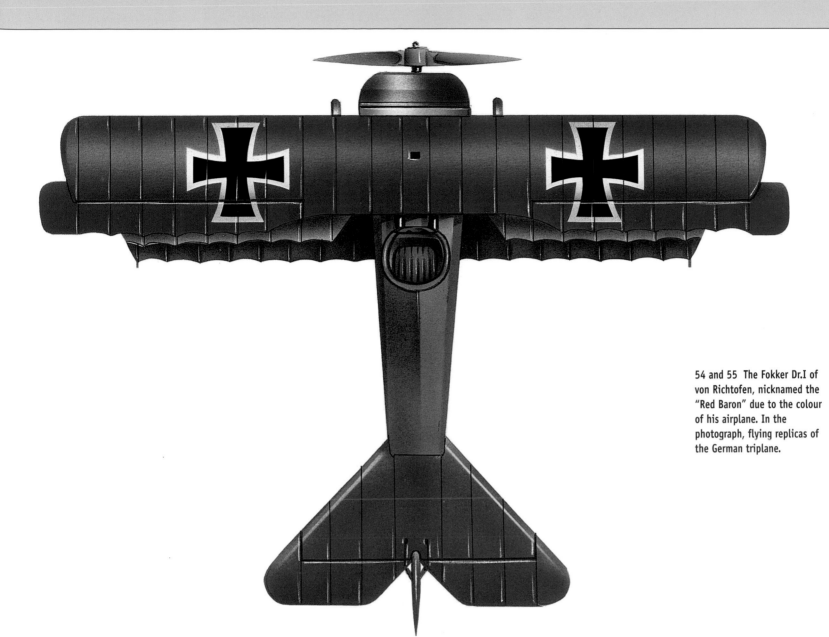

54 and 55 The Fokker Dr.I of von Richtofen, nicknamed the "Red Baron" due to the colour of his airplane. In the photograph, flying replicas of the German triplane.

Fokker D.VII

GERMANY

Toward the end of 1917, Reinhold Platz returned to the biplane formula with another excellent design, which resulted in the Fokker D.VII, unanimously considered the best German fighter of the war. The V.11 prototype was presented at a contest held by the German Ministry of War in Adlershof in January–February 1918. The airplane far surpassed the other participants (around 30) and pilots were very impressed, in particular von Richtofen, who himself suggested some changes to be made to the airplane before mass production commenced.

Large orders were made: 400 airplanes were ordered from Fokker, in addition to significant quantities from both Albatros and O.A.W., for a total of 2000 aircraft. However, only 1000 of these were completed before the end of the conflict.

The first D.VIIs entered service in April 1918 and the first were assigned to the "Flying Circus" of the Jagdgeschwader 1, following a practice whereby the elite units and, within them, the most experienced pilots, were the first to receive delivery of new airplanes.

One month before the Armistice, around 800 of these biplanes were in service at the front. The main characteristics

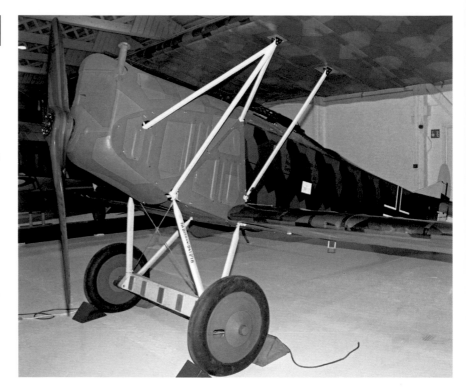

of this excellent fighter were its robustness, its horizontal and climbing speeds, and above all its performance at altitude, reaching maximum levels in the F version, which appeared in the month of August. This version was driven by a 185 hp BMW IIIa engine which maintained full power at up to 19,000 ft (6000 meters) and ensured a significant increase in climbing speed: it took the D.VII just 14 minutes to reach 16,000 ft (5000 meters), against the 38 minutes and 5 seconds of the same plane equipped with a standard 160 hp Mercedes D.III engine.

57 top A formation of Fokker
triplanes in flight, all flying
replicas produced in recent years.

57 bottom The Siemens-Schuckert
D.III was a highly manouvrable
and fast aircraft, fitted with a 160
hp rotary engine.

The war years saw 1348 airplanes built in 1914, 4532 in 1915, 8182 in 1916 and an impressive 19,746 and 14,123 in the last two years of hostilities—impressive figures, which took the total to 48,537 aircraft of all types. The quantity and quality of the products was accompanied by an extreme rationalization of the air force, which reached its peak in autumn 1916, when the combat units were grouped exclusively by specialty. This led to the birth of the famous "Jasta" (*Jagstaffeln*) composed only of fighters, the *Schlachstaffeln*, ground attack units, and *Bombelstaffeln*, bombers. The first of these were undoubtedly the most famous and, in addition to becoming a real breeding ground for pilots of exceptional quality, exalted the role of the pure fighter created precisely by the Germans in 1915.

Airplanes such as those of Fokker, Albatros, and Pfalz marked the phases of the conflict and showed themselves to be among the best in absolute terms. No less important were the great strategic bombers realized by German industry and widely used in devastating raids: names such as Gotha, Zeppelin Staaken, and Friedrichshafen became synonymous with death and destruction. The first two in particular, together with large Zeppelin airships, struck fear into the inhabitants of London during the long, terrible raids over the English capital in 1917.

AUSTRIA

Direct adversary of Italy, this country had a similar situation to that of its antagonist. At the beginning of hostilities, the combat potential of the Austrian air force consisted of a paltry collection of flying machines: one airship, 10 balloons, and 36 airplanes (mainly of the Taube type, purchased some years before, together with a few Lohner biplanes). Even if there had been some interest in the airplane between 1907 and 1910, the political and military authorities had never shown excessive enthusiasm for aviation, and had an extremely suspicious attitude towards technological development in general, and airplanes in particular. Among the reasons for such scepticism was the uncertainty in evaluating the costs and benefits that could be obtained from the new weapon. Not even the passion of the many enthusiasts helped break down the barrier of indifference. In 1907, a group of officers particularly interested in flight set up a pioneering group, but their activities led to nothing. It is indicative that the first airplane donated to the army, as well as the first airport, was the result of civilian contributions.

Between 1911 and 1916 an initial program of development of military aviation finally started, thanks to the drive of General Franz Conrad von Hetzendorf, Imperial Chief of Staff from 1906 to 1917, which provided for the organization of at least 15 squadrons of airplanes by 1914. The outbreak of the war, however, created a number of difficulties, forcing the army to work on fre-

netic restructuring and development, and for a long time to depend on supplies from its German ally. In this phase, however, Austria was advantaged by the availability of excellent nationally produced engines, such as the Daimler and Hiero. This domestic supply of engines helped accelerate production rates. Another element that helped the Austrian army was the sorry state of Italian aviation at the declaration of war in 1915; it was unlikely to cause Austria excessive concern, due to the relative inadequacy of its material. At the beginning of the conflict, Austrian attacks were performed using seaplanes stationed at Pola and Kumbor in the Gulf of Cattaro; subsequently, other water airports were provided for their use. The aircraft used were Lohner seaplanes, alongside land-based planes such as Taubes, Aviatiks, and Agos.

Soon, the Austrian situation improved and it was able to deploy good nationally produced machines, such as various Lohners, Brandenburgs, and Lloyds, alongside others of German origin built under licence. The military potential of Austrian aviation increased again in 1917, with the appearance of fighters such as the Aviatik D.I designed by Julius von Berg, which was the best Austrian airplane of its category made during the war, together with the Albatros D.III by Oeffag, and the Gotha G.IV. The year 1917

58 top A detail of the Aviatik C.II.

58 center The Austro-Hungarian Lloyd C.IV, a two-seater scout much-used on the Italian front.

58 bottom The Gotha G.IV strategic bomber driven by two 160 hp Mercedes engines; it could carry over 1750 lb (800 kg) of bombs.

59 top A Hansa Brandenburg C.I on an airfield in Trentino. This scout was mass-produced in Austria by the companies Phönix and Ufag.

59 bottom A line-up of Albatros D.III fighters at an Austrian airport.

60 top and center The Phönix D.IIs deployed at Pergine airport which flew against the Italian aircraft. These biplanes were the last developments in a series of brilliant Austrian fighters.

61 top The large Russian four-engined Ilya Mourometz.

also witnessed a radical restructuring of the Austrian air force, which was divided into three categories:

- *Aufklarungskompagnien*, for reconnaissance and observation, equipped with 8-10 type-C two-seaters and three or four fighters for escort duties;
- *Jagdkompagnien*, fighter units with 16-20 airplanes;
- *Geschwadern* or *Fliegerkompagnien*, for bombing duties, composed of ten bombers and four fighters for escort duties.

In the last year of the war, moreover, five new national products appeared: the Phönix C.I, the Ufag C.I, and the Phönix D.I, D.II, and D.III. This made it possible to increase the number of fighting units to 13.

Camouflage

The climate of competition and enthusiasm which was dominant in fighter units, despite the horrors of war, directly affected the appearance of the airplanes. These ceased to be anonymous machines and were personalized to the extreme, in violation of every rule of camouflage.

The pilots enjoyed decorating their airplanes with emblems and colors, convinced that this helped raise morale and acted as a psychological deterrent to the enemy. The most striking example was von Richtofen's "Flying Circus", whose airplanes were all painted in bright colors and highly decorated, in order to express the unit's esprit de corps and awareness of their complete superiority over the enemy.

This was an anticipation of what would happen during the Second World War.

However, the rules of camouflage were extremely strict. The need to make the airplane less visible both on the ground, to avoid detection, and in the air, to get as close as possible to the enemy unobserved, had been perceived right from the beginning of the conflict. Initially, little attention was paid to camouflaging aircraft, but gradually, as suitable paints began to be produced, each nation studied the problem in depth, at times coming up with original solutions.

Except for a few exceptions, the colors soon became standardized: dark green or brown for the upper parts and beige or sky-blue for the undercarriage.

It was later discovered that striped painting in two or more colors caused an optical effect which helped

RUSSIA

The development of military aviation in Russia was conditioned by various factors, not least the 1917 revolution, which threw the country into chaos and blocked any initiative aimed at improving the unexceptional situation of the air force. However, aeronautical knowledge had developed extremely early, especially in the military field. In 1910 two flying schools had opened and many officers were sent to France and Great Britain to be trained as pilots. The first military aviation meeting was held in Gatchina in 1911, and was followed by army manouvres in which airplanes were used for the first-time. At the outbreak of war, the Imperial Air Service had 244 airplanes, 12 airships, and 46 balloons, with units at the front equipped with 145 aircraft overall. At the beginning of the war, the level of the Russian air forces was more or less equivalent to that of the other nations in the conflict, and during the war there were no significant changes. The Russian aeronautical industry did not flourish, and mainly produced French aircraft under licence. Dux in Moscow built Voisin, Nieuport, Farman, and Morane airplanes, and the Russian-Baltic factory built Henri and Maurice Farman biplanes. Engines were a problem and Russian industry depended on imports or those built elsewhere in Europe; it also built engines under licence, including Gnomes and Hispanos. To strengthen the units, they used combat aircraft provided directly by France and Great Britain (RAF B.E.2e, Vickers FB.19,

break up the airplane's profile, and this approach was adopted by the French and Germans. In particular, the Germans designed a complicated system of camouflage, composed of lozenges of or five colours grouped in a pre-ordered sequence for the lower and upper surfaces. Their research even led them to experiment with a type of transparent paint, in the hope that the airplane would become almost invisible.

Needless to say, this didn't work. The only exceptions admitted and codified in the rules of camouflage were national insignia and unit markings. The former almost always clearly stood out on the camouflaged surface and in many cases became targets for the aim of enemy weapons.

To allow rapid identification, the Allies had chosen a circular base for the insignia of the various countries, while the Germans opted for a square base, on which had been placed the Black Cross, symbol of the Teutonic Knights.

This appeared in various forms, and became increasingly stylized as the war progressed.

Unit markings were

National insignia.
1. Great Britain;
2. Italy;
3. France;
4. United States;
5. Belgium ;
6. Russia.

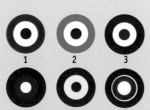

composed of combinations of letters and numbers or, in some cases, simply of unit emblems.

The various German black crosses used in the years of the conflict
1 - 1914-15;
2 - 1915-17;
3 - 1917-18;
4 - 1918.

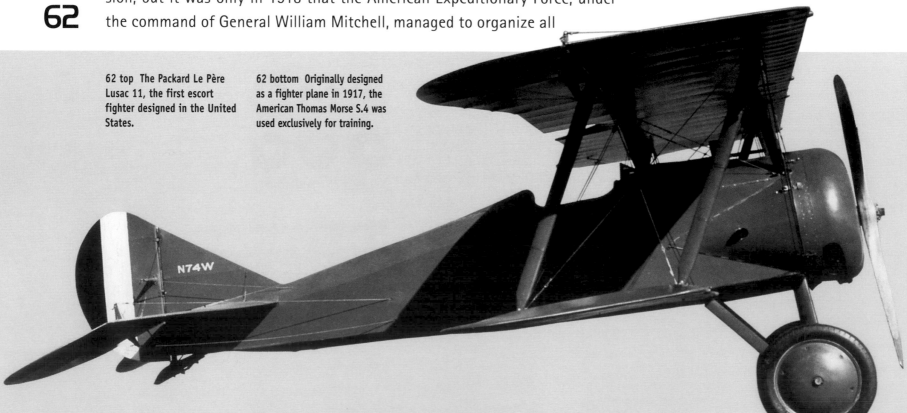

Sopwith 11/2 Strutter), and by the United States, above all Curtiss seaplanes. Russia was, however, temporarily at the international forefront with the products of famous designer Igor Sikorsky in the field of large multi-engine bombers, and their use in a strategic role. Machines such as those of the Ilya Mourometz series, the first four-engined bomber in the world, marked important milestones in the history of aviation, not only starting a tradition of aeronautical gigantism that would be followed by future Soviet designers, but also introducing a category of combat aircraft that would prove fundamental in subsequent decades, and would witness incredible development.

UNITED STATES

The story of military aviation in the United States is an unusual one, after the series of ups and downs which led to the American Army's purchase of the Wright brothers' Flyer. Up until March 1911, when the necessary funds were found for another five airplanes, this single machine represented the entire American air force. On July 18, 1914 the military air force was established as a permanent organization, as the Aviation Section of the Signal Corps, with a staff of 60 officers and 260 men. It was only in the following two years, faced with inadequacies, that an extensive reorganization plan was implemented, with aircraft production programs, extra staff, and the setting up of flying schools. However, when the United States joined the war on April 9, 1917, their aeronautical potential comprised only 131 officers (83 of whom were pilots), 1087 troops, and fewer than 250 airplanes, none of which were adapted to the standards of combat that had prevailed for the previous three years, and had been bloodying the skies of Europe in the battle for supremacy.

The awareness of qualitative and quantitative inferiority gave rise to a huge effort of expansion, but it was only in 1918 that the American Expeditionary Force, under the command of General William Mitchell, managed to organize all

62 top The Packard Le Père Lusac 11, the first escort fighter designed in the United States.

62 bottom Originally designed as a fighter plane in 1917, the American Thomas Morse S.4 was used exclusively for training.

its units at the front rationally and independently. They were equipped exclusively with French aircraft, Nieuports and Spads of various types for the fighter squadrons, Breguet 14s for the bomber units, and Salmsons for the reconnaissance units. At the end of the conflict, in November 1918, General Mitchell had 45 combat squadrons at the front, with a force of 740 airplanes, around 800 pilots, and 500 observers.

The experience of war on European fronts was particularly useful for the American armed forces, since it gave them an awareness of the enormous potential of aircraft and laid the foundations for what would become the most powerful military air force in the world.

FROM THE SCOUT TO THE FIGHTER

At the outbreak of war, in August 1914, the airplane was still in a phase of transformation and development. Despite the fact that the use of the airplane as a combat machine had already been planned, there was great uncertainty in military circles about what tasks the new weapon would be able to perform . Consequently, with a vision still based on the traditional concepts of warfare, the initial role of the "heavier than air" craft was simply that of an "eye" for ground troops, similar to the other airborne craft of the time, the captive balloon and

63 top A flying replica of the Morane-Saulnier AI fighter with the high parasol wing.

63 bottom An Italian S.V.A.5 on a reconnaissance flight.

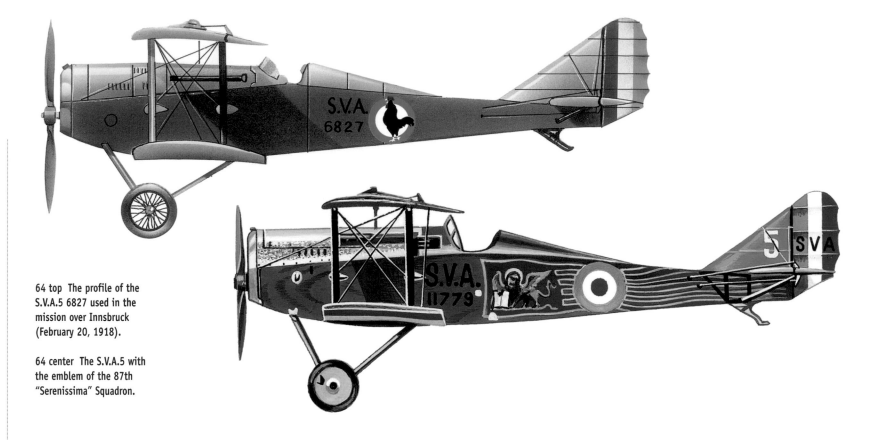

64 top The profile of the S.V.A.5 6827 used in the mission over Innsbruck (February 20, 1918).

64 center The S.V.A.5 with the emblem of the 87th "Serenissima" Squadron.

the airship. Scouts could fly over enemy troops with a certain amount of impunity and subsequently communicate their coordinates, initially by dropping written messages and later by radio. In a war of position such as the First World War, artillery was a weapon of vital importance and discovering how effectively it was being used could be just as important as possessing large-caliber guns. This led to reconnaissance aircraft being equipped with photographic equipment for reporting on artillery fire: damage could be easily evaluated and gun range calculated with a precision that until then had been unimaginable.

On the other hand, the capabilities of the airplanes available at the time restricted use to slow reconnaissance flights, out of range of the ground troops' weapons, and close to their own lines. Fragile and unarmed, with limited autonomy and unable to fly at much over 60 mph (100 km/h), the first machines showed clear traces of their origins, derived as they were from pre-war designs not conceived for the battlefield.

Despite these serious limitations, their initial use highlighted all their advantages. It was precisely thanks to aerial reconnaissance, for example, that the French army discovered the eastward shift of

64 bottom and 65 bottom Two British lightweight scout bombers, the Vickers F.B.5 "Gunbus" (64 left) with its characteristic machine-gunner pit at the prow, and the R.E.8 of the Royal Aircraft Factory (65 right). Originals have been preserved of both the aircraft; the first is on display at the Imperial War Museum, the other at the RAF Museum in Hendon.

German troops on the Marne in September 1914, in contradiction with the original Schiffen plan. This allowed them to block the advance and perform an effective counter-attack which saved France from capitulation. A month previously, on the Eastern front, aerial reconnaissance had determined the German victory at the Battle of Tannenberg, where the Russian General Alexander Sansonov ignored his pilots' warnings on German movements, while General Paul Von Hindenburg planned his moves purely on the basis of reports from his aerial reconnaissance, allowing him to surround the foreign army. His comment after the victory was telling: "Without the air force there would not have been any Tannenberg."

Reconnaissance and observation would remain fundamental roles for the airplane, and this is evidenced by the number of missions completed, which widely exceeded the overall number of all others. How can we forget the most famous and celebrated reconnaissance mission of the entire conflict, performed on August 9, 1918 over Vienna by eight Italian Ansaldo S.V.A.5s, led by Gabriele D'Annunzio, to launch propaganda leaflets and take photographs? It was an historical flight of 675 miles (1126 km) and more than two-thirds of it in enemy territory. Undoubtedly, exploits of this kind were also the result of technological progress fuelled by the war machine. This revolution started in the early years, since operational needs fuelled rapid change aimed at overcoming the initial inadequacies of aircraft.

The first scouts, whose task was the observation of enemy troop movements or the adjustment of artillery fire, ended up meeting and, inevitably, fighting each other. These were not armed aircraft, and the crew could only rely on personal weapons, such as rifles and pistols, whose use was rarely effective. In this situation during the first months of the conflict, pilots and observers tried to increase the offensive capacities of their airplanes and made recourse to a wide assortment of portable weapons, ranging from standard-

issue rifles to shot guns, standard automatic pistols, and others specially modified with a lengthened butt and higher capacity magazines.
Some were even fitted with a kind of metal basket designed to collect
the expelled cartridge cases and prevent them ending up between the
propeller blades and damaging them. These specialized mini-arsenals
also involved the use of somewhat unorthodox methods, sometimes
naive and bizarre, such as a hook hanging from a long metal cable
designed by Captain Alexander Alexandrovic Kozakov, who intended to
latch it onto enemy aircraft during combat and thus make them lose control, or the steel darts that the French and British threw at the wings and canvas covering of enemy aircraft flying below them, or the bricks that were thrown for
the same reason. Some pilots even thought of ramming their adversaries, thus endan-
gering their own lives. This was how Kozakov (the leading Russian ace during the war)
claimed his first victory: not having had any success with his unusual hook system, in
September 1915 he made his adversary crash by ramming him on purpose in flight.

   The newspapers of the time were full of stories and anecdotes of
episodes of this kind, and demonstrate the terrible inadequacy of contemporary airplanes to face the heat of battle. Despite the drama of such moments, these stories
may bring a smile to our faces, used as we are to imagining combat aircraft as deadly machines, equipped with sophisticated instruments, and a combat potential greater
than a First World War warship.

   The appearance of the machine-gun in October 1914 put an end to this
heroic phase of the war and led to armed scouts. The first shooting down with the new
weaponry was on the October 5 near Reims: the victor was a French two-seater Voisin
3, the victim an Aviatik B.I biplane. It is strange to consider that the first experiments

66 top The French pilot Dorme
in the cockpit of a Nieuport.

66 bottom The twin-engined
Caudron G.4 bomber was an
improved and more powerful
version of the single-engined
G.3. In addition to its use in
France, it was also adopted by
Great Britain and Italy, where it
was produced under licence.

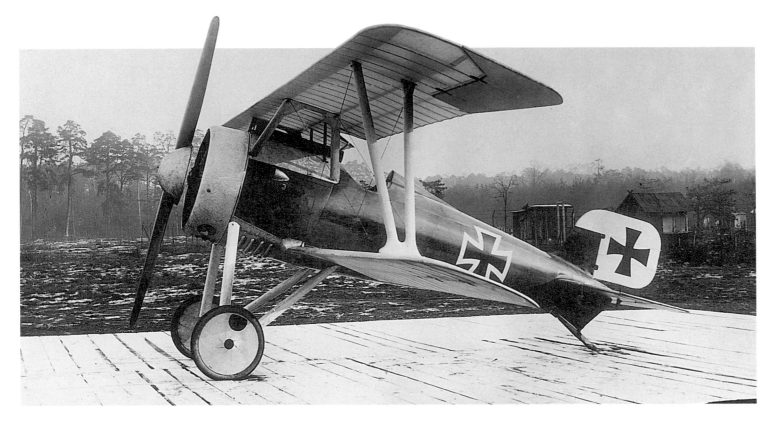

with the machine-gun dated back to a couple of years previously and that its development had been so long and complex. For example, in Great Britain in November 1912, Vickers received a contract for the development of an experimental aircraft equipped with the new weapon. The airplane, the E.F.B.1 nicknamed "Destroyer", was a two-seater with the gunner's pit placed in front of the pilot's, in order to allow unrestricted fire towards the front. The machine-gun was a German Maxim type, but its weight caused the failure of the first flight, as the airplane nose-dived at takeoff, and was written off. Experiments continued and only culminated in 1914 with the F.B.5, nicknamed "Gunbus" because of the extremely advanced position of its weapon. This aircraft may be considered the first attempt at a fighter and, in reality, from February 1915 onwards it equipped the first British squadron expressly created for this role: the No. 11 Squadron of the Royal Flying Corps, which began operations on July 25, 1915. But its use did not prove to be a great success; aiming a mobile machine-gun from an airplane in flight against another airplane was anything but simple. Moreover, the F.B.5 was not agile or fast enough to be an effective fighter.

67 top A biplane Siemens-Schuckert.

67 bottom A replica of the Breguet Br.14. The airplane, which began production in early 1917, gave a significant boost to the Allied war effort: it carried 960 lb (300 kg) of bombs and over 5500 were produced.

The main limitation was the airplane's very set-up. In those early years of the war, stability of flight and observation capabilities were considered the main characteristics of an aircraft, precisely in view of the specific tasks required of it. This was taken into consideration in the training of the pilots, who only flew for a few hours before being qualified and sent to fight. The standard aircraft, therefore, was a two-seater biplane with a pusher propeller (i.e. with a rear engine), and relatively low performance. In the case of airplanes with a front engine, in which the machine-gunner sat behind the pilot, the range of fire was severely limited by the fuselage and the tail and, even more seriously, made defence from head-on attacks impossible. The ideal configuration seemed to be the opposite: a one-seater airplane with a tractor propeller, whose reduced size and weight could provide decidedly superior performance in terms of speed and handling. Thanks to the front-mounted fixed machine-gun, aiming was more effective and intuitive, since the pilot attacked by orienting the entire airplane towards the enemy.

In theory, it seemed the ideal solution, but in practice serious problems immediately emerged: how could a machine-gun fire through the propeller disc without breaking the propellers or causing other serious damage?

The first answer was a compromise: installing the weapon on the upper wing of the airplane, by means of a support which allowed a line of fire passing over the propeller. But this solution also had disadvantages, in that it was difficult to aim and control the weapon, especially when it had to be reloaded or unblocked. An example of this was the terrible experience of British pilot Captain Lewis A. Strange, the commander of No. 6 Squadron of the Royal Flying Corps. On May 10, 1915 Strange, who was flying in a Martinsyde S.1 scout, started to pursue an Aviatik B.II which was observing the British positions. When it was

The machine gun

Among the weapons used on airplanes, the machine gun had a fundamental role.

All the countries at war developed original types, almost always derived from weapons used by ground troops, but adapted technical and construction features for use on board an airplane.

Hotchkiss, Lewis, Spandau, Schwarzlose, Revelli, and Vickers were the most recurrent names, synonyms of military efficiency and arbiters of victory or defeat.

The Hotchkiss was used by the French in the early years of the war on board the Voisins and Farmans. It was an 8-mm calibre weapon, with metal magazines containing 25 rounds or feed belts held in a drum. The Lewis, which was invented by American Colonel Isaac Newton Lewis and built in Belgium, became one of the Allies' standard weapons. With a 0.303-inch calibre, it was lightweight, fed by magazines containing 97 rounds, and had a firing rate of 850 rounds per minute. The latest versions

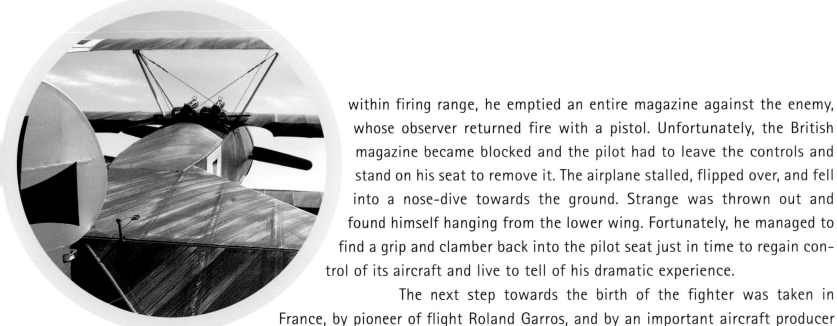

within firing range, he emptied an entire magazine against the enemy, whose observer returned fire with a pistol. Unfortunately, the British magazine became blocked and the pilot had to leave the controls and stand on his seat to remove it. The airplane stalled, flipped over, and fell into a nose-dive towards the ground. Strange was thrown out and found himself hanging from the lower wing. Fortunately, he managed to find a grip and clamber back into the pilot seat just in time to regain control of its aircraft and live to tell of his dramatic experience.

The next step towards the birth of the fighter was taken in France, by pioneer of flight Roland Garros, and by an important aircraft producer Morane-Saulnier. In early 1915, Garros examined the firing problem with Raymond Saulnier, the designer of the monoplane in which he flew, and both reached the conclusion that a simple device could provide the solution: steel triangular plates fixed to the propeller blades at the height of the line of fire and oriented so as to deflect forwards any bullets which hit them. Roland Garros tested the system for the first time on April 1, 1915, and recorded an immediate success by shooting down a foreign scout. Exploiting the advantage of his new weapon, in the first three weeks of the month, the French pilot managed to shoot down another four adversaries. The French equipped a number of airplanes with the device and also gave some to the British RFC.

The "deflecting plate" system made the Morane-Saulnier L the first real "fighter" in the history of flight, and turned Roland Garros into the first "ace" of military aviation, but this was still an imperfect and rudimentary mechanism, not without its setbacks, above all for the engine, whose mechanical components were under excessive stress from deflected bullets. The final solution was that of fitting the machine-gun with a mechanical interrupter switch connected to the propeller shaft, which prevented the gun firing when there was a propeller blade in the line of fire. The device had been tested by Morane-Saulnier since before the outbreak of war, but experiments had been unsuccessful and had been abandoned. Similar studies

were also fitted with a round counter and electric heating for high altitudes. The Spandau, which derived its name from the town where it was built, was the archetypal machine-gun of German airplanes. With a 7.62-mm calibre it could fire 550 rounds per minute and, once equipped with a synchronization device, became the main factor in German supremacy.

The 8-mm Schwarzlose was the standard gun on Austrian airplanes, while the 6.5-mm Revelli equipped the majority of Italian scouts.

The 0.303-inch Vickers, lastly, was the first to be fitted with a Costantinesco-type hydraulic synchronizer, in mid-1917. This ensured a high degree of reliability and efficiency.

68 top A replica of the Avro 504.

69 top A replica of a Fokker Dr.1.

The weaponry of some First World War aircraft:
68 bottom left 7.7-mm Lewis mounted on the upper wing of a Nieuport fighter,
68 bottom right The traversable gun (again 7.7-mm)
69 bottom left An Aviatik scout and a 12.7-mm machine-gun mounted on a German Gotha G.V. bomber.
69 bottom right The weapon of a Caproni.

70 top The British RAF S.E.5a fighter.

70 bottom The S.V.A.5 production line in the Ansaldo factory in Genoa.

had been made in Russia, above all by Captain Victor Poplavko, and in Great Britain; in 1913 Franz Schneider had gone so far as to patent a similar mechanism, although the idea had never been put into practice. But it was the Germans who took up the idea and perfected it and, ironically, it was precisely Garros who gave them the help they needed.

On April 19, 1915, the French pilot (who would be killed in action on October 5, 1918) was forced to make an emergency landing behind enemy lines. Before being captured, he tried to set fire to his airplane to protect its secret, but the Germans managed to recover the Morane-Saulnier and immediately passed it on to Fokker for examination. The idea was to copy the device and adopt it on Anthony Fokker's new monoplane. But the great Dutch designer went further: in only 48 hours he built an effective synchronization device and installed a perfectly functioning synchronized machine gun on one of his M5K monoplanes.

Engines and construction techniques

Airplane engines and construction techniques underwent interesting developments during the war.

In engine development in 1914, France and Germany were at the forefront. At the outbreak of hostilities, in fact, Great Britain did not have a nationally produced airplane engine worthy of consideration, and was forced to equip its airplanes with French products imported or built under licence. France and Germany, meanwhile, were focusing on two completely different sectors.

After the appearance of the rotary engine, France had developed this technology to heights of extreme efficiency. Compact, light, and with a higher weight-power ratio than all the other engines of the period, the rotary engine was ideal for fast, lightweight airplanes.

It was widely used by the Allies, and the British company Sopwith equipped its planes with it longer than anyone else, up until 1918. The rotary engine was also developed in Germany, where the most widely used, the Oberursel, was simply a copy of the French Le Rhône. The choice was, however, temporary and dictated in 1915 by the need to beat the enemy: it was no coincidence that the Fokker monoplane was fitted with a rotary engine. Such engines, however, always had one great limitation: the power delivered never exceeded 200 hp. Moreover, in the more powerful double-row engines, cooling problems were almost insurmountable.

Germany, meanwhile, gave industrial priority to the development of liquid-cooled fixed engines, with cylinders in line. A high level of technology was achieved, and the products of companies such as Mercedes, Benz, and Austro-Daimler were also of excellent quality. Their engines were certainly heavier than rotary models, but also stronger and more reliable and, above all, able to deliver significantly more power.

Great Britain started engine production slightly later, but immediately earned a reputation for the exceptional quality of its products. In 1915 Henry Royce presented his first V-12, called the Eagle, which was the first in a series of successful airplane engines. These would continue to be used up until the Second World War, when they would be replaced only with the advent of the jet.

In this period, the new technologies and the increasingly wide use of metals and lightweight alloys led to even more reliable versions. An important development was marked by the Hispano-Suiza V-8. Thanks to a cylinder block in aluminium with steel liners, it boasted a weight-power ratio previously unheard of. From the initial 140 hp of the prototype, the engine performance rose to 200 hp, and finally reached 300 hp. This amount of power was exceeded by the latest wartime versions from Rolls-Royce, and by the 400 hp delivered by the V-12 Liberty, designed in 1917 in the United States by the Packard Motor Company, which was one of the most powerful engines in the war.

Increased engine power influenced aircraft design and construction techniques. Traditional materials—wood for the framework and canvas for the covering—were first replaced by a partial or total covering in plywood, then by monocoque structures, and finally by metal tubing covered in canvas and partially in aluminium. The Germans in 1915 made the world's first entirely metal airplane. This was the Junkers J.1, in which the steel tubing structure was covered with sheets of duralumin. This aircraft served as the basis for the development of a two seater, the CL.I, which appeared in the last months of the conflict and was among the best airplanes of the war.

Monoplanes, however, were clearly in the minority, and after the years of wartime experience, the biplanes emerged as the most popular form. The archetypal fighter plane, which would remain unchanged until the 1930s, was a biplane with a tractor propeller, an open cockpit, fixed front undercarriage and front-mounted synchronized machine-guns. Naturally, as the years passed, engine power and performance increased, but in 1918 the average fighter plane was already equipped with an engine of around 220 hp, could reach speeds of over 125 mph (200 km/h) and had an operating altitude

71 top The first airplane engine designed and built by Fiat in 1908: the SA8/75 provided power of 50 hp.

of around 19,200 ft (6000 meters).

The four years of war gave a decisive boost to the development of aviation. The incessant contest to overcome the enemy had fully engaged Europe's industrial resources. From a few hundred airplanes present at the front in the two rival camps at the outbreak of hostilities, by Armistice day the number of combat aircraft in service had risen to almost 13,000.

Between 1914 and 1918, the countries involved in the conflict produced a total of 177,000 planes of all types, almost 18 times more aircraft than were produced in the whole world between 1903 and 1914. In Great Britain alone, 55,000 were built by an industry that provided jobs for 350,000 men and women.

Italy, the other pioneer in this field, began to make intensive use of its "giants of the air" designed by Caproni straight after its entry into the war, performing the first raid on August 20, 1915. The airplanes of the Ca.3 series were the most widespread and widely used by the Corpo Aeronautico Militare (Military Aeronautical Corps), and their missions became increasingly important and difficult, continuing without interruption for the entire duration of the war. In February 1916 the first long-distance raid was performed, with a bombing attack against Lubiana, and in the same year there was a total of 540 missions. In 1917, the large three-engined aircraft were also used in tactical roles, such as support for ground troops, particularly during the various battles of the Isonzo.

The Germans, who for the first two years of the war had performed strategic bombing with large Zeppelin airships, also converted to the airplane, first with the twin-engined AEGs, Gothas, and Friedrichshafens, and then with the giant Zeppelin Staakens. The Gothas and the Friedrichshafen, in particular, proved themselves to be top

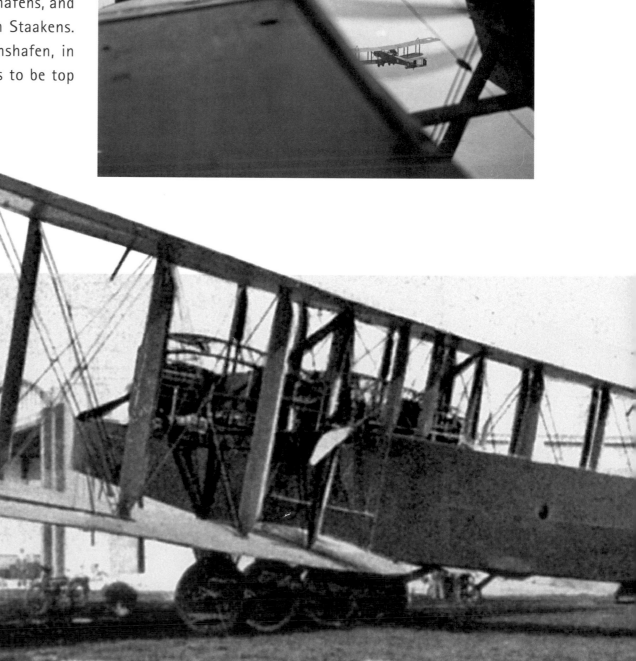

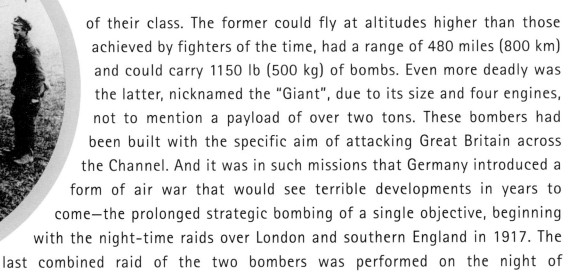

of their class. The former could fly at altitudes higher than those achieved by fighters of the time, had a range of 480 miles (800 km) and could carry 1150 lb (500 kg) of bombs. Even more deadly was the latter, nicknamed the "Giant", due to its size and four engines, not to mention a payload of over two tons. These bombers had been built with the specific aim of attacking Great Britain across the Channel. And it was in such missions that Germany introduced a form of air war that would see terrible developments in years to come—the prolonged strategic bombing of a single objective, beginning with the night-time raids over London and southern England in 1917. The last combined raid of the two bombers was performed on the night of October19, 1918.

It was precisely the continuous threat of German airships which drove Great Britain to build heavy bombers. In 1914, the Zeppelins were extremely difficult to intercept, and it was decided that the best strategic move was to destroy their bases. While the light bombers already in service were used for this purpose, work started on a series of Handley Page twin-engined aircraft—ordered and designed with the single aim of striking Germany—to be used for night-bombing. The initial 0/100 version came into service in November 1916 and in March of the following year the bombing missions started-ed. The increasingly devastating raids into German territory began in February 1918, and continued until the end of the war.

Unlike fighters, whose growth was particularly fast, and conditioned by that of the enemy, the sector of bombers was fairly static during the war years. The general approach was to develop and upgrade existing aircraft which had given good results in the field, rather than to design new machines.

The last years of the conflict saw the offensive capabilities of bombers increase at an amazing rate: from the initial small bombs of a few pounds in 1914, the airplanes ended up carrying and

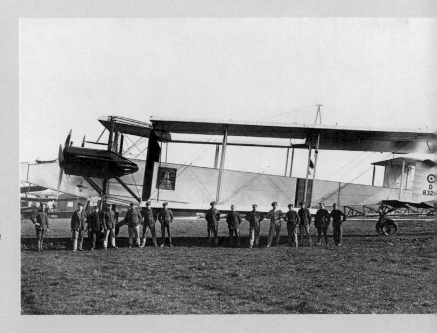

74 top and 75 top In spring 1917, the British twin-engined Handley Page 0/400 entered service on the Western Front (74, top: the machine-gunner pit), replacing the previous 0/100 model (75, its bomb load) which had been transferred to night-time missions. Seven squadrons of the Royal Flying Corps were equipped with this bomber, which was used up until 1920.

74-75 and 75 bottom right The English Handley Page V/1500 bomber had the particular feature of foldable wings, allowing it to be kept in normal-sized hangars.

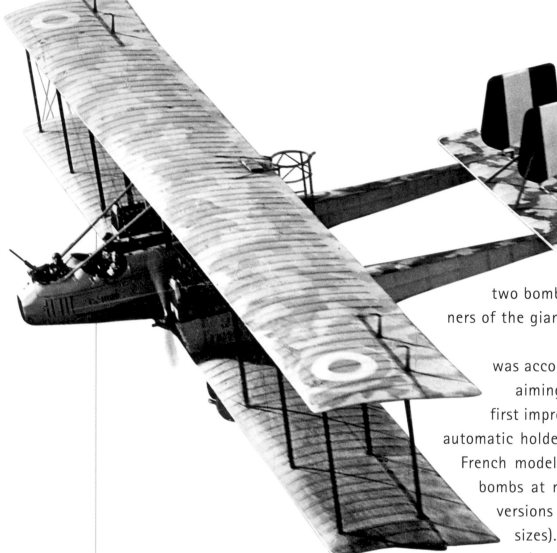

dropping high-potential incendiary and fragmentation bombs whose weight varied between 230 lb (100 kg) and 2300 lb (1000 kg). The Handley Page V/1500 of 1918 was able to carry two bombs of 3443 lb (1497 kg) each, real forerunners of the giant bombs of the Second World War.

Naturally, the development of the aircraft was accompanied by a rapid evolution in bombs and aiming, transport, and release devices. From the first improvized holders under the wings or fuselage, automatic holders were gradually introduced (such as the French model produced by Michelin, which could drop bombs at regular and predefined intervals. The later versions were able to hold and manage bombs of all sizes). When the capacity of the airplanes had become suffcent to hold bombs inside the fuselage, racks able to hold a large number of bombs in the position considered most suitable for dropping were adopted.

The aiming systems—no less important than the bombs—were transformed from primitive clockwork mechanisms (the pilot or navigator first had to calculate the speed compared to the ground and the attack angle using rudimental methods) to the telescopic sights used in the last two years of the war.

76 top In October 1918, units began to receive the new Ca.5 series Caproni with a greater payload, and in which the 150 hp Isotta Fraschini engines had been replaced by the more powerful 300 hp Fiat A.12s.

76 bottom One of the first great heavy German bombers was the Siemens-Schuckert R.I, a three-engined aircraft with a wingspan of over 90 ft (28 meters): in this highly original design, the three engines were enclosed within the fuselage and drove two propellers mounted between the wings.

THE BEGINNINGS OF NAVAL AVIATION

Ever since its early pioneer age, the airplane had displayed its potential in the naval field, arousing great interest. This interest grew with the outbreak of war, since battles were also fought on the sea. Seaplanes soon became commonly used in the navies of the major players in the conflict, almost always with reconnaissance tasks. As operational procedures and combat techniques developed, a similar course to land-based aviation was taken, and reconnaissance aircraft began to be flanked by fighters, or rather "sea-fighters". Especially in the Adriatic, the Italians and Austrians made great use of the specialty, in a direct and bloody confrontation.

The role of naval reconnaissance, however, was conditioned by a series of factors, fundamentally linked to the characteristics of the airplanes of the period, such as poor autonomy and reduced performance caused by the large floats. This, together with the fact that the aircraft operated from naval bases, made them unsuitable for following the movements of the fleet in open sea. Ideally, airplanes would be stationed directly on the decks of the larger ships, as advance "eyes" in navigation or combat. It was precisely this need that led to the concept, albeit in a rudimentary form, of the aircraft carrier, a category which would undergo extensive development in subsequent decades and would prove to be fundamental in the strategies of the Second World War.

The first experiments in the naval use of the airplane were performed by Eugene Ely in his Curtiss biplane between 1910 and 1911 on board the ships of the US Navy. The first deck landing in history took place on January 18, 1911 on the battleship *Pennsylvania*. It had been preceded two months earlier, on November 14, 1910, by the first takeoff from the deck of the light cruiser *Birmingham*, off Hampton Roads, in Virginia. The ship had been equipped with a long wooden platform at the bows, inclined 5° downwards to facilitate takeoff which, albeit with difficulty, was successful.

But a definitive solution to the problem was still a long way off. The military technicians of the time had concluded that Ely's experiments could not be reproduced on a ship during navigation. The United States,

77 bottom On July 6, 1918, the seaplane of German ace Karl Christiansen attacked the British C25 submarine in the North Sea.

untouched by the first signs of the war which tormented Europe, did not give particular priority to developing this specialty. In Great Britain, it was a different story; it was the only European combatant to develop the idea of marine aviation systematically and with conviction, thus laying the foundations for the Royal Navy's important future role in this sector.

The many experiments performed on ships fitted with special platforms led to an initial conclusion: take-off was technically possible, albeit with important restrictions on the weight of the airplanes; landing, meanwhile, was practically impossible. The Royal Naval Air Service temporarily abandoned the idea of using land-based aircraft and thought it best to further exploit seaplane using special support ships. These took on board a small number of seaplanes which could be placed in the water with a crane. On completion of the mission they would land on the sea beside the ship and be taken back on board.

The first of these ships was the old converted cruiser Hermes, which was sunk by the Germans in November 1914. Another three ships were soon converted: the Engadine, the Riviera and the Empress, originally ferries used in cross-Channel services. Their baptism of fire was not long coming; it was from these ships on Christmas Day, 1914, that raids were performed against the Zeppelin bases in Cuxhaven and Wilhelmshaven. This mission was the first in which aircraft on board ships were used in an offensive role, and even if it was not a success in terms of damage inflicted on the enemy, it proved the practicality of this type of operation, which became increasingly popular.

The British Royal Navy fitted out other ships of this type: in 1915 the Ben-My-Chree entered service along with the Ark Royal (the second ship to bear this illustrious name in naval history, first given to a galleon in the sixteenth century which had fought against the Spanish Armada. It would be used again for another aircraft carrier in the Second World War). The former, also a converted ferry, was the ship from which, on August 12, 1915, C. H. K. Edmonds became the first pilot to sink a ship with a torpedo (in this case a Turkish merchant ship).

The battle of Jutland, on May 31—June 1, 1916, saw the Engadine operate alongside English cruisers. When Admiral David Beatty received the first reports of the enemy fleet, he did not hesitate to launch a

79 top Seaplanes of various types were widely used in the Regia Marina (Italian Royal Navy) air service. Italy did not have any aircraft carriers, but seaplanes were loaded onto a specially equipped ship or attached off-board to a support ship, as in the photo (the ship is the Europa).

reconnaissance aircraft in order to have a more precise picture of the situation. While in difficulty due to the low clouds, the airplane, piloted by F. J. Rutland, encountered four enemy light cruisers, which opened fire on him. The observation mission did not determine the outcome of the battle, but in his report Admiral Beatty highlighted the great value of aerial reconnaissance in circumstances of this kind.

Other navies used similar ships, in particular Russia, which stationed them with the Black Sea fleet, and deployed them aggressively in the campaign to block the Bosphorus. The most successful raid was that of February 6, 1916, when nine M-9 seaplanes from the ships *Emperor Aleksandr I* and *Emperor Nikolai I* attacked the port of Zonguidak and sank the Turkish ship *Jamingard*, in addition to causing other damage.

But the Royal Navy remained the armed force which most extended the field of operations of seaplanes. Another task performed successfully by the Royal Naval Air Service was fighting German submarines, the deadly U-Boats that revealed their tremendous effectiveness during the First World War.

In these reconnaissance missions both airplanes and non-rigid airships were used; even though the latter were slower, they could transport the heavy radio transmission apparatus that could not be carried on aircraft. These operations had a double objec-

78-79 The Iron, as the Argus aircraft carrier was nicknamed, started life as an Italian liner, the Conte Rosso, until being transformed into the first British ship with a continuous deck, and entered service in October 1918. It was equipped with an entire squadron of Sopwith Cuckoo torpedo-bombers.

tive: to discover the U-Boots; and to force them to stay underwater as long as possible, making them more vulnerable to attack when they surfaced to recharge their batteries.

Techniques became increasingly refined and anti-submarine operations intensified as the war progressed. On May 20, 1917 the first submarine was sunk, and another two followed in July and August.

It was the need to combat the serious threat of airships, that led to the next development. It was clear that the seaplanes in service at the time, heavy and weighed down by their floats, did not have the necessary performance, especially at altitude, to intercept the Zeppelins and deprive the German fleet of its most effective means of reconnaissance. It was necessary to go back to the idea of using land-based aircraft on wheels taking off from the decks of the largest ships and to solve the problems of landing.

In terms of aircraft, the solution was found in the Sopwith Pup, a small but effective biplane which had all the characteristics required: high climbing speed and good performance at altitude, and which moreover required extremely limited space for take-off: against a wind of 20 knots it only needed 20 ft (6 meters) to take off from the deck. For the return flight, there were only two alternatives: landing on the coast or, if that was not possible, landing on the sea. The Sopwiths were equipped with special inflatable floats which allowed them to stay afloat until they were picked up by the ship. Once these operational procedures had been defined, take-off platforms were installed on light cruisers. The solution was found to be effective, although there was a great risk of losing the airplane and the pilot.

On August 21, 1917 a Sopwith Pup flown by Lieutenant B. A. Smart took off from one of these ships,

the *Yarmouth*, which was escorting a fleet of mine-layers during the Battle of Heligoland Bight. Having climbed to 4600 ft (2000 meters), Smart attacked a Zeppelin L23 from above and managed to shoot it down. He then landed the airplane on the sea and was successfully recovered by the *Prince*.

Experience and success led the Royal Navy to implement a more advanced approach when it decided to change the design of the *Furious*, originally built as a light cruiser. The bow gun turret was eliminated and in its place a 160 x 35 ft (70 x 15 meter) flight deck was installed with a crane, connected by a passageway to a hangar below which could hold four seaplanes and six normal airplanes.

81 top Small-caliber bombs attached to the fuselage of an Italian Navy FBA torpedo-bomber.

81 bottom One of the first Short seaplanes in service with the Fleet Air Arm, the type 184. This became the most famous aircraft produced by the British company for the next two decades (over 900 were built).

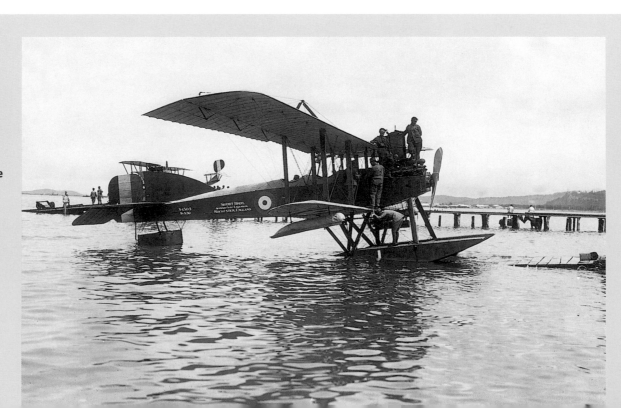

The commander of the flight unit on the *Furious*, E. H. Dunning, thought he had also found a solution for landing. He maintained that, if the ship sailed at 21 knots with a wind of 19 knots, the combined speeds would cancel the landing speed of the Sopwith Pup, which was 40 knots.

The demonstration of how to land on a flight deck took place on August 2, 1917. Dunning flew alongside the ship and, as soon as he turned down the engine, he basically had a relative speed of zero with respect to the flight deck. The airplane was literally dragged down by a group of sailors, who hooked on to it using cables. The operation was a complete success, but had a dramatic epilogue. Five days later, Dunning asked the crew not to intervene, and to let him try and land on his own. Something went wrong and the engine suddenly jammed; the airplane flipped on to its side, fell into the sea, and the pilot drowned. This accident brought experiments to an end.

But there were further attempts to find a solution, by once more modifying the *Furious*. The rear turret was removed and in its place a second 200 ft (87 meter) landing deck was installed behind the funnel. At the same time the hangars were equipped with lifts connecting them to the decks. The landing deck was fitted with a braking system composed of tensed elastic cables that the airplane had to hook on to. However, none of these changes was successful, since they worked when the ship was still, but not during navigation. The main problem was the funnel, which not only blocked the head-on wind, creating an area of calm unsuitable for landing aircraft, but generated an area of strong turbulence with its exhaust, having an even stronger effect on the manouvre.

After these attempts any idea of landing on the Furious was abandoned, and only the take-off deck

was used. On July 19, 1918 it served as the base for an important operation against the Zeppelins: six Sopwith Camels attacked the airship base of Tondern, destroying two airships, and putting the facilities out of use until the end of the war. One of the pilots on this mission was the same lieutenant Smart who had shot down the L23 airship a year previously. This time, he landed on the sea near the fleet and was successfully picked up together with his airplane. Of the other pilots, one had a similar experience, and another three landed in Denmark. One failed to find his way back, and was lost at sea.

But the experience with the Furious was ultimately useful, and in the end yielded results. In the fall of 1918, the Navy launched its first real aircraft carrier, the Argus, which marked the beginning of a new phase in the evolution of naval aviation. Mindful of previous problems, the engine exhaust gas was channelled towards the stern, the small bridge was lowered and the ship could thus be equipped with a large deck free of obstacles for take-off and landing, 386 x 49 ft (168 x 21 meters).

The first successful deck landing took place in October 1918, and the new procedures were officially adopted. Admiral Beatty immediately planned a daring attack against the German fleet at anchor in port using the new Sopwith Cuckoo torpedo-bombers. The Admiralty did not approve the mission, but the seed for a new naval strategy had been sown. On the night of November 11, 1940, 22 years later, the English fleet would implement a similar plan against the Italian fleet at Taranto, marking a turning point in the war in the Mediterranean.

82 bottom The deck landing of Commander Dunning's Sopwith Pup on the Furious: this photo would become part of aviation history, as it documented the first experiment of this kind on a warship (August 2, 1917).

83 top A replica of the aircraft.

83 bottom The Italian Navy performed initial tests launching a torpedo from a three-engined Caproni Ca.3, but experiments were not followed up.

of March, showed their exceptional characteristics to the full in the battle of Verdun. From that moment the balance returned once more in favor of the Allies, also thanks to the appearance of another exceptional biplane, the Spad S.VII, the best aircraft of its time.

However, the German response was not slow in coming, and arrived on two fronts. The first was technical, with the production of fighters such as the Albatroses and the D-series Halberstadts; the second organizational, with a complete restructuring of the combat units, which took place in the fall of 1916. The results were felt immediately, and for the second time the arrival of winter coincided with German supremacy in the air. Apart from the intrinsic superiority of the German airplanes, the most important factor was the deadly firepower of the two front-mounted synchronized machine-guns, which had become a standard weapon, able to fire a thousand rounds without reloading. To put themselves once more on an even footing, the Allies had to wait for spring–summer 1917, with the appearance of fighters such as the British Sopwith Camel and Triplane, the Royal Aircraft Factory S.E.5 and Bristol Fighter, and the French Spad S.XIII.

From that period until the end of the war, however, control of the situation remained in Allied hands. Even though the Germans made a last effort to step up production near the end of the war, introducing impressive machines such as the Fokker D.VIIs and D.VIIIs, the Roland D.Vis, and the Pfalz D.XIIs, any air superiority they achieved was limited and temporary. The disadvantage was no longer one of quality, but quantity: in the spring and summer 1918, with a force of around 2390 combat airplanes, the German air force found itself facing no fewer than 10,000 Allied planes. It would only be a matter of time before the inevitable Allied victory.

86 Replicas of the Fokker
Dr.1.

87 One of the most widely
used fighter planes of the
First World War: a Nieuport 11
Bébé, here in service with the
Italian Air Force.

Ni 2140

strongly felt the need for reconstruction and to follow the path of economic and social progress. In a significant reversal of previous trends, the discovery and use of the airplane as a means of transport became the new driving force behind aeronautical development.

This climate of growing interest, fuelled by the brutal laws of competition, gave the industry a real boost, and replaced the needs of war as a driving force for growth. At the same time, intense sporting activity, which reawakened the adventurous spirit and enthusiasm of the pioneer years, encouraged research and experimentation in the field of materials, structures, and engines.

This was a golden age for the airplane—the age of heroic solo crossings, of the exploration of far-off lands in search of new destinations for civil airlines, of

90 top Another English fighter of the 1920s, the Hawker Hart biplane.

90 bottom 1927 was the year of the Atlantic. The most famous exploit was the solo crossing by Charles Lindbergh (left). In addition to his great personal qualities, he could also count on his extremely reliable Ryan Spirit of St Louis (right).

91 top left The Douglas seaplane. In March 1924, four of these airplanes from the US Army Air Service flew round the world in legs: the total flight time was over 365 hours.

91 top right The prow of the Vickers Victoria.

91 bottom During the revolution in Afghanistan in late-1928, the twin-engined English Vickers Victorias transported troops to the area, and were also used for the evacuation of European civilians.

heated competition, records, and challenges involving entire nations and industrial sectors for the conquest of records which displayed not only technological superiority, but prestige in the international arena. The many exploits of the period included the unforgettable flights of Jean Mermoz, Henri Guillaumet, and Antoine de Saint-Exupéry over unexplored territories in South America where the Aéropostale wanted to extend its network of connections, and the solo flight of Charles Lindbergh, who paved the way for North Atlantic crossings between America and Europe.

   While all of these feats had immediate consequences, they also represented the surmounting of technical and technological problems, and became small but important milestones marking the progress of machines and engines. Among the many competitions, the Schneider Cup in Europe and the National Air Races in the United States gave the most important contribution to this progress.

THE EVOLUTION OF ENGINES

The most significant evolution was in the field of engines. The rotary engine disappeared for good, as the challenge of speed and the search for ever greater power demanded liquid-cooled "fixed" engines with V-cylinders. All the most advanced nations in the aeronautical field who competed for conquest of the Schneider Cup, followed this technological trend: France adopted the later versions of the famous Hispano-Suiza "V-8" for the competitions; Great Britain improved and perfected the formidable family of Rolls-Royce engines that in following years would represent the utmost expression of aeronautical piston

92 top A typical training aircraft of the early 1930s, the Avro Tutor.

92 bottom left The 12-cylinder Hispano-Suiza in-line engine, which equipped another Britishmulti-purpose aircraft,the Fairey Fox biplane.

92 bottom right Airplane engines were not particularly successful. In the round picture: an example of a Clerget radial engine developed in 1929.

engines; Italy, albeit experimentally, produced the Fiat A.S.6, which allowed Francesco Agello to conquer the world speed record for seaplanes in his Macchi M.C.72; and the United States, after the Liberty's debut in the war, developed the more sophisticated and powerful Curtiss engines, the "heart" of their Navy and Army racers.

It was, in fact, North American industry of the 1920s that ensured the widespread

93 top Rolls-Royce technicians fine-tuning one of their most successful engines, the R-type, which equipped the winner of the Schneider Cup in 1931.

93 bottom The Boeing F4B-2 biplane of the US Navy.

use and commercial success of radial engines, whose reliability and relative simplicity made them an extremely valid alternative to traditional models.

Thanks to the products of companies such as Wright and Pratt & Whitney, this started an uninterrupted evolutionary line which would characterize the future development of military aviation around the world, not only in America.

94 top The Italian Macchi M.C.72 racing seaplane (in the photo above with its predecessor, the M.39, both conserved at the Museum in Vigna di Valle), set the world seaplane record in 1934.

94 bottom The Schneider Cup was perogative of the English, with the Supermarine S.6B (bottom), fitted with the prestigious Rolls-Royce R. engine.

THE BIRTH OF THE MONOPLANE

Sporting competitions gave a major boost to the development of components and structures. Examples included propellers, built in metal and fitted with increasingly efficient mechanisms for variable pitch during flight; and landing gear, which saw a change from fixed to retractable devices due to the need for increased aerodynamic performance. However, the most significant development was without doubt the affirmation of the monoplane formula over the biplane. This was made possible only by research into more sophisticated construction techniques, such as the introduction of metal structures and coverings, made necessary by contests such as the Schneider. The most famous result was triggered by the English participation in the Trophy with the Supermarine seaplane, laying the foundations for the creation of the Spitfire, one of the best fighters of the Second World War.

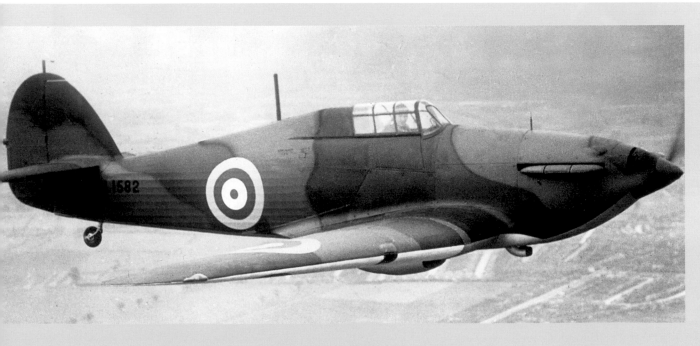

95 Thanks to the development of military air forces all over the world, construction techniques also improved. The transition to monoplanes was already underway by the mid-1930s. An American assault aircraft, the Curtiss A-12 Shrike (top). The British Hawker Hurricane fighter (bottom).

There were similar examples in the United States: the Republic P-47 Thunderbolt, one of the best and most widely used combat aircraft of the war, and the fighter which was built in the largest numbers, derived from a monoplane, the Seversky P-35. This was a military prototype that had been modified into a civil version, and won the Bendix Cup in 1938, piloted by the famous aviatrix Jacqueline Cochran.

The contribution of sporting competition to the evolution of the airplane was enormous, albeit a contribution that took some time to filter through to the military field. The situation began to change with the first signs of a new world war. The First World War had taught everyone the importance of superiority in the air. And to achieve this, it was necessary to have the best machines. Strategists and politicians were once more interested in the aircraft, and the race for rearmament gained speed, as all the progress and conquests of the years of enthusiasm was immediately absorbed and assimilated by military production. The nations prepared for the conflict, and above all worked on developing two basic types of airplanes: fighters and bombers.

Fighters had to be fast and manouvrable, and technological advances had also radically changed their appearance. Monoplanes built entirely in metal came onto the scene towards the mid-1930s, and in Europe, Great Britain, and Germany—the countries most directly involved in the imminent conflict—led the way. The RAF brought the Hawker Hurricane and the Supermarine Spitfire into service. The former, which was still a transition machine,

98 Replica of one of the last fighter biplanes used by the US Army Air Service, the Boeing P.12 of 1925.

The aces in Spain

As in all modern wars, the Spanish conflict also had its aces. The Regia Aeronautica (Italian Royal Air Force) and the Luftwaffe sided with the Nationalists; the Soviet air force with the Republicans. These units, however, did not contain only Spanish and Russian pilots. French, Soviet, American, and Yugoslavian aviators fought to the end. There follows a list of the main aces on both sides and the number of victories they achieved in air combat.

REPUBLICANS
M. Zarauza Claver **23**
L. Morquillas Rubio **21**
M. Aguirre Lopez **11**
A. Garcia de la Calle **11**
J. Maria Bravo Fernandez **10**
J. Comas Borrás **10**
E. Ramirez Bravo **10**
M. Zambudio Martine **10**
A. Arias **9**

NATIONALISTS
J. Garcia-Morato y Castano **40**
J. Salvador Diaz-Benjumea **24**

M. Vasquez Sagastizábal **21**
A. Garcia López **17**
A. Salas Larrázabal **16**
M. Guerrero Garcia **13**
M. Garcia Pardo **12**
C. Bayo Alessandri **10**
J. Velasco Fernández Nespral **11**

RUSSIANS
A. Stepanovich Osipenko **51**
L. Levovich Shestakov **39**
S. Ivanovich Gritsevets **37**
I. Alexeevich Lakeev **32**
I. Yevgrafovich Fedorov **23**
P. Vasilievich Rychagov **20**

GERMANS
W. Moelders **14**
W. Schellmann **12**
H. Harder **11**
P. Boddem **10**
O. Bertram **9**

ITALIANS
B. di Montegnacco **14**
G. Presel **13**
A. Mantelli **9**
G. Nobili **9**
A. Zotti **9**
G. Cenni **7**
A. François **5**
G. Aurili **5**
G. Baschirotto **5**
G. Caselli **5**

had two merits: it had brilliantly displayed the potential of the new Rolls-Royce Merlin engine, and had proved in battle the deadly effectiveness of its machine-guns. These were eight in number, installed far from the propeller in the wings, and could provide a constant flow of bullets towards the adversary. The Spitfire, with its high speed and excellent manouvrability, significantly improved on the performance of the Hurricane. The German reply was the Messerschmitt Bf.109, an airplane which was tested in combat during the Spanish Civil War. It had the smallest body compatible with the most powerful German engine of the time, the V-12 Daimler-Benz and, with its excellent flight characteristics proved to be a deadly machine. The evolution of the conflict led to the direct technological confrontation between the Spitfire and the Bf.109. In a continual race of one-upmanship, increasingly powerful versions of each were produced, in order to combat the enemy's temporary superiority.

In the early 1930s other nations also developed excellent fighters, while not technologically comparable to English and German planes, that marked the beginning of change. A case in point was Poland, with its high-wing PZL P.11, the first of a long series, which displayed its brilliant qualities in various speed competitions. The Soviet Union, meanwhile, brought out the stumpy yet deadly Polikarpov I-16 monoplane, also tested in combat conditions during the Spanish Civil War. In Asia, Japan created an impressive air force practically from nothing and produced its first modern fighters, such as the Mitsubishi A5M and the Nakajima Ki-27.

Bombers also witnessed rapid evolution, incorporating all the military theories expounded during the First World War, from those of the Italian Giulio Dohuet to the American William Mitchell, the real

99 top Curtiss developed a family of powerful V engines which were adopted for the first time on the R3C-2 seaplanes used to compete for the Schneider Cup.

99 bottom A P-6E of the US Army 17th Pursuit Squadron in 1932–33. This was the last representative of the great family of Hawk fighter biplanes produced by Curtiss.

Apart from providing an opportunity for experimentation in the field, the conflict also served as a testing ground for new operational tactics for fighters and bombers that would be used in the Second World War.

ITALY

After the end of the First World War, the Italian air force went through a period of deep crisis, which ended only in 1923 when it was reformed as an independent armed force (March 28 marked the birth of the Regia Aeronautica). From then on, interest in the airplane revived and the industry, after four years in the doldrums, was urged to step up the rate of production. There were two main stimuli: on one hand, the need to reconstruct an air power which placed Italy among the great technologically advanced nations; and on the other, the need to participate directly in the development of commercial aviation.

The recovery took place in a climate of great enthusiasm. The Regia Aeronautica, its pilots, and aircraft became leading protagonists in all the major international competitions. The challenge to set records and achieve victories fuelled memorable exploits, which would never be repeated, such as the fight for the

106 top Before fighting in the skies over Spain, the Italian air force had been busy in the Ethiopian conflict. In the round picture: The Fiat C.R.1.

106 bottom The Fiat C.R.20.

107 bottom The IMAM Ro.37bis reconnaissance biplanes were also widely used in eastern Africa.

Schneider Cup, which continued passionately until 1931 and culminated in 1934 with the historic record of Francesco Agello and his Macchi M.C.72 racing seaplane; or Italo Balbo's cruises and transatlantic flights of 1930 and 1933, which earned international admiration; or the great endurance and distance flights made by De Pinedo and Ferrarin in 1925 and 1928.

This "golden period" undoubtedly served to fuel the development of military aviation, but marked the beginning of crisis which would have profound effects in the following years. The combat operations in which Italy took part in those years were conducted in conditions of almost total superiority (until 1927 in Libya for the reconquest of colonial territories; the Ethiopian campaign in 1935; and in 1936 the intervention in Spain, in which around 6000 men took part, along with 763 aircraft, including 418 fighters, 190 bombers, and 112 scouts-assault planes, trainers and seaplanes).

This led strategists to overestimate the real potential of the Regia Aeronautica, and fuelled their conviction that the air force was able to withstand the trials of a new world war. This error of judgment triggered off a chain reaction, whose most serious consequences were a failure to start work on new advanced projects and an excessive reliance on maintaining existing product lines which would soon prove to be obsolete. This is shown by the fact that the front-line of Regia Aeronautica fighter units were still based on biplanes or transition monoplanes, completely unable to stand comparison even with the airplanes of its closest ally, Germany.

110 top The three-engined Savoia Marchetti S.M.81. was one of the protagonists in August 1936of the first massive air lift between Spanish Morocco and southern Spain.

110 center The Fiat C.R.32, manouvrable, fast, and sufficiently well-armed, had the upper hand over the varied fleet of the Republican air force in Spain until the arrival of I-16 monoplanes. The ace Garcia-Morato achieved most of his 40 victories in the Italian biplane.

110 bottom Three-engined Caproni Ca.133s used in transport and bombing missions in Ethiopia.

SOVIET UNION

The crisis of 1917 had placed Russia outside the aeronautical world, but the situation improved drastically in 1924. The air force was reorganized and the industrial fabric completely renewed in great secret. These significant efforts brought important results, not only in terms of quantity (in 1935 the size of the Soviet air force was around 4000 aircraft), but above all in terms of quality. The best of the machines were clearly at the international forefront, such as the Polikarpov I-16 fighter and the Tupolev SB-2 bomber. These had been immortalized in the Spanish Civil War, where they helped form the backbone of the Republican Air Force. The Soviet Union did not, however, manage to go beyond this limit before the outbreak of the Second World War.

111 top and center Large numbers of Polikarpov I-15 fighter biplanes served in the Republican air force. A replica.

111 bottom The Soviet Union also provided the Republicans with the fast twin-engined bomber, the Tupolev SB-2 Katiuscia.

114 and 115 It was still many months before the United States would enter the war, but they were preparing to become the world's major military power. The nacelle of an English Bristol Beaufighter (top); a Boeing B-17 (bottom left); the Messerschmitt Bf.109 (bottom right).

The Second World War

Many historians admit that the Spanish Civil War has been underestimated, and overshadowed by the huge tempest that struck the whole world in 1939. In reality, the bloody civil war went on for over three years and was not simply a localized conflict. It was the first conflict to erupt onto a changed geopolitical stage that arose during the 1930s.

It would serve as a dress-rehearsal for the new military power, which was identified with the hegemonic ambitions of Germany and Hitler's Third Reich.The air force was the main instrument of this expansion and the Spanish Civil War, apart from its historical and political significance, marked the beginning of a new evolutionary cycle in military aviation, fuelled once more by the brutal requirements of war. The German Luftwaffe was the first to test it.

It is no coincidence that the airplane returned once more to the center of strategy, and the Spanish Civil War was an ideal testing-ground. The destruction of Guernica on April 26,1937 made history not only because of the massacre of innocent civilians, but because it put into practice mass-bombing aimed at civilian objectives to weaken the spirit of enemy populations, a policy adopted later in the Second World War.

The use of the Junkers Ju.87 Stukas demonstrated the validity of ground-attack aircraft and their cooperation with ground forces, introducing the principles of the German blitzkrieg. Meanwhile, the duels in the Spanish skies

116 top A pilot next to his C.R.32 during the Spanish Civil War.

116 center The Polikarpov I-16.

116 bottom The profile of a Henschel Hs.123 scout with Spanish nationalist insignia.

117 bottom The Morane Saulnier M. S.406.

between Messerschmitt Bf.109s and Polikarpov I-10s made it possible for the Luftwaffe to perfect combat tactics which would later be employed during the Battle of Britain. Superiority in the air became more than ever linked to the efficiency and technological progress of machines and engines.

Only five months passed between the end of the Spanish Civil War and the beginning of Second World War, but this was sufficient for Germany to transform what had been a dress-rehearsal into a deadly show of military power.

The première took place on September 1, 1939, the actors were the waves of Luftwaffe bombers and fighters, and the scene was Poland, the first victim of the blitzkrieg, Hitler's lightning war. For the next six years, the airplane became the great leading player in the immense confrontation, and aviation became the main weapon, sustaining and often superseding the potential of armies of men and fleets of ships.

Its influence, and the role it played in determining the balance of power in the field was so important that it was involved in all the turning points of the war, both in Europe and the Pacific.

As in the First World War, the incessant pursuit of supremacy of the air gave a huge boost to the development of aviation, which grew at unprecedented speed and intensity between 1939 and 1945. Technology and new materials transformed airplanes into formidable war machines with excellent performance and weaponry. Aircraft evolved continuously and there seemed to be no limit to their development.

The most important changes were the moves from propellers to turbines, and from the traditional alternative engine to the revolutionary jet engine; this change marked the end of an era covering the first 40 years in the history of the airplane.

All the main combatant countries felt the effects of this technological evolution, albeit at different times and in different ways. Victories and defeats began to be determined not only by the quantity of aircraft used in combat, but above all by their quality. In the end, the strongest countries proved to be those who had most resources, in human, productive, and industrial terms.

118 top The first Fairey Battle light bombers in flight over France in September 1939.

118 center and bottom The German twin-engined Junkers Ju.88 entered service on the outbreak of war and was one of the most versatile aircraft in the world. Over 16,000 were built.

THE WORLD SPLIT IN TWO

The conflict divided the world into two clearly opposed camps: on one side the forces of the Axis, whose main representatives were Germany, Italy, and Japan; on the other, the Allies, concentrated around Great Britain and its former colonies, the United States, and the Soviet Union. These alliances fought until the end; other countries, such as France, Belgium, and Holland were occupied early on in the conflict and much of the European war was fought on their soil. In the aeronautical field, however, winners and loses all had an important role, which contributed to the history of aviation.

GERMANY In September 1939, when Germany invaded Poland, the Luftwaffe was the most powerful air force in the world, with a front-line made up of an impressive 4840 modern, competitive airplanes. Of these, 1750 were bombers and 1200 fighters. And the German industrial system, which for some time had been running at full

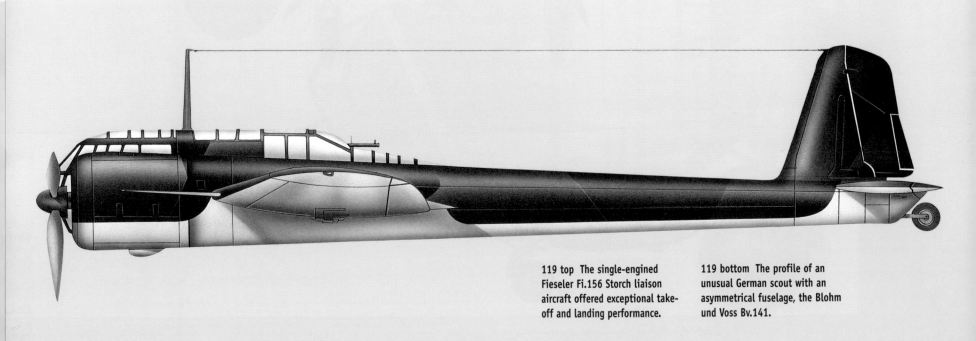

119 top The single-engined Fieseler Fi.156 Storch liaison aircraft offered exceptional take-off and landing performance.

119 bottom The profile of an unusual German scout with an asymmetrical fuselage, the Blohm und Voss Bv.141.

Junkers Ju.88-188

GERMANY

The Junkers Ju.88 was launched in 1936 and remained in production from early 1939 until 1945. Over 16,000 left the assembly lines, and were made in versions increasingly tailored to specific tasks. The twin-engined Junkers was used initially as a high-speed bomber, a night-fighter, a scout, a dive-bomber, a ground-attack aircraft, and a torpedo-bomber. The first version was the Ju.88 A-1, which

entered service in August 1939.

The night-fighter versions were the most successful, since the twin-engined Junkers were extremely effective in this role. The first major variant for night-fighter use was the C, which made its combat debut in July 1940, in Nachtjagdgeschwader 1, established on Göring's orders to deal with raids by the RAF. The Ju.88 C soon displayed great limitations, weighed down by its large and clumsy radar antennae

and heavy weaponry, which compromised manouvrability at low speeds.

The problems were overcome in version G (illustrated in the 3-view drawing), of which around 800 were produced. These appeared in spring 1944 and were extremely successful against enemy bombers. The Junkers Ju.88 family grew in 1942 with a new model, the Ju.188

(in the side view), which started to leave the assembly lines in February 1943. This was the final version of the design.

1076 were built, and over half of these remained in service as scouts until the end of hostilities. The first series, the Ju.188 E, fitted with a pair of BMW engines, became operational in October 1943. This was followed by the F series scouts, G

series bombers, and the H series, also scouts. Versions driven by Jumo engines were developed with a slight delay.

The first was the Ju.188 A, of which deliveries started in mid-1943; second was the Ju.188 D, adapted for reconnaissance tasks. The Ju.188 served as the basis for the final variant, the Ju.388, which appeared in late 1943 and of which only a few dozen were built.

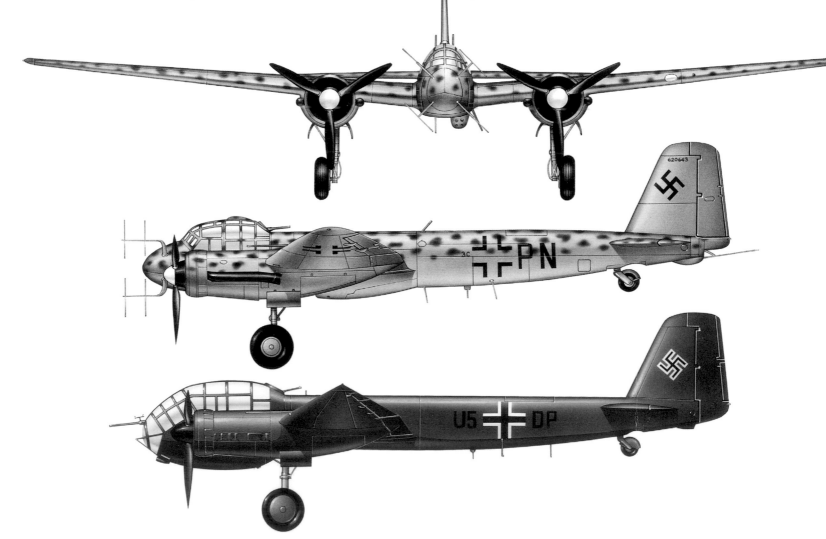

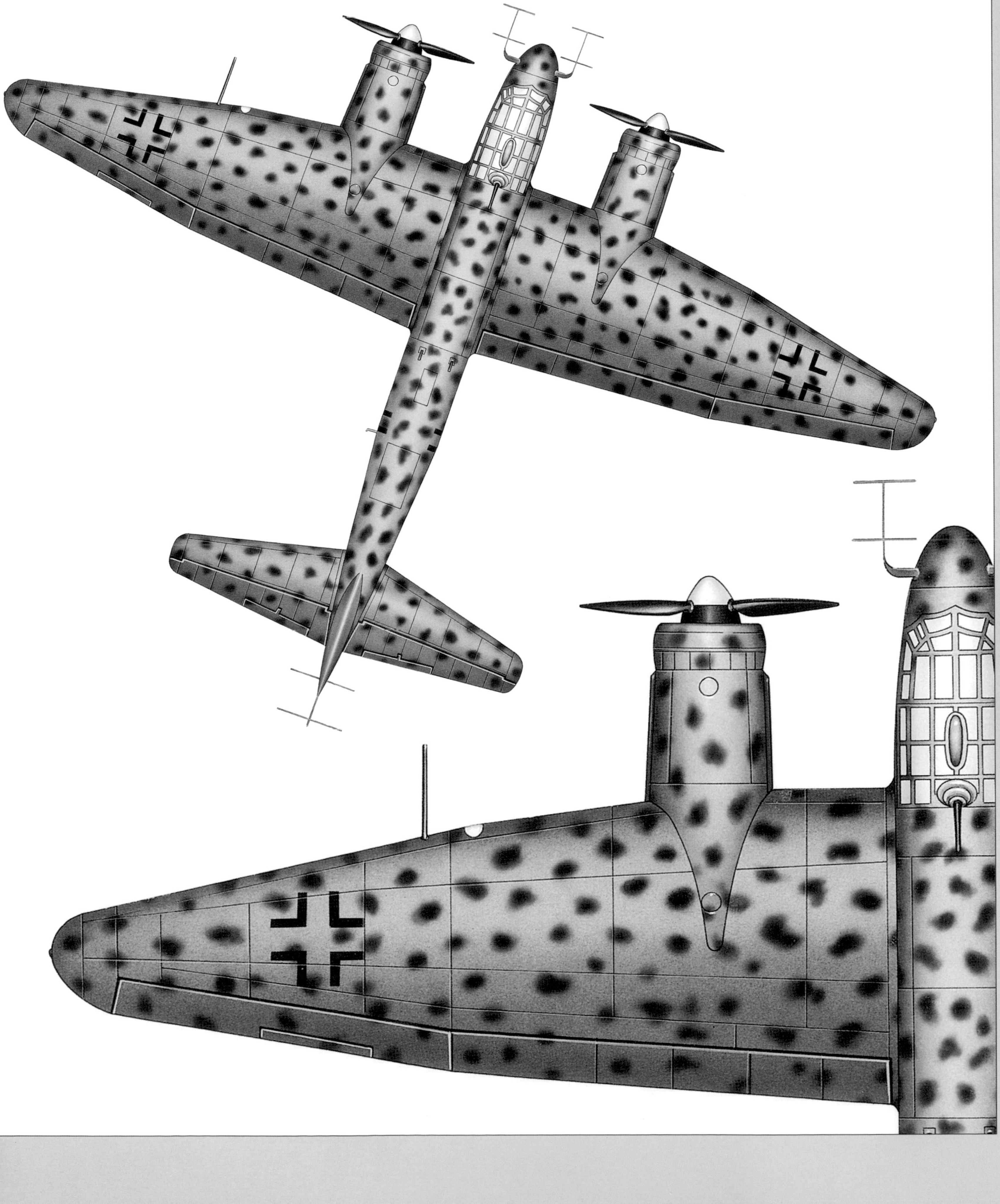

Heinkel He.111

GERMANY

Officially designed as a civil aircraft, like the contemporary Junkers Ju.86 and Dornier Do.17, the Heinkel He.111 was created to perform a dual role of fast commercial cargo aircraft and bomber. It ended up making more of a mark than its two peers due to its combat performance and the large quantities produced. The plane was first built in 1936 and continued to be produced until almost the end of the war, with a total of over 7300 built in a wide range of variants. These operated on all the fronts and in a wide range of roles, demonstrating the great validity of the initial design.

The first prototype made its maiden flight on February 24, 1935 and the first bomber version, the He.111 B, characterized by its two Daimler-Benz DB 600 engines, entered service in late 1936. In February the following year, around 30 of them were assigned to the Condor Legion in Spain, where they made up the core of a large contingent. Military versions soon began to follow one another on the assembly lines. After a few aircraft of the D series had been built, the lack of Daimler-Benz engines led to the development of the next variant, the He.111 E of 1938, in which Junkers-Jumo 211 engines were fitted. Significant changes to the wing structure characterized the He.111 G, but it was in 1938, with the appearance of prototypes of the P and H series, that the bomber was given its final form. In these machines the front section of the fuselage was redesigned. Completely glazed and profiled with the rest of the structure, its characteristic asymmetrical form was designed to give the pilot maximum visibility. The He.111 H version (in the drawings) became the most widely produced: they entered service in May 1939 and around 5000 were built.

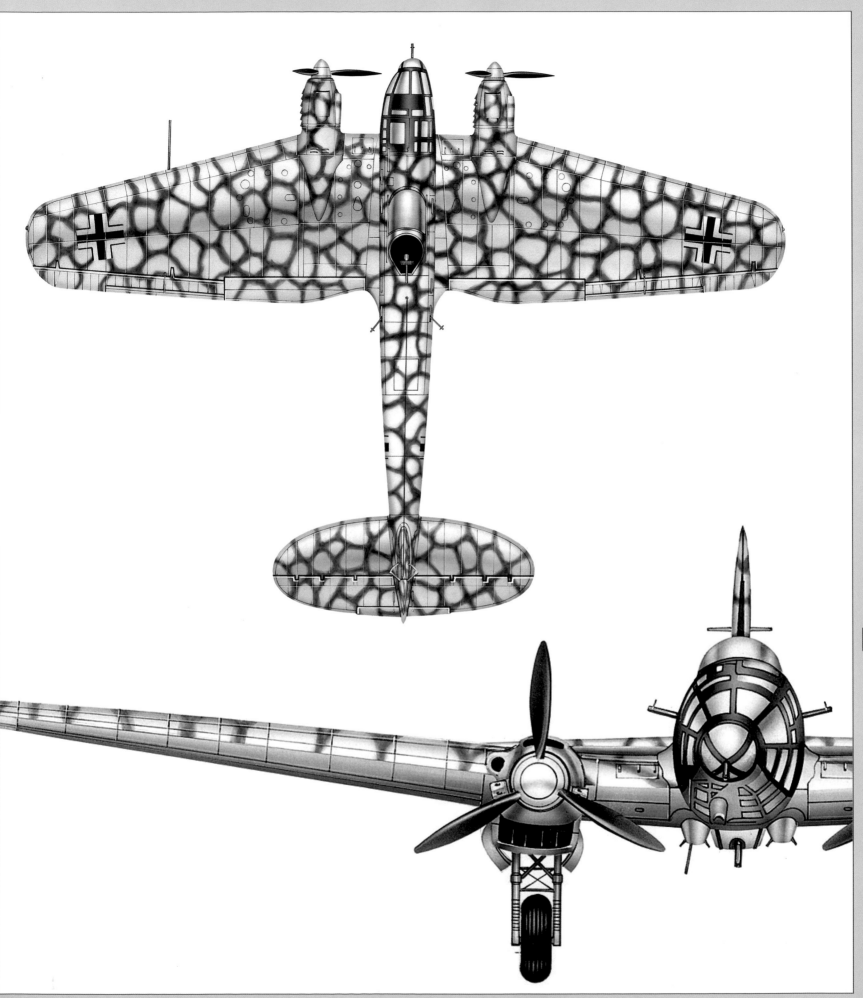

Macchi M.C.202 Folgore

ITALY

After the M.C.200 Saetta, the family of combat aircraft produced by Macchi from the second half of the 1930s onwards was boosted in 1940 with the arrival of a new, more effective model, the M.C.202 Folgore. This airplane is remembered for its characteristics, the high numbers produced, and its extensive use, as the best Italian fighter deployed by the Regia Aeronautica during the Second World War. In service from 1941 onwards, the Folgore operated on practically all the fronts. Between May 1941 and August 1943, more than 1100 were built. The feature which made it possible to exploit to the full the excellent cell of the 200 model was the use of the German Daimler-Benz DB 601 engine. From this point of view, the introduction of the new Macchi fighter marked a fundamental turning point in the design philosophy adopted by the Italian aeronautical industry, which had previously preferred to use radial engines. The prototype made its maiden flight on August 10, 1940, and right from the very first tests displayed excellent performance. In particular, horizontal speed reached 360 mph (600 km/h) and climbing speed was such that an altitude of 19,200 ft (6000 meters) could be reached in 5 minutes and 55 seconds. The only limitation was the weaponry, which was limited to two 12.7-mm machine-guns synchronized to fire through the propeller. There were attempts to improve the armament in later series by adding another two lower-caliber guns in the wings. The Macchi M.C.202 continued to be used after the Armistice, both in the units of the air force fighting alongside the Allies and in those of the Italian Social Republic.

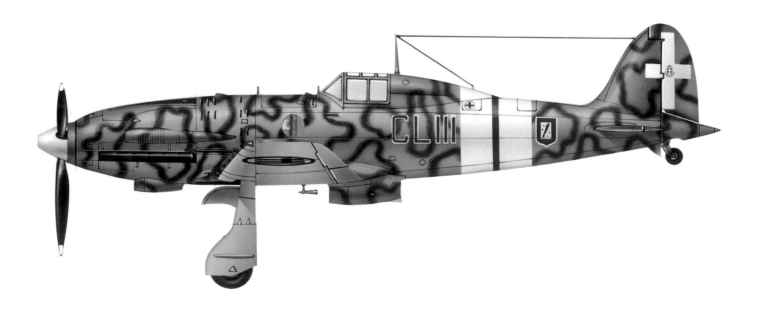

132 top The Italian Fiat C.R.42s were sent to the north with the Italian Air Corps, to support the Luftwaffe's operations against England.

132 bottom The CANT Z.506. These seaplanes proved too slow to be used as bombers, but nevertheless played an important role as naval reconnaissance aircraft and in sea-rescue operations.

Apart from the general inadequacy of the machines (operating in particularly difficult weather conditions and with temperatures well below zero—the fighters still had open cockpits), the lack of training in instrument flight, and the absence of suitable communications apparatus weighed heavily.

The best account of the situation was given by Luigi Gorrin,i the Italian ace (19 victories) who survived the war and who flew in Belgium with the C.R.42s of the 18th Group: "We escorted the bombers, but it was almost possible to keep them together: some fell out of the sky because their engines stopped working. They were B.R.20s, aircraft covered in canvas, designed for flying light and for taking off from dry fields. Instead, they were overloaded with bombs, the landing strips were a sea of mud, and the pilots were untrained.

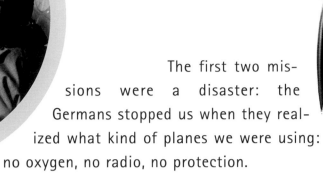

The first two missions were a disaster: the Germans stopped us when they realized what kind of planes we were using: no oxygen, no radio, no protection.

First of all, they gave us catalytic heaters to heat up the engines and then, in only 48 hours, they installed armor where the airplanes needed it. They also gave us their flying suits, gloves, and helmets, seeing that we only had our light ones. To be honest, all we had were eyes to cry with; but nevertheless we fought on in these conditions. We didn't even have maps—even back home in Italy we used to fly by the road maps produced by the Touring Club".

Apart from the great individual bravery of the pilots and crews, the situation soon became unsustainable from an operational point of view, and toward the end of December, with 50 percent of the aircraft damaged or out of use, the order came to suspend operations. On January 3, 1941 what remained of the bomber units and the majority of the fighter units left Belgium.

133

133 top left Benito Mussolini next to a M.C.200.

133 top right and center The Regia Aeronautica's most widely used fighter was the Macchi M.C.200, which performed well in the air despite its somewhat limited engine.

133 bottom The Fiat G.50 monoplane fighter. Only one squadron was equipped with this aircraft, deployed at bases in Belgium with mediocre results.

SIAI Marchetti S.M.79 Sparviero

ITALY

The line of three-engined aircraft introduced by SIAI Marchetti with the S.M.73 achieved fame with the S.M.79 model, the best of the series.

This was better known by its official name of Sparviero (Sparrowhawk) (but affectionately rechristened Gobbo (Hunchback) because of its characteristic form). This airplane played a prominent role in the war, and was to become one of the immortal names in the history of aviation. The S.M.79 fought for Italy on all fronts from the first to the last day of the war. Although it started life as a bomber, it found its true vocation in an even more aggressive role, that of torpedo

bombing, in which it proved to be an unbeatable machine. From October 1936 to June 1943, the assembly lines produced 1217 of this three-engined aircraft, a significantly greater quantity than the production averages of the Italian aeronautics industry at the time. The birth of the S.M.79 dated back to October 1934, when the first prototype flew. It had been designed as an eight-seater civil aircraft, and the manufacturer intended it to take part in the London to Melbourne race.

The S.M.79 debuted in Spain in February 1937 and at the outbreak of war 594 were in service. Their initial role as bombers was soon extended to cover torpedo bombing. After Italy's defeat, the airplanes were kept by the air force of the Italian Social Republic. After the war those which remained were used for a few years as transport aircraft and finally for pulling targets.

Their final withdrawal took place in 1952, with the demolition of the last planes remaining.

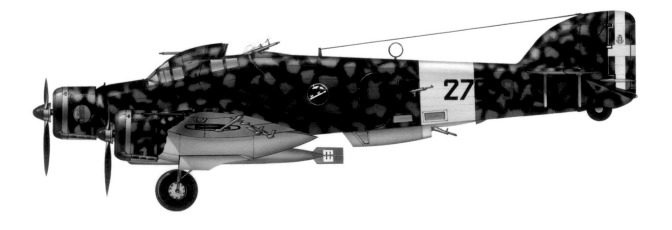

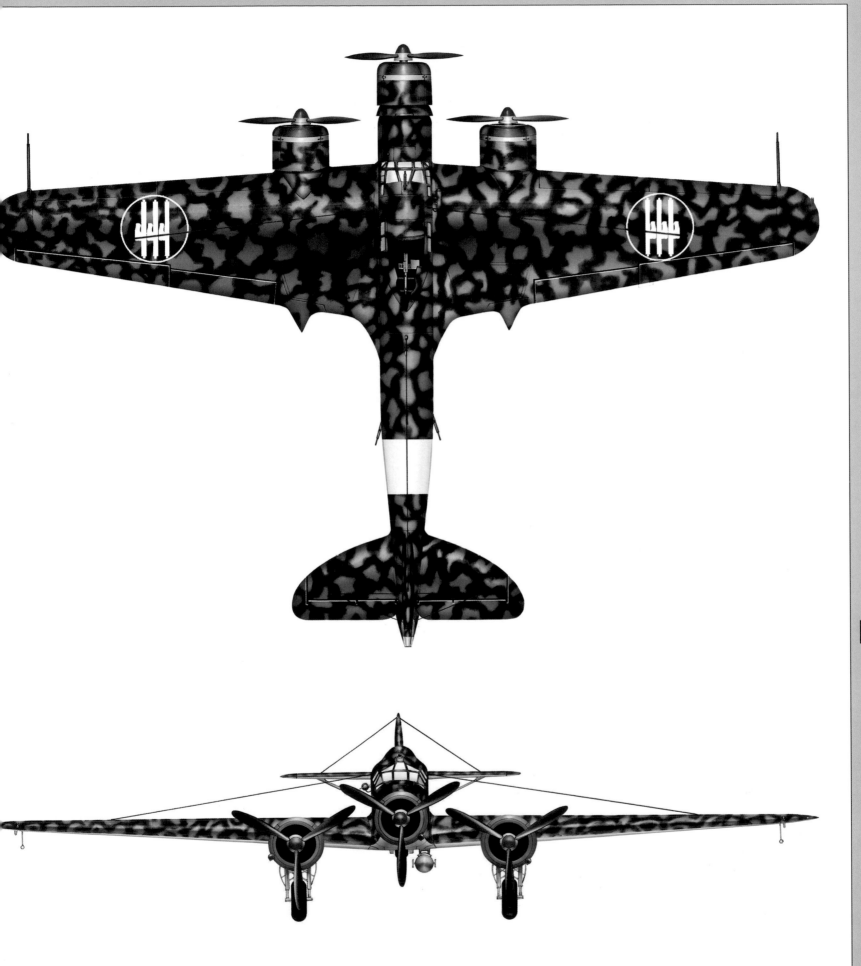

136 top The Fiat B.R.20, which in 1939 flew 2700 miles (4500 km) from Rome to Addis Ababa at an average speed of 242 mph (404 km/h), beating the world record for its category. The airplane, baptized Santo Francesco, was piloted by Maner Lualdi.

136 bottom The twin-engined B.R.20s were also used in night-time missions; the white strip on the fuselage, which characterized Italian aircraft, was masked with black paint to make them less visible.

The expedition over the Channel, totally useless from a military point of view, had cost 38 aircraft and 43 pilots. But above all, it had thrown light on the real conditions of the Regia Aeronautica.

In light of this experience, it became a priority to recover lost ground. The most serious limits which prevented the design of a combat airplane competitive with English and German products was the absence of a valid in-line engine.

Seeing that it was impossible to develop an engine of this kind in time, Italy decided to import the excellent German Daimler-Benz DB 601, which would be used to equip a second generation of fighters. This led to the production of the Macchi M.C.202 Folgore and the Reggiane Re.2001, which entered service in 1941 and which, albeit with different destinies, were the first really modern machines produced by the Italian war industry.

Work continued, although the most significant progress arrived too late. Towards the end of spring 1942, tests began on the three fighters of the "Series 5" (the Macchi M.C.205 Veltro, the Fiat G.55 Centauro, and the Reggiane Re.2005), fitted with the more powerful Daimler-Benz DB 605 engine.

Their seriously inadequate weaponry was also finally overcome. These three machines, which were the best of their kind produced during the war, did not see significant use. In fact, they entered service only in spring-summer 1943, when Italy's fate was already clear, and in extremely limited quantities. The industrial system, tormented by bombing, and with a lack of raw materials, was in a sorry state and was unable to sustain the intense rate of mass production.

Moreover, it had never achieved particularly high production levels: 3257 airplanes in 1940; 3503 in 1941; and just 2818 in 1942. In the first eight months of 1943, 1930 airplanes were produced.

On September 8 that year, with the country split in two, the Regia Aeronautica (whose losses, since June 10, numbered around 10,000 aircraft) ceased to exist. On the day of defeat, it still had 877 airplanes: 247 scouts, 108 bombers, 359 fighters, and interceptors, 61 torpedo-bombers, and 102 light-

137 top and center Initially delivered to bombing units, the three-engined Savoia Marchetti S.M.79 was subsequently used by torpedo-bomber units, where it was fairly successful thanks to its robustness and flying performance.

A great leap forwards in quality and efficiency was achieved with the arrival of the more modern Macchi M.C.202 Folgore fighter.

137 bottom Delivery of the new aircraft to the 4th Division.

weight twin-engined aircraft. Of these, a couple of hundred managed to reach the south, where they formed the basis of a new air force (the Aviazione Cobelli-gerante) which became part of the Allied Balkan Air Force.

There was a similar, but opposite situation in the north, where in October that year the Aviazione della Repubblica Sociale Italiana (Air Force of the Italian Social Republic) was established, and lined up on the side of the Germans.

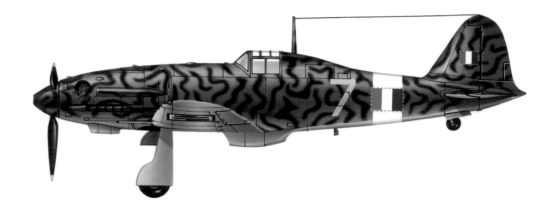

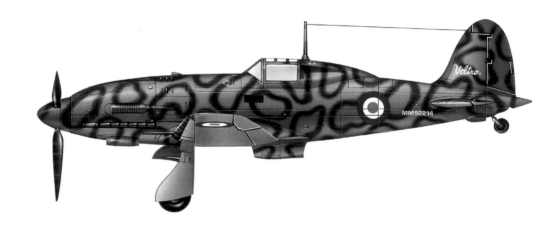

138 top The three aircraft of the so-called Series 5 were the best fighter airplanes produced by national industry but arrived too late and in limited quantities. From top to bottom: The Fiat G.55, the Reggiane Re.2005, and the Macchi M.C.205. They were all fitted with an in-line Daimler-Benz DB 605 engine built under licence in Italy and were armed with 20-mm cannons.

138 bottom A Reggiane Re.2001. Designed as an interceptor, it was principally used as a fighter-bomber.

JAPAN

While Europe was shaken by German military power, on the other side of the world a second, deadly war machine was preparing for action. In 1939, the real extent of Japanese rearmament was still little known in the West, despite the worrying signals coming from it aggression against China. Above all, there was the widespread myth in the West that the development of the military airplane in Japan was taking place at a much slower rate than in the nations traditionally considered at the forefront. On the eve of the United States' entry into the war, experts and strategists were convinced that the Japanese industries were producing obsolete machines, copies, or derivates of foreign aircraft, and that their technology was entirely dependent on that of the main Western suppliers.

Rarely in the course of history has such confidence been so misplaced. Japan's attack followed Hitler's by a little over two years, but it was no less devastating for that. The December 7, 1941 attack on Pearl Harbor revealed the modernity and power of the Japanese armed forces, along with their high level of efficiency. This situation colored the first six months of war in the Pacific and forced the United States to make an enormous effort to regain supremacy in the air, faced with an enemy that posed an increasingly threat.

During the 1930s, the growth of Japanese aviation had gone unnoticed by the rest of the world. Above all, the extensive reorganization of its industrial system had gone unobserved. The process had started toward the end of the First World War, and had led to the creation of an impressive manufacturing infrastructure almost completely oriented toward military production. In this phase, a particularly active role was played the army and the navy, which were in constant competition to produce

139 top The profile belongs to the twin-engined Mitsubishi G4M bomber (Betty in code).

139 bottom The predecessor of the famous Zero, the Mitsubishi A5M (known as Claude in Allied code), was distinguished by its fixed faired landing gear. It was the first fighter monoplane to be stationed on ships by the Japanese Navy Air Corps and was used by Japan in operations against China.

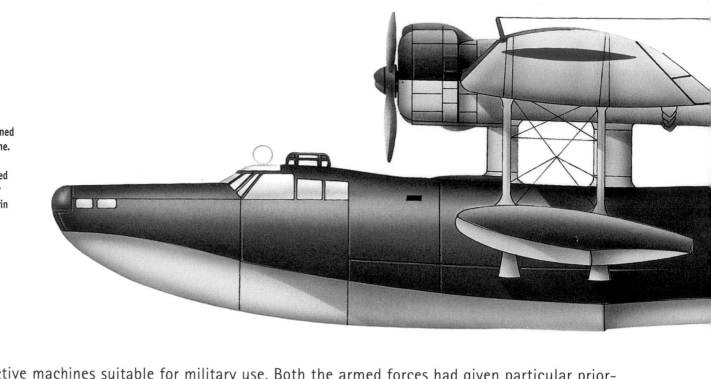

140 top The large four-engined Kawanishi H6K Mavis seaplane.

140 bottom The twin-engined Kawasaki Ki-45 Toryu fighter (codenamed Nick) was used in the defence of Tokyo.

increasingly effective machines suitable for military use. Both the armed forces had given particular priority to developing their air units. The Imperial Navy Air Corps had been in operation since 1912, while that of the army was set up in May 1925.

After its experience of conflict against China, Japan's readiness for the new world war was demonstrated by its aeronautical production figures for the three years prior to the outbreak of hostilities in Europe. From the 445 airplanes built in 1930, the number rose to 1511 in 1937, to 3201 in 1938, and to 4467 in 1939. The acceleration in production was accompanied by further consolidation of the industrial system, which became even more flexible and competitive, enabling it to fully develop its immense potential.

Consequently, by Pearl harbor, the japanese were ready to put into practice weaponry and strategies established long beforehand. The Imperial Army Air Corps, which had around 1500 airplanes ready for use, was given responsibility for operations over land. The Navy Air Corps, with 1400 front-line aircraft, was given the task of neutralizing the American fleet with units stationed on aircraft carriers, and once they had accomplished this, to

141 top Allied aircraft attacking an enemy airfield in Borneo, using delayed-action bombs. In the foreground: a Japanese twin-engined Mitsubishi Ki-21 Sally.

Over 200 of these aircraft were built.

141 bottom A side view of the Kawasaki Ki-48-IIB.

support expansion with the land-based units. After Pearl Harbor and until mid-1942, the two air forces fought with great success, and like the German Luftwaffe, Japan's victories fuelled the myth of Japanese invincibility. But it was not to last.

What historians have called the turning-point of the war in the Pacific came with the great air and naval battles of spring–summer 1942, particularly that of Midway. At Midway, the two small islands which represented the advance sentry post of American territory, Japanese power received its first great defeat.

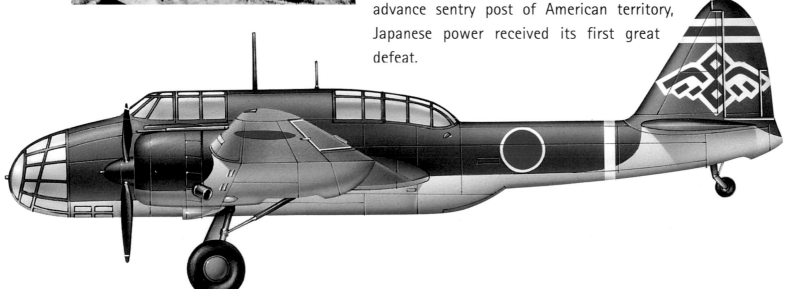

The insignia of Japanese airplanes

The aircraft insignia system used in Japan was complex and different for the army and the navy. In the army, from 1932 onwards, each aircraft was identified by a construction serial number (Kitai) followed by suffixes in Roman numerals and letters to indicate the variants and derived series. It also had a type number, based on the last figures of

the Japanese year in which the airplane had been completed. Lastly, there was often a popular name, assigned for propaganda reasons. In the navy, in addition to an experimental number (Shi) based on the year of the Emperor's reign, each airplane was identified by a group of letters and numbers. The first letter indicated the role; the first

number, the serial number for airplanes of the same type; the second letter, the manufacturer; the second number, the version of the aircraft. Lastly, there was a number based on the figures of the Japanese year and often a popular name.

The main abbreviations indicating the function of navy aircraft
A = on-board fighters

B = on-board attack aircraft
C = scouts
D = on-board bombers
E, F = naval scouts
E, F = naval scouts
G = attack aircraft
H = seaplanes
J = land-based fighters
K = trainers
L = transport
M = seaplanes for special purposes
N = fighter seaplanes
P = bombers
Q = observation aircraft
R = land-based scouts
S = night fighters

Allied identification code
The aircraft insignia system used in Japan by the army and navy was complex. For this reason, the Allies created a particular code, assigning a name to each Japanese airplane in service. Men's names were given to fighters and seaplane-scouts; women's names to bombers, scouts, and seaplanes; names of trees to trainers; and names of birds to gliders.

Nakajima Ki-43 Hayabusa

JAPAN

The successor to the Nakajima Ki-27 as the standard fighter of the Imperial Army, the Ki-43 arrived on the scene more or less at the same time as the Mitsubishi A6M Zero and, as its counterpart in the navy, was the first modern Japanese combat aircraft used in the Pacific.

Christened Hayabusa (Peregrine Falcon), the Ki-43 had a long and intense career, which continued until the end of the war. The height of its success came in the first year of the war when, faced with weaker adversaries, the Nakajima fighter earned a reputation for being invincible. Work on the project was started in December 1937 and, in January 1939, the first of the three prototypes was taken on its maiden flight.

The initial variants (Ki-43-Ia and Ki-43-Ib) entered service in June 1941. 716 were built. After its initial success, a significantly improved version of the Nakajima was developed, the Ki-43-II, which became the most widely produced model (in the drawings). In 1944 the final version, the Ki-43-III appeared and proved to be the best of all, even if only 10 prototypes were built. In total, 5919 Ki-46 Hayabusas came off the assembly lines.

Their career ended in the desperate suicide attacks of the last months of the war.

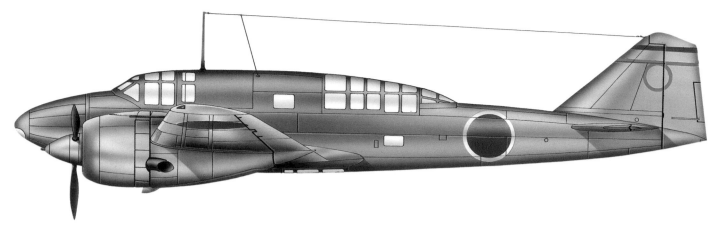

The clash, on June 4–7, 1942 in which Japan took part with a force of over 180 ships and 599 airplanes, sharply redressed the balance. The Imperial fleet lost four of its precious aircraft carriers, all its air groups, and, worst of all, most of its best trained and effective crews, the most difficult component to replace. Midway also had important strategic consequences: Japan finally gave up its plans to conquer the Fijian Islands, Port Moresby, Samoa, New Caledonia, and Australia. Japan was forced to abandon the offensive and had to defend itself much sooner than its strategists had forecast.

146 top and center The profiles show the Mitsubishi Ki-46 and the Nakajima Ki-84 Hayate.

146 bottom A twin-engined Japanese airplane with excellent performance was the Mitsubishi Ki-46 scout.

147 top After purchasing
the licence for the German
Daimler-Benz DB 601 inline
engine in 1942, Japanese
industry began to produce
the Kawasaki Ki-61 Hien
fighter, but the aircraft did not
reach the units until 1943, and
its operational use was
extremely limited.

However, this did not mean that the war effort slowed down. In the aeronautical field, progress continued at an extremely high level: 5088 airplanes of all types (including 1080 fighters and 1461 bombers) and 12,151 engines were built in 1941; in 1942 production almost doubled, with a total of 8861 aircraft (2935 fighters and 2433 bombers), and 16,999 engines.

Just as Pearl Harbor had marked the beginning of the war in the Pacific, and Midway had characterized its turning point, the third phase which led to the defeat of Japan, started in summer 1944. A vital strategic element was the American taking of the Marianne Archipelago. From this outpost, the Allies for the first time had the possibility of operating within the range of the brand-new B-29 heavy bombers, taking the war directly onto Japanese territory. Japan's reaction, however, continued to be tenacious until the end. Japan's final effort into which all available resources were thrown, consumed what was left of the powerful military apparatus. The glorious Imperial fleet was by now non-existent, and the air forces of the Army and Navy sustained the greatest burden of the struggle, but were decimated. In the campaign of Okinawa alone, from April to June 1944, 7830 aircraft of all types were lost, many in desperate suicide attacks per-

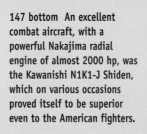

147 bottom An excellent combat aircraft, with a powerful Nakajima radial engine of almost 2000 hp, was the Kawanishi N1K1-J Shiden, which on various occasions proved itself to be superior even to the American fighters.

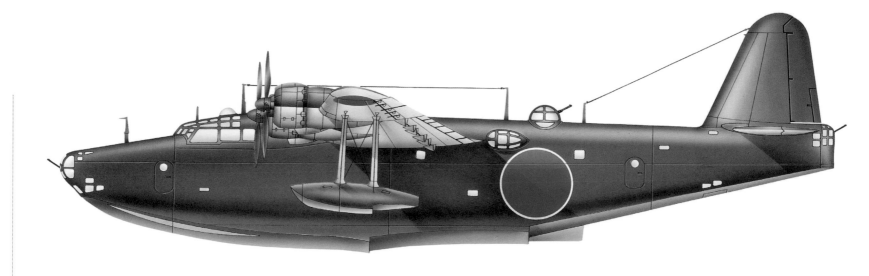

formed in an attempt to destroy enemy ships. From then on, the limited reserves were used mainly in defence of the homeland.

The Japanese aeronautical industry made a last-ditch attempt to produce an interceptor able to deal with the threat of the B-29s. It was a determined effort, with the last prototypes test-flown in the final weeks of the war (on July 7, 1945 the Mitsubishi J8M Shushui jet interceptor, a copy of the German

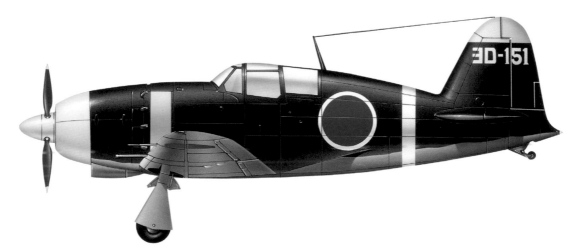

148 top The Kawanishi H8K reconnaissance seaplane.

148 center The Mitsubishi J2M Raiden fighter of the Japanese navy.

148 bottom Camouflage on a Ki-61 Hien fighter.

149 top and center The Nakajima Kikka combat aircraft fitted with a jet engine and the Yokosuka MXY7 flying bomb. Both came into service in the last months of the war.

Messerschmitt Me.163B, and on August 3, the original Kyushu J7W Shinden "canard"), but also a useless one. Equally useless was the massive boost given to industrial production: in the first eight months of 1945, Japan managed to produce 11,066 airplanes of all types (including 5474 fighters and 1934 bombers), and 12,360 engines. It is worth noting that in 1943, 16,693 airplanes were built (7147 fighters and 4189 bombers), with 28,541 engines; in 1944 the number rose to 28,180 airplanes (13,811 fighters and 5100 bombers), and 46,526 engines.

Japan surrendered on September 2, 1945 only after two atomic bombs were dropped by the Americans on the cities of Hiroshima and Nagasaki on the August 6 and 9 1945 respectively.

149 bottom A Japanese copy of the Messerschmitt Me.163, the Mitsubishi J8M Shusui was tested in July 1945 with disastrous results. Only seven prototypes were built.

GREAT BRITAIN

At the outbreak of war, the only European nation able to compete with Germany on an aeronautical level was Great Britain. In October 1939, 1500 aircraft were stationed around the country, with more or less the same number of reserves. From May onward, production of aircraft was maintained at fairly high levels, with monthly rates of 700 airplanes.

The development of the war and its expansion subsequently demonstrated the great vitality of the British air force and the solidity of its tactical and strategic base.

The end of the First World War had seen the Royal Air Force emerge as the most powerful air force in the world. But this position had not lasted long. With the drastic cuts to the military budget, the air force had been sharply reduced in size. From 188 squadrons, the number was cut to 33. The situation of the naval air force was the same. The Royal Naval Air Service at the end of 1919 had only three units: one fighter, one

150 top left The Hurricane, the Spitfire, and the Lancaster (in the round picture) were the most important aircraft produced by British industry.

150 top right A modern replica of the Hurricane Mk.IIC.

150 center and bottom The Gloster Gladiator was the Royal Air Force's last fighter biplane. The airplane shown on the left bears the insignia of the Norwegian Air Force, to whom it was given at the beginning of the war.

reconnaissance, and one for torpedo-bombers. In January 1924, three months before the RNAS became the Fleet Air Arm, the airplanes in service numbered 78; they became 144 in September 1930, and 156 in 1932. The lack of resources also had direct consequences on provisions and, consequently, negative repercussions on industry. In fact, up until the first half of the 1930s, the evolution of the combat airplane had slowed down. This was the age of the biplane. Significant examples of this tendency were the Gloster Grebe and Fairey Flycatcher fighters, among the best representatives of the first post-war generation, or the Bristol Bulldog and the Hawker Fury, machines which remained in service for many years, characterizing an entire period in the history of the RAF.

151 top The Westland Lysander liaison and reconnaissance aircraft, which could take off and land in restricted spaces.

151 bottom The large Short Sunderland seaplane, robust and well-armed, operated in the North Sea and the Mediterranean, the Atlantic, and the Indian Ocean. It remained in service for over 20 years.

Hawker Tempest

GREAT BRITAIN

The Hawker Tempest represented the final version of the design which had led to the Typhoon in 1940. It proved to be disappointing as an interceptor, but an excellent attack aircraft. The Tempest was one of the fastest propeller-driven aircraft deployed by the RAF in the last year of the war. It distinguished itself above all in two particular duties, which it shared with the Spitfire Mk.XIV: the interception of the Messerschmitt Me.262 jets and attacking V-1 flying bombs.

The success of this extremely particular role can be demonstrated by a few statistics: from June 13 to September 5,

1944, around a third (638) of the 1771 V-1s destroyed by the British air defence were shot down by Tempests.

A precise combat tactic was perfected: fitted with supplementary tanks which allowed them a maximum patrol-time of 4.5 hours at altitude, fighters flew at an altitude of 9600 ft (3000 meters), remaining in constant contact with the radar stations on the ground which provided them with information on the trajectories of the V-1s. Since the bombs flew at altitudes of 960–7700 ft (300–2400 meters), the Tempests usually attacked in a dive, allowing them to achieve significant speed margins. The heavy on-board

weaponry did the rest, even if in some cases, pilots who had run out of munitions managed to pull up alongside the V-1s and make them dive into the sea by flipping them over with their wing tip. The main production variant in the war period was the

Mk.V, illustrated in the drawings, of which 800 were built up to August 1945. It made its maiden flight on September 2, 1942, and entered service in April 1944. The Tempest Mk.VI (142 built), in which a different engine was fitted (a 2300 hp

Napier Sabre) and the radically different Mk.II (764 built), with its 2526 hp Bristol Centaurus radial engine, arrived too late to take part in the war. These last two versions of the Tempest remained in service until 1949 and 1951 respectively.

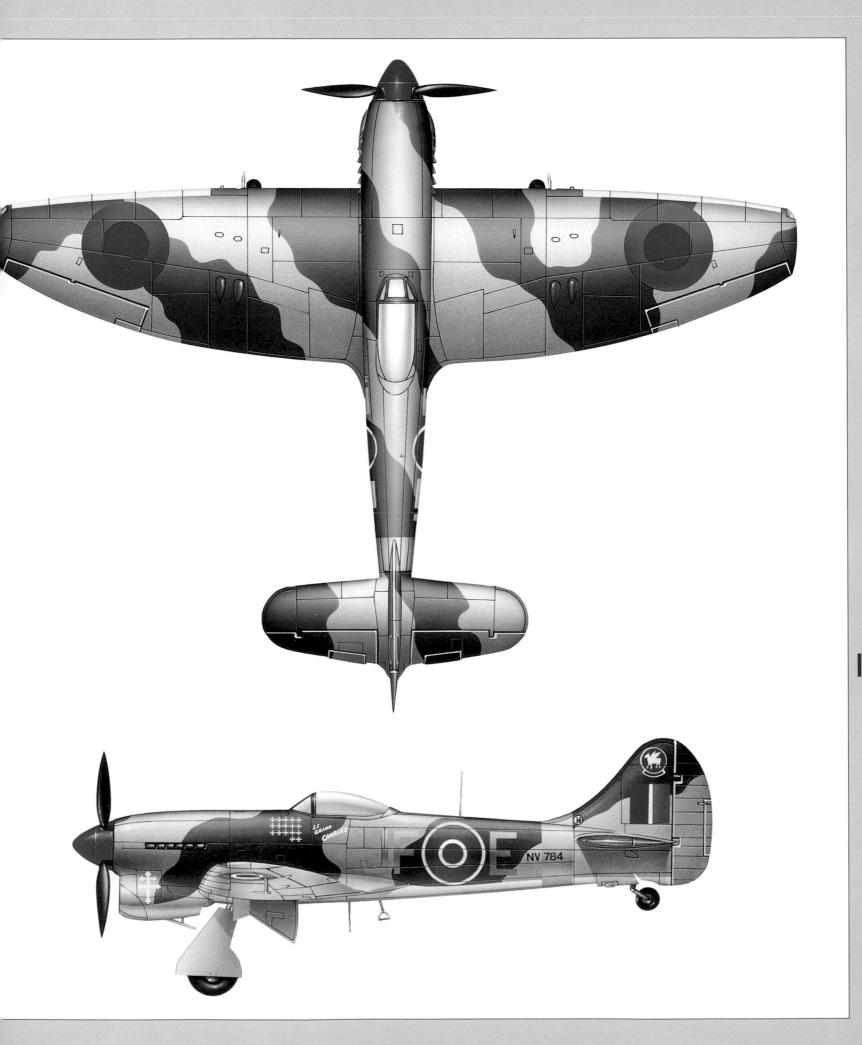

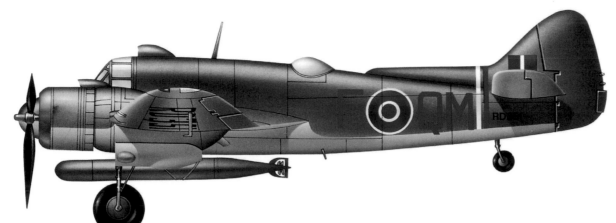

154 The powerful and versatile Bristol Beaufighter was used as a fighter-bomber, night-fighter, and torpedo-bomber for the entire duration of the conflict.

With the first signs of the coming conflict, alarm bells began to ring. By the end of 1933 the force was equipped with a front line of only 850 airplanes, many of which were old. That year the Air Chiefs of Staff implemented a series of measures which would turn out to be extremely timely, requesting industries to produce a single-seater fighter equipped with eight machine-guns. Then in 1934 long-range heavy bombers were commissioned and in 1936 the first four-engined strategic bombers. Industry sprang back to life and took this sudden surge in demand in its stride: by 1938 it managed to produce 4000 airplanes, which became 7000 the following year, and an impressive 15,000 in 1940.

The direct comparison with the enemy took place during the Battle of Britain. Between August 13 and October 31, 1940, the full potential of the RAF (whose main components were Fighter Command, Bomber Command, and Coastal Command) was put severely to the test. The British victory, however, was not only down to the fighter pilots and their machines, but also to the perfect organization of the operational control system, based on the use of what was a revolutionary instrument at the time—radar. From 1935, a chain of radar installations had been set up on the south coast of Britain, and by July 1939 the network comprised 20 stations. Radar was able to detect aircraft up to 120 miles (200 km) away, at altitudes of over 9600 ft (3000 meters), and to transmit their course well in advance directly to the com-

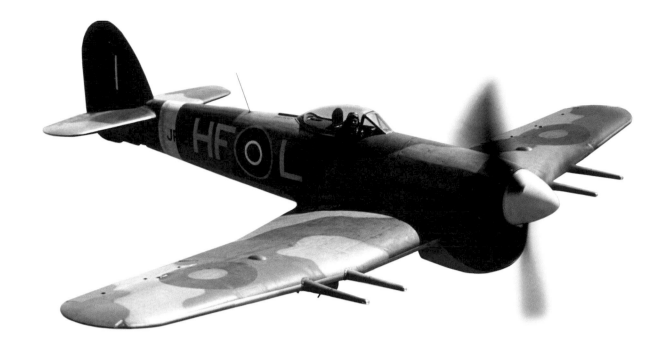

mand center. Thanks to this information, enemy formations could be "seen" even before they had left the French coast, and the RAF could optimize the use of fighter units against the incessant large-scale German raids. The end of the direct threat to national territory marked the beginning of a new phase of development for the RAF. Industry had a chance to reorganize itself to deal with the growing demands which came from theaters of war throughout the world, and production was maintained at high levels, and would remain so for the entire duration of the conflict. In addition to the three strategic bombers, this period also saw the creation of the most prestigious machines of the RAF: the Bristol Beaufighter, the de Havilland Mosquito, and increasingly powerful versions of the Spitfire.

The overall development of the war machine, however, did not simply affect the RAF, but also affected the Fleet Air Arm, whose modernization programs were significantly behind schedule. Only in May 1939 did the Fleet Air Arm achieve complete autonomy as an armed force and, at the outbreak of war, the aircraft stationed on the units of the Royal Navy (including the six aircraft carriers Courageous, Furious, Glorious, Eagle, Hermes, and Ark Royal) numbered only 225, out of a total of 340. These were not

155 top The Hawker Typhoon was a great failure as a fighter, but proved to be a valid ground-attack aircraft. It played a vital role in the operations in Normandy.

155 bottom The units of the Fleet Air Arm were equipped with the Fairey Fulmar, a fighter with firepower compatible to that of the Hurricane and Spitfire.

North American B-25 Mitchell

UNITED STATES

Among the best medium bombers of the entire conflict, the North American B-25 Mitchell was one of the leading protagonists of the air war. Over 11,000 in a number of versions left the assembly lines between 1940 and 1945, continuously improved and with more powerful engines. The intense career of this versatile and efficient twin-engined aircraft continued long after the Second World War. After having served on all fronts, not only under the insignia of the Air Services of the US Army and the US Navy, but also with the British RAF, and with the air forces of the Commonwealth and the Soviet Union, in the post-war years, the B-25 remained operational until the 1960s, above all in some minor air forces.

The prototype made its maiden flight in January 1939, and the first definitive B-25 on August 19, 1940. Full speed production started on the two B-25C and B-25D variants, which started to be delivered from late 1941 onwards, and of which 1619 and 2290 were built respectively.

In 1942 the G variant was introduced. This saw a radical change in weaponry, the first step towards subsequent modifications which would transform the Mitchell into a sort of flying cruiser: the installation in the prow of a 75-mm cannon. This piece of artillery had 21 shells and was designed to be used to attack ships in the Pacific theater. 405 B-25Gs were built, but due to a series of practical problems linked to difficulties in cannon loading and performance, production shifted in favor of the H version (of which 1000 were built). The first B-25Hs (in the drawings) arrived at the front in February 1944.

The subsequent version, the B-25J, was also the most widely produced (4390, 295 of which went to Great Britain), and represented the final evolution of the cell.

In this variant, there was an initial return to the classic set-up of a horizontal bomber with a glazed nose, then to that of a ground-attack aircraft with a basic armament of 12 heavy machine-guns.

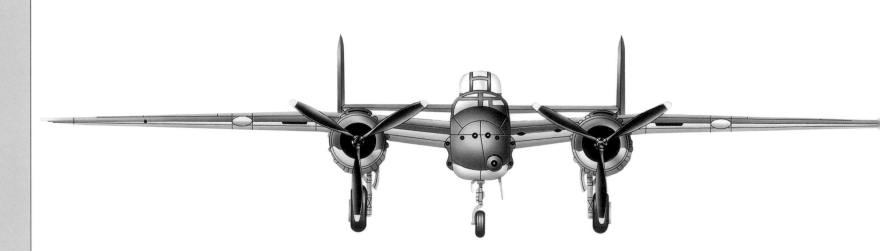

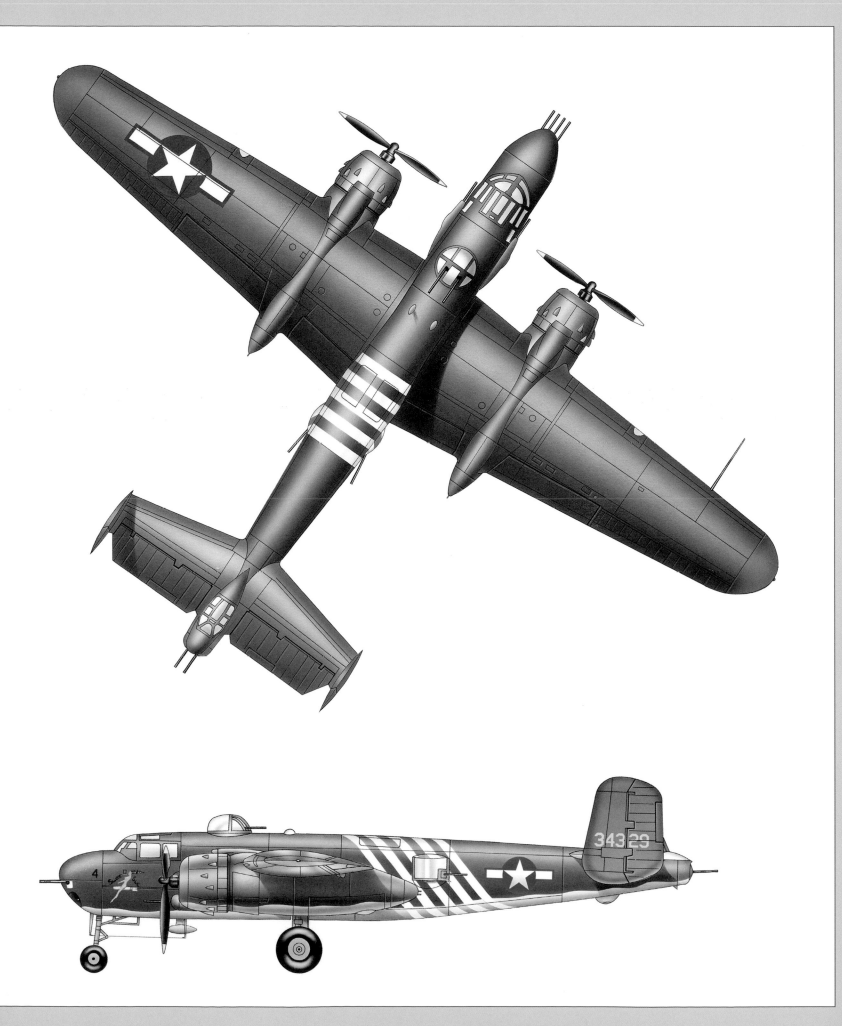

After the end of the First World War, in which the United States had taken part with a force headed by General William Mitchell, the autonomy that the air force had enjoyed as the Air Service since May 20, 1918, ended sharply with demobilization. On June 4, 1920 the air force once more came under control of the Army and its size reduced from 87 to 27 squadrons. On July 2, 1926 the US Army Air Corps (USAAC) was set up, and a rearmament and development plan was launched, which progressed extremely slowly. Only on March 1, 1935 was a single command for the USAAC set up, while the final reorganization arrived during the war, in June 1941, when the air force was renamed US Army Air Forces, USAAF, and achieved semi-independence. The parallel process of expansion in the naval air corps had been more uniform. The restrictions of the inter-war years had not affected the vitality of the Naval Flying Corps (set up on July 1, 1915), which by November 1918 had (together with the Marine Corps) around 40,000 men, 2107 airplanes, and 15 airships. Further structural consolidation took place in 1921, with the creation of the Bureau of Aeronautics, a co-ordinating body within the Ministry of the Navy, responsible for everything related to naval aviation.

On the eve of the Second World War the American air force was unprepared. The aircraft (in 1939 the USAAC had 2400 airplanes of all types, the US Navy 2500, of which 600 on board ships) were not

160 top left The long-range twin-engined Lockheed P-38 Lightning.

160 top right While being designed in 1936, the Douglas A-20 Havoc bomber (named the Boston by the English) showed itself in war to be a cutting-edge aircraft with exceptional performance.

160 bottom Originally designed for civil passenger transport, the Douglas C-54 was adapted for military use.

161 top The Vought OS2U-1 Kingfisher was the US Navy's most widely used on-board reconnaissance aircraft.

161 center The twin-engined Curtiss C-46 Commando shared with the C-47 Dakota duties of troop transportation for the entire duration of the war.

161 bottom Winner of a seaplane contest, the Consolidated PBY Catalina was subsequently produced in an amphibious version and developed for the protection of convoys and in anti-submarine operations. In the round picture: A detail of the side floats.

of great quality, and production levels were also extremely low compared to the country's industrial potential: in 1938, 1800 combat airplanes were built, and a few more (2195) the following year.

In September 1939 the US recommenced the exports of military material (until then prohibited under the Neutrality Act of 1935), in response to desperate requests from France and Great Britain. This support became increasingly significant after the approval in March 1941 of the Lend-Lease Act, which for the duration of the war provided for the needs of the Allied countries. The reaction came only after America was attacked by the Japanese at Pearl Harbor. Direct involvement in the brutal reality of combat was like a whiplash. With its entrance into war, the nation's energies were galvanized to the full, and all its

resources were channeled into the needs of the country and those of the Allies. There were the first, significant increases in production: from 6028 airplanes built in 1940, the number rose to 19,445 in 1941. The following year, America's involvement became global. The challenge of Germany in Europe had been joined by that of Japan, as their direct enemy in the Pacific, and the assembly lines recorded a sharp rise in output: 47,836 airplanes, of which 10,769 were fighters and 12,627 bombers.

In 1943, the American war machine was running at full capacity and the weight of the United States in the conflict began to be felt. Aeronautical production leapt to 85,898 aircraft; that of engines to 227,116. Quantity was accompanied by an equally exceptional increase in quality, above all in the sector of fighters. During this period emerged the best aircraft produced by American industry, those which succeeded in regaining supremacy in the air for the Allies and which remained in the history of aviation as absolute champions of aeronautical technology: the North

162 top The aggressive prow of the Lockheed P-38 shows the heavy armament of this American fighter.

162 bottom The Bell P-63 Kingcobra, a fighter-bomber for tactical support, was used above all by the Soviet Air force.

The insignia of American airplanes

The system of classification for American military aircraft was extremely complex and different for the army and the navy.

There briefly follow the letters which indicated the role of the airplane.

US Army Air Service
From 1924 to 1948, the system of classification was

composed of the following elements:
1) a prefix to be used only when special indications were required, such as on prototypes and experimental aircraft
2) one or more letters indicating the type of airplane
3) a serial number indicating the model
4) a suffix composed of a letter of the alphabet indicating

the production variants
5) a number (from 1942 onwards) indicating the production sub-series
6) initials indicating the manufacturer and factory.

Lastly, there was almost always a nickname.
The letters indicating the main types of aircraft are as follows.

A = attack or light bomber
AT = advanced training
B = medium and heavy bombers
BT = basic training
C = transport
CG = transport glider
F = reconnaissance
L = liaison
O = observation
OA = observation (amphibious)
P = fighter
PT = basic training
R = rotary wing

TG = training glider
UC = light transport

US Navy Air Service
From 1923 to 1962 the identification system of the US Navy included:
1) a prefix to be used only when special indications were required
2) one or more letters indicating the type of airplane
3) a number indicating the sequence of airplanes accepted by the Navy for each

163 top The Northrop P-61 Black Widow owed its nickname to its use as a night-fighter.

163 bottom A Douglas A-26 Invader, a twin-engined ground-attack aircraft and tactical bomber. Renamed as the B-26 in June 1948, it also took part in the Korean War.

American P-51 Mustang and the Republic P-47 Thunderbolt for the USAAF; the Grumman F6F Hellcat and the Vought F4U Corsair for the US Navy.

The war against Japan entered its final phase in summer 1944, when it became possible to attack the country directly. Parallel in intensity and effectiveness was the role played by the B-17s and by the B-24s in Europe against the Third Reich. Germany was the first to surrender, followed three months later by Japan. In terms of production, the figures of this huge effort are unbelievable: 96,318 airplanes and 256,911 aircraft engines built in 1944 alone; 297,199 airplanes (99,742 fighters and 97,592 bombers, of these 35,743 four-engined and 35,369 twin-engined), and 789,947 engines from 1941 to 1945.

individual manufacturer
4) a letter for the manufacturer's name
5) a number indicating the subsequent versions of the airplane.

Also in the Navy, the airplanes almost always had an additional name The letters indicating the main types of aircraft are as follows:
B = bomber
F = fighter
G = transport (single-engine)

H = rotary wing
J = multi-purpose
L = glider
N = training
0 = observation
P = reconnaissance
R = transport (multi-engined)
S = scout
T = torpedo-bomber

Consolidated B-24 Liberator

UNITED STATES

The second strategic bomber deployed by the United States, the B-24 Liberator shared with the Boeing B-17 the honor and burden of the Allied attack against the Third Reich. 18,188 were built up to May 1945 in a wide range of variants. This large four-engined aircraft served not only under American insignia, but also with the RAF (the second largest user, who received 1694), as well as the Australian, Canadian, and South African air forces.

Deployed intensively on all fronts, the B-24 proved to be extremely versatile and, thanks to its impressive operating range, was able to perform brilliantly tasks beyond the scope of its basic roles, ranging from transport to naval reconnaissance and anti-submarine warfare.

Consolidated started work on the project in January 1939, and the prototype XB-24 first flew on December 29. The first important production version was the B-24D (in the drawings), which was ordered in large numbers (a total of 2738) in 1940. The B-24Ds (called the Liberator Mk.III by the RAF and the PB4Y-1 by the US Navy) were used by the USAAF as bombers from June 1942 onwards. Their initial activity was concentrated in the Middle East and the Pacific. The subsequent B-24E version was similar, while the G variant underwent a significant modification, with the addition of a mechanically controlled turret on the nose, to provide greater defence against head-on attacks. These variations were the last of any significance, and from mid-1943 onwards the gigantic industrial machine that produced the B-24s at full capacity produced aircraft whose exterior appearance was practically identical. Similar to the B-24Gs were in fact the subsequent B-24Hs, of which 3100 were produced.

It was on this version that the most numerous version, the J, was based. From 1943 onwards, 6678 were built. The B-24Hs and B-24Js provided to the RAF under the Lend-Lease Act were renamed Liberator Mk.VIs. Further improvements in the on-board systems characterized the last L and M versions, of which 1677 and 2593 were built respectively up to May 31,1945.

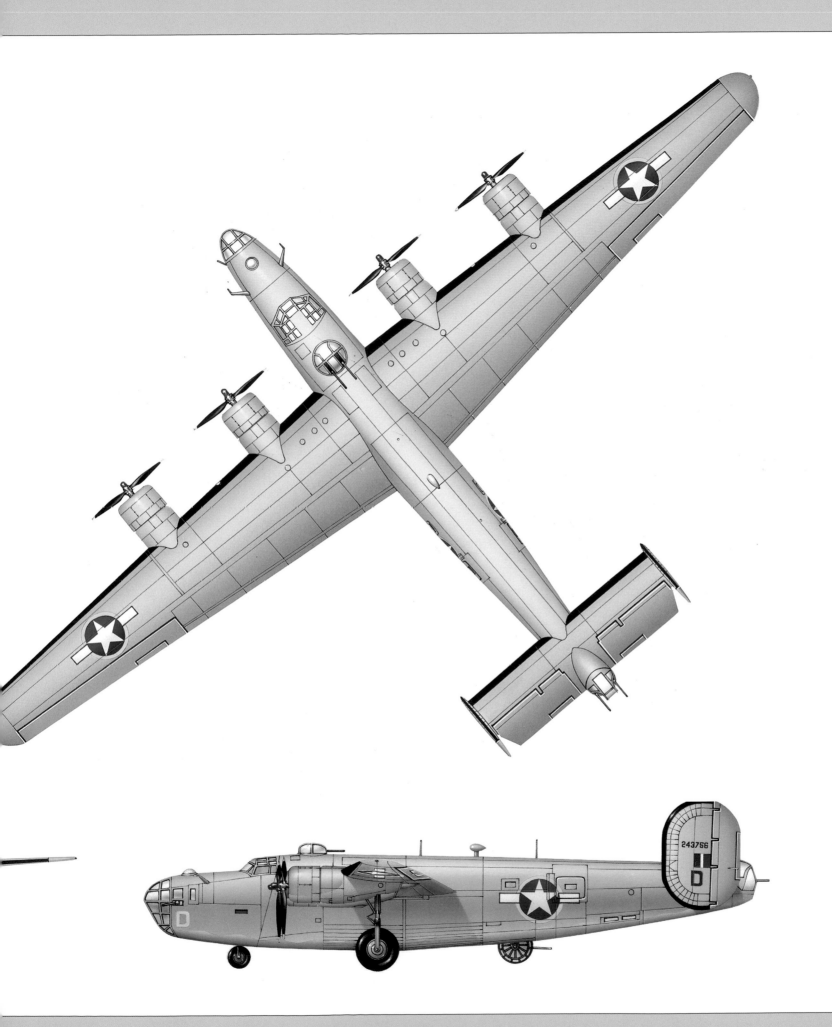

de Havilland Mosquito

GREAT BRITAIN

Rarely has a combat aircraft proved as versatile and effective as the de Havilland Mosquito. This streamlined, powerful twin-engined aircraft built entirely in wood was exceptional as a fighter, reconnaissance aircraft, and bomber, to the point that the later versions remained in service long after the end of the Second World War. Only in 1951 did the units of Bomber Command replace the old "Mossie" with the two-jet English Electric Canberra. In all, from 1941 to 1950, 6439 Mosquitoes were built in Great Britain, in over 10 different versions, while another 1342 were built in Canada and Australia. The project was started privately by de Havilland in 1938, with the aim of producing a bomber-reconnaissance aircraft able to fly so high and fast as not to require defensive weaponry.

The proposal, initially rejected by the Air Ministry, was taken into consideration immediately after the declaration of war. On November 25, 1940 the first prototype took its maiden flight, and from the very beginning it was clear that this was a real thoroughbred, highly manouvrable and with excellent performance in terms of horizontal and climbing speed (during test flights, a peak of 384 mph (640 km/h) was achieved). The first operational version was the PR.Mk.I reconnaissance model, in September 1941. In 1942, this was followed by the Mk.IV bomber (in the drawings) and the Mk.II night-fighter. These three initial types were the basis for many other series, which were constantly updated and improved.

The most widely deployed Mosquito was the Mk.VI (2584 built, adapted as a fighter-bomber and in service from 1943 onwards).

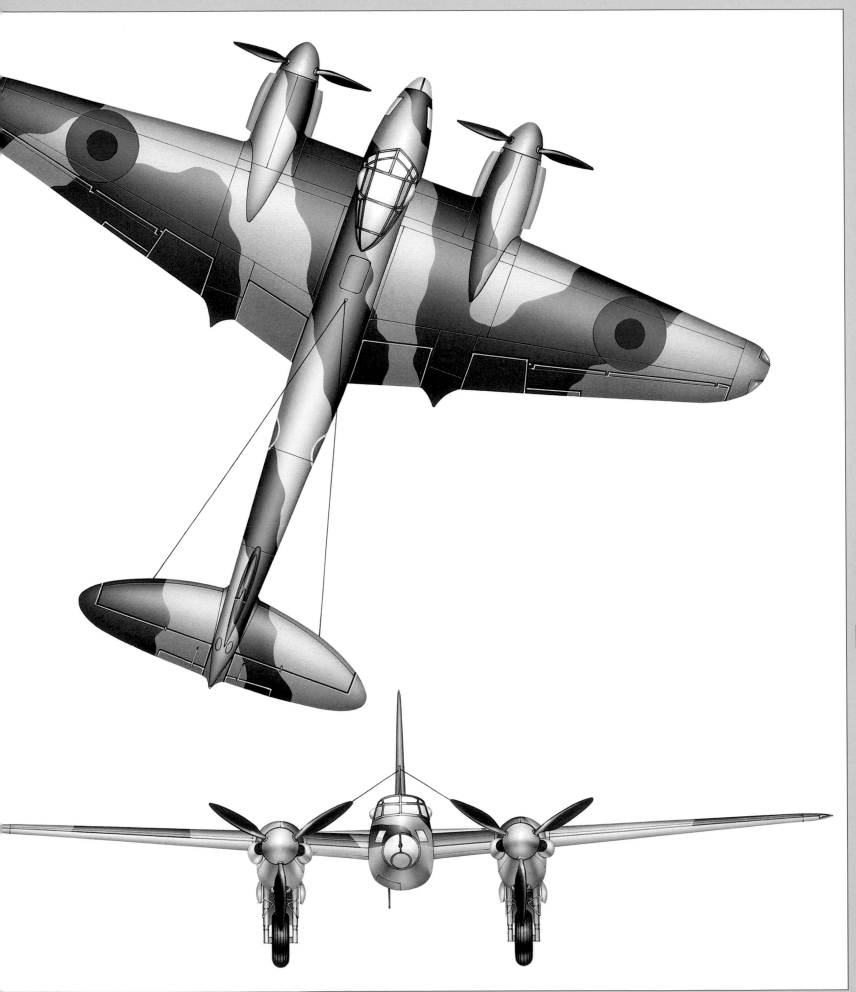

Boeing B-17 Flying Fortress

UNITED STATES

Rarely in the history of aviation has an airplane been both a symbol of military power and a legend for pilots and crews. Such a plane is the Boeing B-17 Flying Fortress, the first strategic bomber deployed by the United States during the Second World War, the machine that, perhaps more than any other, contributed to the destruction of the Third Reich and the end of hostilities in Europe. Overall, 12,731 B-17s were built throughout the war. The first flight of the prototype took place on July 28, 1935 and the first order of 39 B-17Bs in 1938; there followed in 1939, 38 B-17Cs and, in 1940, 42 B-17Ds. These last two versions were the first to see combat; from May 1941 bearing British insignia and immediately after Pearl Harbor with those of the US. In 1941, the B-17E variant appeared; the entire tail section had been radically changed to provide greater stability and to allow the installation of defensive weaponry in the tail. The armaments were thus improved, with two turrets, one on the back and one on the undercarriage, equipped with 12.7-mm machine-guns. 512 of the B-17Es were built, followed by 3400 B-17Fs (maiden flight on May 20, 1942), with even more powerful weaponry.

Much larger numbers were produced of the last variant, the B-17G (in the drawings), which in 1943 began operations on the European front. In all, 8695 airplanes left the assembly lines.

These Fortresses had improved defensive weaponry with a remote controlled turret in the nose section.

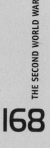
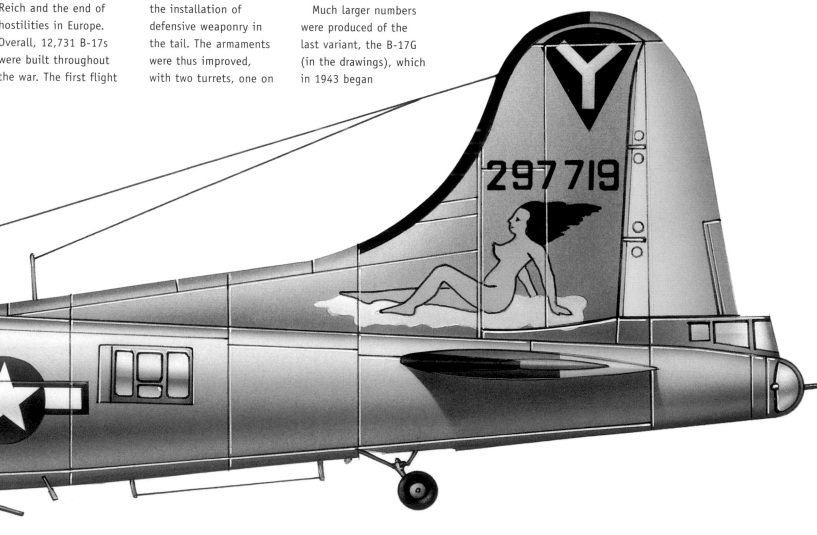

SOVIET UNION

The development of military aviation in the Soviet Union started after direct involvement in the war. The great progress seen in the 1930s had fooled strategists with regard to the effective potential of the air force. At the time of the German attack, on June 22, 1941, what was considered one of the most powerful air forces in the world was literally swept aside by the superiority of the Luftwaffe. At that time, modernization programs were still being discussed, units of the VVS (Voenno-Vozdushnye Sili, the military air force) were in the middle of being reorganized, and were equipped with obsolete machines clearly inferior to those of the enemy. An official Soviet report dramatically described the effects of this lack of preparedness: in the first nine hours of Operation Redbeard, the Germans destroyed 1200 Russian airplanes, 800 of which were still on the ground, and decisively gained supremacy in the air.

Nevertheless, for the whole of the 1930s the development of aviation in the USSR had been extremely significant. Of particular importance was the complete reorganization of the industrial system and the creation of an important center for research and co-ordination, the Central Institute of Aerodynamics (TsAGI), whose tasks were to design machines and engines, carry out study and research, recruit engineers and technicians, and co-ordinate their work. In this fervor of activity, a great many products were developed, and many bore the names of technicians of great talent, such as Tupolev, Polikarpov, Grigorovich ,and Yakovlev—designers who would become famous throughout the world, some to this day, and would leave their mark as major players in the history of aviation. The reaction to the first, crushing strike by the Luftwaffe, however, was not long in coming. The winter was on the Russians' side, and drastically slowed

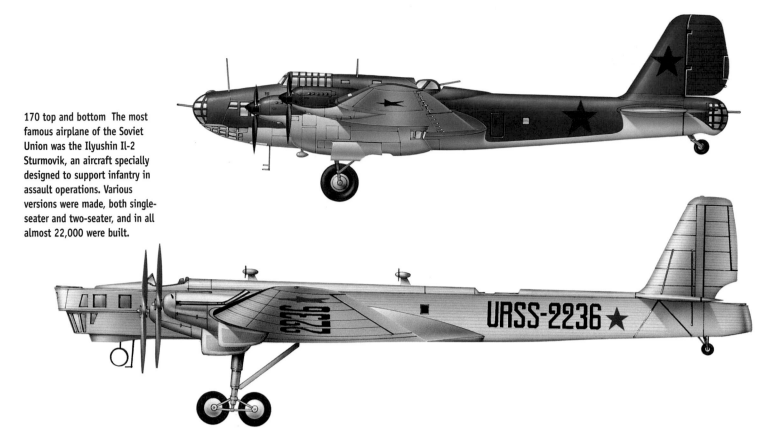

170 top and bottom The most famous airplane of the Soviet Union was the Ilyushin Il-2 Sturmovik, an aircraft specially designed to support infantry in assault operations. Various versions were made, both single-seater and two-seater, and in all almost 22,000 were built.

down the intensity and effectiveness of German airborne operations. It also made it possible to implement an emergency plan which many considered desperate, but seemed to be the only possible way of continuing with the programs of industrial reorganization, and with them, the design and production of new models: the transferral of the war industry to locations far from the front. The process, which was long and complex, required an immense effort, but it was finally completed and gave the hoped-for results. Over 600 plants were moved to areas considered out of danger because they were beyond the range of the Luftwaffe: the Volga, the Urals, and western Siberia. Entire factories of airplanes and engines were dismantled and reassembled, and study and research centers were transferred with them. The immediate effect was negative, considering its direct consequences for aircraft production. Even though a total of 15,735 airplanes of all types were built in 1941, the second half of the year saw a real collapse, which continued in early 1942, with 1039 aircraft completed in January, 915 in February, and 1647 in March. But recovery was just round the corner.

171 top and center Two Soviet four-engined bombers, the Petlyakov Pe-8 and the giant Tupolev TB-3.

171 bottom Another prestigious Soviet-produced aircraft, the twin-engined Petlyakov Pe-2.

Ilyushin Il-2/Il-10

SOVIET UNION

One of the most effective series of combat aircraft produced in the Soviet Union during the Second World War was that of the Ilyushin Shturmoviks. Starting with the initial Il-2 model of 1940 up to the final Il-10 version in 1944, these robust and efficient single-engined ground-attack aircraft represented a formidable weapon in the hands of Soviet pilots, and their role in the conflict can be summarized in Stalin's comment in 1941 on the use of the first mass-produced aircraft: "The Shturmovik is at least as essential to the Red Army as oxygen and bread".

Deliveries of the Il-2 fu started in April 1941. Right from the beginning, it proved to be extremely effective against the German armoured units. The originality of the design resided in the fact that the entire front section of the aircraft (from the engine housing to the cockpit) was built in a single armoured shell, which also had a

structural function. This solution, in addition to ensuring maximum defensive protection for the engine unit and the crew, also allowed significant weight savings compared to a traditional structure subsequently armoured. Additionally, the entire fuselage was protected with steel plating and thick duralumin, making the Il-2 a real "flying tank",

practically invulnerable to light weapons. This potential was completed by heavy offensive weaponry, which included two 20-mm cannons and up to 1400 lb (600 kg) in bombs.

Overall, over 36,000 were built (setting a production record for combat aircraft), and the final variants continued to be produced until 1955 (the drawings show the

Il-2M3 of 1942).

After the war, the Il-10 was supplied to the air forces of the satellite countries of the Soviet Union (Hungary, Romania, communist China, North Korea, Albania, Czechoslovakia, Bulgaria, and East Germany). It was also used in the Korean War, then withdrawn from the units of the Soviet VVS in 1956.

Yakovlev Yak-9

SOVIET UNION

The Yakovlev series of fighters, originating with the Yak-1 of 1941, was one of the most important families of combat aircraft produced in the Soviet Union during the Second World War. Of the over 30,000 built, 16,769 were of the Yak-9 variant, which served as the basis for the final model, the Yak-9P of the post-war years, the last and highest expression of the cell. The Yak-9 was originally a development of the 1941 Yak-7 fighter, of which 6399 were built.

In particular, it was from the experimental Yak-7D variant that the new model was derived. The decision to produce an improved series of this machine had been dictated by the need to increase its range.

Production began in summer 1942, and the Yak-9 was delivered to fighter units in October. One year later, the 9D variant entered service, with a more powerful engine. This was used as a long-range escort fighter. The increased range (which managed to exceed 780 miles/1300 km) was obtained by reducing the offensive weaponry to a 20-mm cannon and a 12.7-mm gun.

These airplanes were used to escort American bomber formations, flying from bases in Great Britain to make raids on the oil facilities in Romania.

The last variant produced in the years of conflict was the Yak-9U, which appeared in December 1943. In this model, Yakovlev radically renewed the cell, redesigning the entire basic structure— now entirely in metal— and perfecting the aerodynamics. Additionally, the wingspan and wing area were increased, while the more powerful 1650 hp Klimov M-107A engine was fitted, significantly improving performance, with peaks of 420 mph (700 km/h) at altitudes of 17,600 ft (5500 meters).

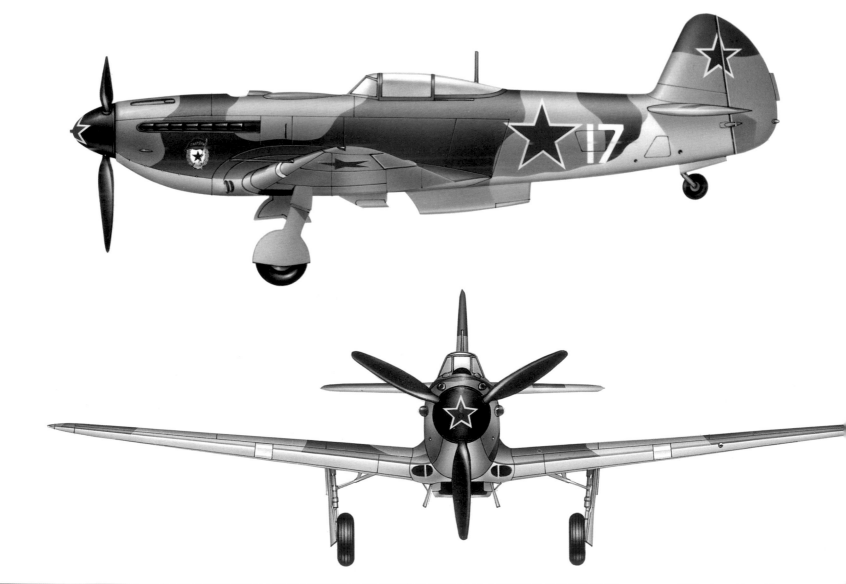

In 1942, 25,400 airplanes left the assembly lines, in addition to 38,000 engines. And this manufacturing drive, along with new designs, especially of fighters and attack aircraft, contributed to the gradual reconquest of air supremacy. In the last two years of the war, the results were even more significant: 35,000 airplanes (and 49,000 engines) built in 1943, 40,300 in 1944, and 20,900 in the first half of 1945. At the same time, the process of industrial transformation continued, with the increased mechanization and rationalization of assembly lines and production units, and with a gradual shift from traditional construction methods using wood to more modern approaches based on the use of metal not only in the structures, but also in the covering.

The Allies provided a vital contribution to this evolution, by supplying means, materials, and technologies. Between 1941 and 1945, the United States alone sent the Soviet Union around 15,000 airplanes of all kinds, and no less than $500 million in machinery, plant, and raw materials such as steel, copper, and aluminium. Thanks to this impressive outside help, the aeronautical industry managed to achieve complete autonomy and full competitiveness.

The process of expansion, however, did not stop at the end of the war, during which the USSR managed to produce an enormous total of 125,000 airplanes, with a production rate of 41,800 units per year achieved in 1945. While in the United States and Great Britain the end of hostilities led to a drastic reduc-

tion in military production programs (and above all airplanes), the Soviet Union experienced the exact opposite. The industry of weapons, particularly relating to the world of aviation, did anything but slow down. By now consolidated in its role as an antagonist of the Western bloc, the USSR took advantage of the relative and temporary weakness of its former allies to recover lost time and to acquire the technology it lacked, in particular the jet engine, which, unlike Germany, Great Britain, and the USA, it did not possess at the end of the war.

The USSR received a vital boost from the West in 1946, when Great Britain agreed to supply Moscow with some models of its most advanced turbo reactor, the Rolls-Royce Nene and their production under licence. In one fell swoop, the Soviet aeronautical industry made up all the time it had previously lost.

176 top A Lavochkin La-5.

176 bottom and 177 bottom right The Yak-1, the first in a line of successful Soviet fighters. It was also supplied to the Yugoslav Air Force.

177 top The Yakovlev Yak-3 was used not only by the Soviets, but also by the French and Polish. It was considered one of the best designs produced by Yakovlev.

177 bottom left In the Russian Air Force, women pilots also became famous.

The insignia of Soviet airplanes

Up until the end of 1940, the identification codes of Soviet aircraft were essentially composed of a prefix indicating the function of the aircraft and a serial number.

The main ones were as follows:
ARK = Arctic service
BB = short range bomber
DB = long range bomber
SB = medium bomber
TB = heavy bomber.
I = fighter
KOR = onboard aircraft
PS = transport
U and UT = training

From 1941 onwards, the names of the designers were also indicated with an abbreviation.
ANT = Tupolev
Il= Ilyushin
La = Lavochkin
MiG = Mikoyan and Gurevich
LaGG = Lavochkin, Gorbunov and Gudkov
Pe = Petlyakov
Po = Polikarpov
Su = Sukhoi
Tu = Tupolev
Yak = Yakovlev

FRANCE

Birthplace of aviation in Europe, France had emerged as one of the major air powers in the First World War, but arrived on the threshold of the Second World War unprepared. The Armée de l'Air, established on the basis of the organizational plan in 1933 and officially made the third armed force the following year, only began to operate as a structure in 1936. It would have had time to consolidate its position if its needs had been recognized and satisfied with the necessary haste, but this did not happen for a series of political, strategic, and industrial reasons, which largely diminished its role and potential, particularly compared with the modern and organized German war machine.

Immediately after the Armistice in 1918, the Aviation Militaire had been subjected to significant cuts. The 100 squadrons remaining operational still represented a significant air force, and were considered necessary to impose compliance with the peace treaty, and to control colonial territories. But the situation did not last

178 top The French twin-engined Bloch 174 light bomber.

178 bottom At the outbreak of the Second World War, the Morane Saulnier M.S.406 fighters were used extensively, but results against the more agile and faster German Bf.109s were disappointing.

179 top: a derivation of the Morane Saulnier M.S. 406 resulted in the Finnish Mörkö Moraani, with 41 lanes refitted with Klimov M-105Ps Soviet engines captured by the German.

179 bottom Better performance was provided by the Dewoitine D.520, although only a few dozen were used in operations.

long. Towards the end of the 1920s, convinced that the League of Nations was able to deal with the international disarmament issue, French politicians and strategists shelved development of the air force and decided to give priority to strengthening the army.

The Maginot Line, the pride of military engineering at the time, cost enormous sums of money, and gave a false sense of security; behind this barrier an impressive 110 divisions could be mobilized in a short time, and this was judged more than sufficient to block any attempt at aggression from Germany. No one realized the extreme weakness of this strategic line, which was the result of obsolete theories dating back to the First World War. Events provided a brutal demonstration of this. At the time of the offensive, the defensive line was simply ignored by the Germans, and its entire potential cancelled by Luftwaffe bombing.

The delay in the establishment of the Armée de l'Air was made worse by the effects of the far-reaching process of reorganization which preceded slowly and with difficulty while the rearmament program was being developed. Starting from 1936 the logistical and functional structure of the units was radically changed, together with their organization. The Air Regiments disappeared, and were replaced by the Escadres (Air Divisions), each composed first of two, then three Groupes (Air Brigades), each in turn structured in two to three Escadrilles (Flights). The national air forces were divided into four Regions, each in turn sub-divided into two Zones, while a fifth air Region dealt with North Africa. The Navy, lastly, had the on-board air force (aircraft of the aircraft carrier Béarn and the airplane support ship Cdt. Teste and those on board the larger units) and the Coastal Air Corps.

In theory, this new structure was more modern and organized than the previous one. In practice, however, it was precisely this which restricted the relaunching of the aeronautical industry. In previous years, this had produced a large number of good prototypes, but had not been able to start mass-production due to the uncertainty of the operational framework. Further delays were caused by the process of nationalizing the industries which produced airplanes and aircraft engines, implemented by the government in the conviction that this was necessary to co-ordinate the sector and restore competitiveness. But not even this worked. The uncertainties remained and production levels were seriously affected. The programs provided for the construction of 200 airplanes per month, but until the end of 1938, deliveries managed to satisfy at best only a fifth of the demand, no more than 40 aircraft per month.

Stalemate ensued and in order to buy time, it became necessary to purchase foreign machines. France was the first European nation to make widespread use of American products. In late 1938 the first 100 Curtiss Hawk 75A fighters were ordered, and in the field of light bombers, they requested Martin 167 Marylands and Douglas DB-7s. For training, they chose Italian Caproni Ca.313s and Nardi FN.305s. At the end of 1939 the French authorities urgently requested from the United States a hundred Consolidated B-24 heavy bombers, whose prototype had only just made its maiden flight, on December 29.

But such efforts were largely futile, since the rapidly deepening crisis meant that foreign orders could only be partly met. On September 3, 1939, when it entered the war against Germany, France had 1200 modern combat aircraft (of which 826 were fighters, some not yet operational), and around 1500 airplanes dating back to the early 1930s (of which almost 400 were fighters).

The fighter units were equipped with Morane-Saulnier M.S.405s and 406s, Curtiss Hawk 75As, and Potez 63s, in addition to the extremely old Dewoitine D.500s and D.510s. Reconnaissance, in addition to the same Potez 63, was based on particularly obsolete airplanes, such as the Les Mureaux 113s

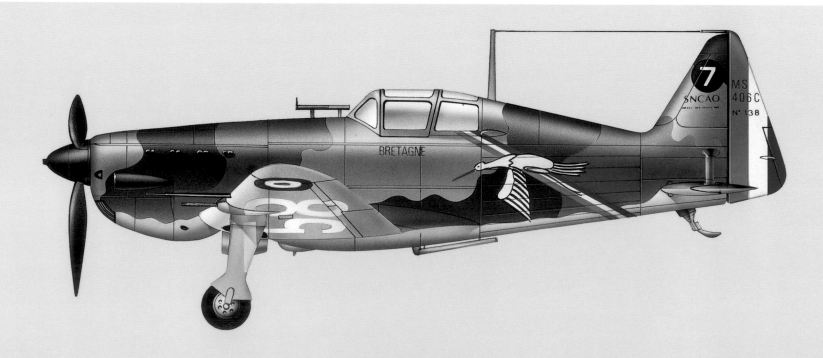

180-181 The Lioré et
Olivier LeO.45 twin-engined
bomber.

180 bottom and 181 bottom
The profiles illustrate two
aircraft of the Armée de l'Air:
the Morane-Saulnier M.S.406
and the Potez 63.

and 115s, and Potez 25s and 39s. The bombing units were even worse off, since in practice they could only rely on the old Bloch 200s and 210s, and Amiot 143s.

On May 10, 1940 the size of the front line had risen to 1501 aircraft, including 784 fighters. In the face of the enemy's immense superiority, the Armée de l'Air fought with great honor and sacrifice, but could not stop the inevitable. On June 14, German troops entered Paris. On June 22, the armistice was signed. Afterwards, some of the men and materials went to the Vichy air force, while other pilots escaped to Great Britain, where they continued to fight with the RAF, under the insignia of the Air Force of Free France.

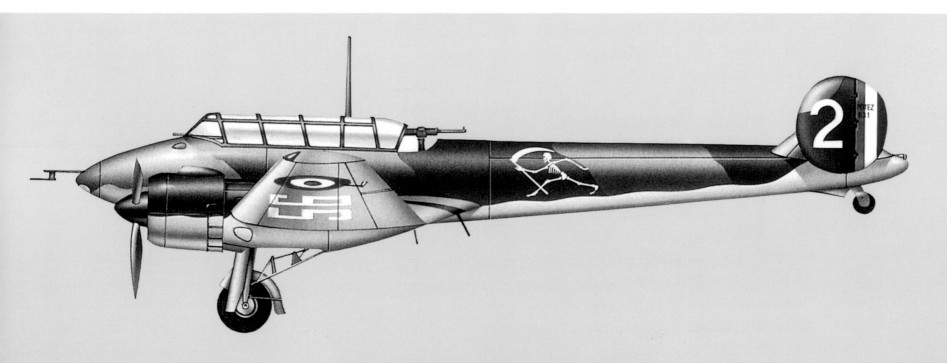

Dewoitine D.520

FRANCE

Small, agile and powerful, the Dewoitine D.520 fighter was the only airplane of the Armée de l'Air able to successfully counter the more powerful aircraft of the Luftwaffe.

The very small number operational at the moment of the German attack fought with great determination. They were unable to prevent the inevitable, but went down in history as the best French combat aircraft of the war.

Emile Dewoitine, the "father" of the D.520, had privately started work on the project in 1936. The well-known airplane builder, appointed director-general of the new Société Nationale de Construction Aéronatiques du Midi (SNCAM), was convinced he could produce a modern fighter able to fly at over

312 mph (520 km/h). But amidst the general uncertainty about relaunching military aviation at that time, the development phase was shelved for almost two years. It was only on April 3,1938 that he was authorized to produce three prototypes, the first of which made its maiden flight on October 2 and the last on May 5, 1939. The tests revealed excellent performance, especially in terms of speed, with peaks of 330 mph (550 km/h) at an altitude of 16,650 ft (5200 meters), and with a climbing time of 12 minutes and 53 seconds to 25,600 ft (8000 meters). Evidence of its excellent aerodynamic and structural characteristics was provided on February 8, 1939, when the first prototype achieved a speed of 495 mph (825 km/h) in a nosedive. The potential of the D.520 received

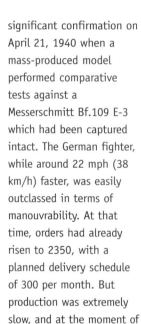

significant confirmation on April 21, 1940 when a mass-produced model performed comparative tests against a Messerschmitt Bf.109 E-3 which had been captured intact. The German fighter, while around 22 mph (38 km/h) faster, was easily outclassed in terms of manouvrability. At that time, orders had already risen to 2350, with a planned delivery schedule of 300 per month. But production was extremely slow, and at the moment of

the German attack, only 36 D.520s were operational. The number increased gradually and during the Battle of France, they managed to equip five fighter units.

By the time of the French occupation, of the 437 Dewoitines completed, 351 had actually reached the fighting units. These airplanes achieved 108 confirmed downings and a further 39 probable strikes.

The occupation of France did not stop the fighter's career. In April 1941 the

Germans recommenced production, which continued up to December 1942, taking the total built to 775.

These served in the Vichy Air Force, the Luftwaffe, the Regia Aeronautica, and in the air forces of other Axis countries. At the end of the war, after the re-establishment of the French Air Force, some D.520s which had survived the war were given dual controls and used as trainers. The last flight was made on September 3, 1953.

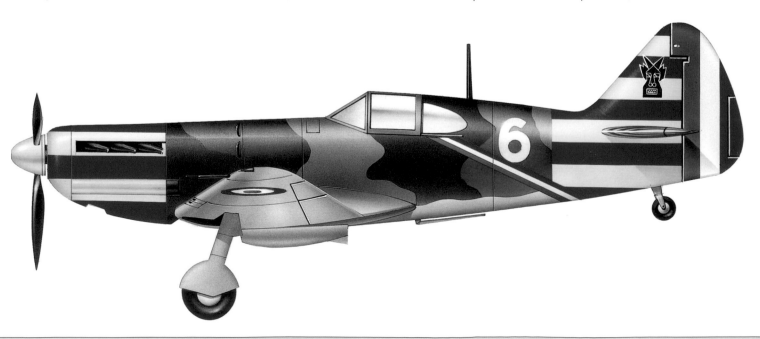

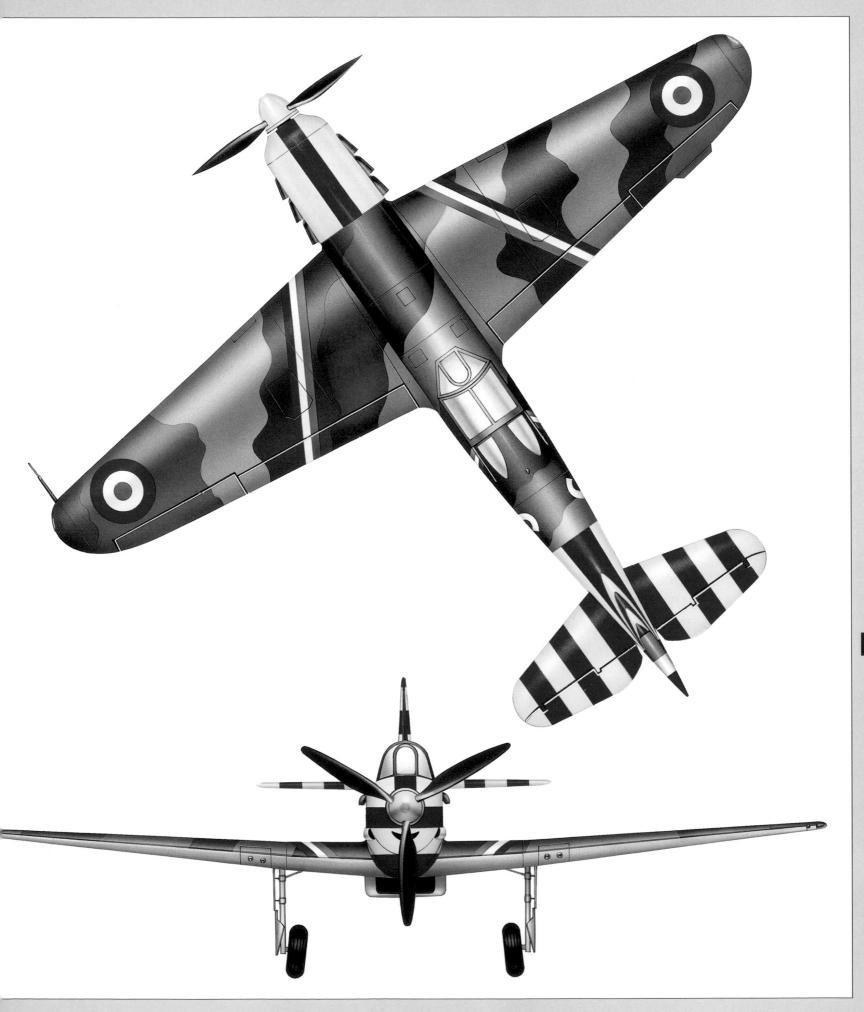

planes. This force was wiped out: around 330 airplanes were destroyed, while the Luftwaffe lost 258, with another 263 damaged. As had happened in Czechoslovakia, many Polish aviators fled to Great Britain, where they distinguished themselves, above all, in the Battle of Britain.

The superiority of the Luftwaffe rapidly swept aside Yugoslavia and its air force, which was not particularly competitive, despite the appearance of some good designs (such the Rogozarski IK-3 fighters). On the day of the German attack, April 6, 1941, the Yugoslavian air force had around 600 airplanes in the field, almost all obsolete. Its spirited display of courage did nothing to delay the moment of surrender on April 17.

The alliance with the Axis powers influenced the development of military aviation in Romania. The Army's first air corps had been formed at the time of the First World War and, subsequently, the air force had adopted French and British airplanes. These aircraft were soon replaced by Italian and German models and this dependency slowed down the organization of an independent aeronautical industry. The only valid original design, the I.A.R.80 fighter, arrived in the early years of the war.

The situation in Finland was much more dramatic. The air force of this small Nordic country, after having fought for three years against the Soviets, was forced by the clauses of the Armistice to turn its weapons against its former ally Germany. Its material was extremely varied: in the fighter and bomber units there were English, Dutch, Italian, French, German, and even Russian airplanes. Despite this, Finnish

industry managed to add an entirely national product to this heterogeneous arsenal: the Myrsky II fighter, which entered service in 1944.

Amidst the incredible upheaval in the rest of Europe, Sweden managed to remain neutral. Its air force, Svenska Flygvapnet, had been established in 1926 and had in service a number of combat airplanes, mostly English and Italian, used for the defence of its national frontiers. In the war years, the Swedish industries also produced original designs, including the Saab 18 bomber and the F.F.V.S. J.22 fighter, and laid the basis for a brilliant post-war future.

On the other side of the world, Australia deserves particular mention. Despite its almost total dependence on English and American supplies, it made a crucial contribution to the Allied forces. The central nucleus of the military air force had been formed in 1913 and, after its experiences in the First World War, the Australian Flying Corps evolved into the Royal Australian Air Force (RAAF) on March 31, 1921. Up until the mid-1930s, the RAAF was fuelled by British supplies, but in 1935 the threat of Japanese expansionism drove it to free itself, at least partly, from this restriction.

In 1936 the first national aircraft industry was established (the Commonwealth Aircraft Corporation), which produced the American trainer North American NA-33 under licence. In 1939, a new factory (the Government Aircraft Factory) built an improved version of the English twin-engined Bristol Beaufort. In following years this policy bore fruit: not only did it mean the RAAF could be supplied with good equipment, whilst awaiting for Allied provisions, but it also made it possible to produce original designs, including that of the CA-12 Boomerang, a fighter that, for a certain period, was the only combat airplane of any value available to fight the Japanese.

186 and 187 top Among the aircraft which faced the Japanese air force in Malaya (now Malaysia), were the Australian Commonwealth CA-12 Boomerang fighters, designed and produced nationally (Commonwealth Aircraft).

187 bottom The F.F.V.S. J.22, a modern Swedish fighter built between 1941 and 1942, which remained in service until the 1950s, and the Yugoslav Rogozarski IK-3.

Messerschmitt Bf.110 Zerstörer

GERMANY

The failure of the Messerschmitt Bf.110 as a heavy fighter (the airplane had been christened Zerstörer [Destroyer] by Göring himself) emerged sensationally during the Battle of Britain.

But the Bf.110 still achieved success in its role as fighter-bomber, reconnaissance aircraft, and night-fighter, to the point that it became irreplaceable. Between 1938 and 1945, around 6050 were built in numerous versions, serving on practically all fronts from the first to the last day of the war.

Towards the end of 1941, when it became clear that the program of the Messerschmitt Me.210 (designed as a successor to the Bf.110) was still far from finished, it became necessary to produce a new, more powerful version of the twin-engined aircraft. This was the Bf.110 G, fitted with a pair of 1475 hp Daimler-Benz DB 605Bs and improved from an aerodynamic point of view.

From this was developed the definitive version of the night-fighter, the G-4; production started in June 1942.

A further variant for night missions (the H4) was derived from the last production version, the Bf.110 H, built in small quantities starting from 1942 alongside the version G.

These airplanes bore the brunt of the defence of the Third Reich during 1943, and the use of the Bf.110 in this role reached its peak at the beginning of the following year, when 60 percent of night-fighters in service with the Luftwaffe were twin-engined Messerschmitts.

The front-line aircraft numbered 320 at most. The drawings show a Bf.110 C.

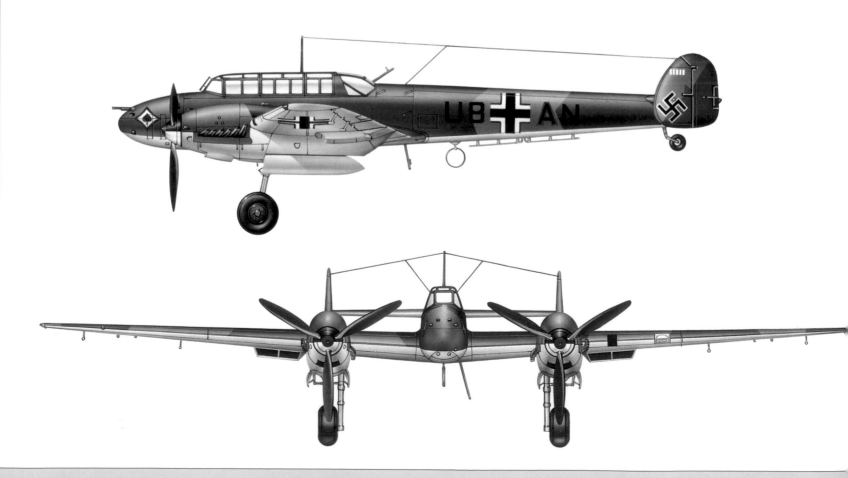

Heinkel He.219 Uhu

GERMANY

Still considered the best night-fighter deployed by Germany in the Second World War, the Heinkel He.219 Uhu ('Owl') never managed to obtain full approval from the chiefs of staff of the Luftwaffe, who were overly concerned with the idea of avoiding wasteful production and of developing radically new models. Consequently, an extremely low number of these powerful, fast, and effective combat machines reached the front line (just under 300).

Moreover, production was suspended in May 1944 bringing to an end all the promising development programs.

The first prototype flew on November 15, 1942 and was followed in December by numerous other experimental versions, in which various types and combinations of offensive armament and radar systems for night search were tested. The aircraft was a streamlined high-winged monoplane, the first in the Luftwaffe to use front tricycle landing gear, and was driven by a pair of 1750 hp Daimler-Benz DB 603 A engines, equipped with annular radiators.

The cockpit was entirely glazed and the two crew (seated shoulder to shoulder and for the first time in aviation history, in ejector seats) enjoyed exceptional visibility. The basic armament consisted of 20-mm and 30-mm cannons installed in the undercarriage fairing, in the wings and subsequently also on the back of the fuselage, set obliquely upwards. After the A-1 reconnaissance version, the first definitive fighter version was the A-2/R1.

The major production variant was the He.219 A-7 (in the drawings), with its formidable firepower: six 30-mm MK 108 cannons and two 20-mm MG 151 cannons.

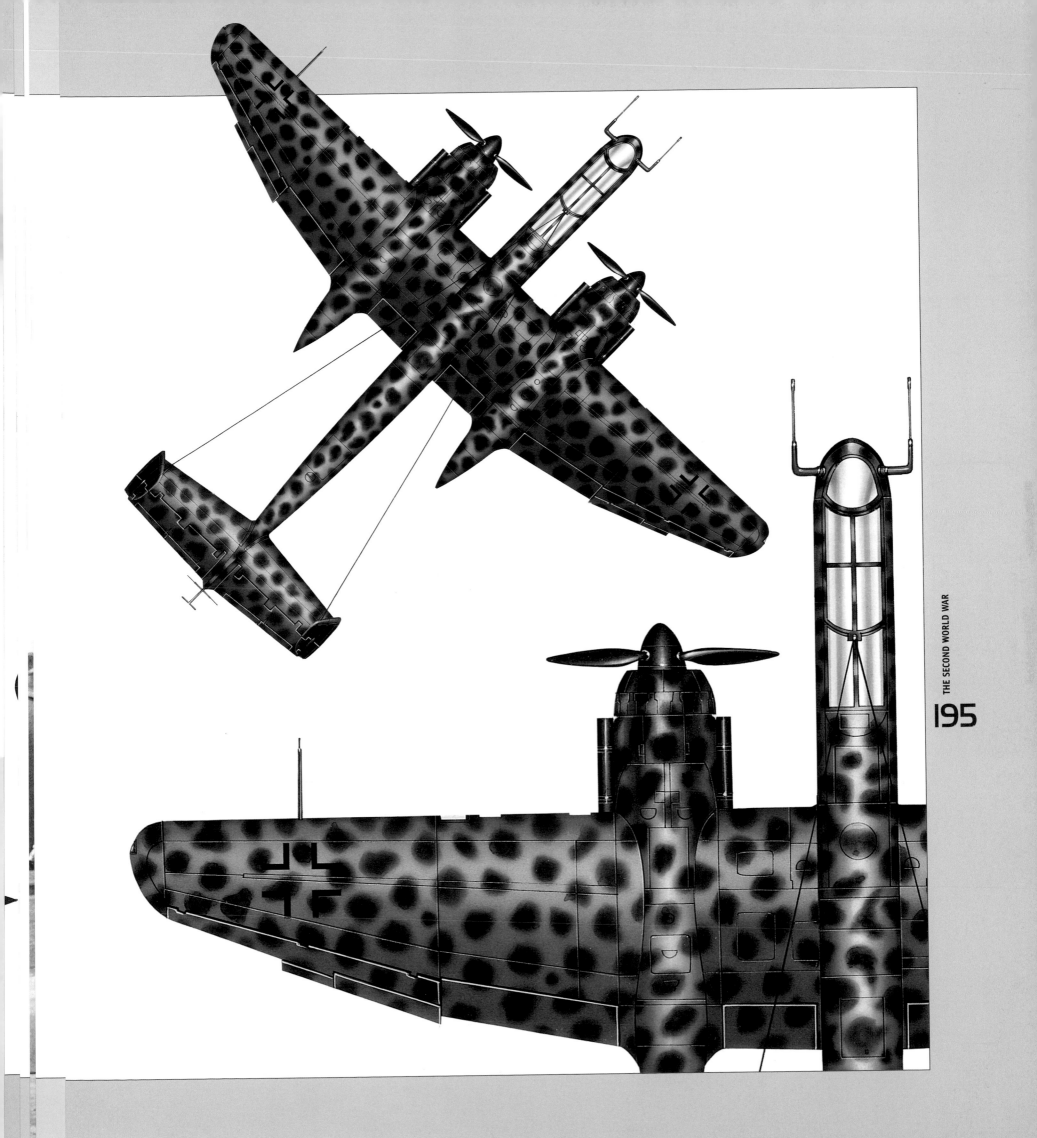

Arado Ar.234 Blitz

GERMANY

The Arado Ar.234 (christened Blitz [Lightning]) was the first jet bomber in the history of aviation. In theory it could have changed the course of the war, in practice it remained a dramatic example of the enormous potential of the German air force, since only a few hundred were built and its use was extremely limited.

The first pre-production version, the B-0s, were delivered in June 1944, and were followed on the assembly lines by the B-1 sub-series (photo-reconnaissance), B-2 (bomber), B-2/1 (search and target identification), B-2/b (reconnaissance) and B-2/r (fitted with auxiliary fuel tanks). The payload of the Arado bombers was held in racks under the nacelles, while the offensive weaponry consisted in a pair of MG 151/20 20-mm cannons housed in the belly of the fuselage which fired towards the tail of the aircraft. The first to enter service was the Ar.234 reconnaissance version.

In July, two airplanes assigned to an experimental unit performed a number of missions, showing themselves capable of eluding enemy fighters. In September, a special unit was set up (the Sonderkommando Götz), with reconnaissance duties to prevent the Allied invasion of Holland.

Two months later there followed another two units (the Sonderkommando Hecht and the Sonderkommando Sperling) which were given the task of evaluating the bomber version. This entered service for the first time with the Stabstaffel of the 76th KG; among the missions in which the Ar.234 B-2 took part, the most well known is that against the bridge of Remagen, on the Rhine, in March 1945.

210 top The Cant Z.1007 bis Alcione was deployed by the Regia Aeronautica as a front-line bomber, and served on all fronts.

Since the beginning, in the ambiguous situation which had seen the Luftwaffe use the commercial activity of Deutsche Lufthansa as a cover, the three main German bomber manufacturers, Junkers, Heinkel, and Dornier, had concentrated on producing twin-engined and single-engined models. The one exception in the following years was the four-engined Heinkel He.177, the only strategic bomber deployed by Germany. And even this was only a relative exception, since the He.177 was really a traditional twin-engined aircraft, with the four engine units grouped in pairs in two nacelles. Nor did its use, for a complex series of reasons, mark a change in tendency. The front-line aircraft continued to be the twin-engined Dornier Do.17, Junkers Ju.88, and Heinkel He.111, and the single-engined Junkers Ju.87. While these machines evolved significantly during the conflict, they were never replaced by equally valid new models.

In Italy, the Regia Aeronautica had prepared itself on the basis of its combat experience in Spain, which had given it a misleading view of the effective potential of its force. Unlike its ally, the Luftwaffe, the quantity and quality of Italy's bombing units had not been significantly improved. At the outbreak of hostilities, the main types were the twin-engined Fiat B.R.20 and the three-engined Savoia Marchetti S.M.79 and CANT Z.1007 bis which, while substantially similar to their international counterparts, in practical terms were poorly defended and extremely vulnerable. These airplanes remained basically unchanged for the entire duration of the war and continued to represent the front-line standard. Italy was extremely late in producing a real strategic bomber, the four-engined Piaggio P.108. This was an excellent, modern machine, but arrived too late when the war was practically over, and in very small quantities.

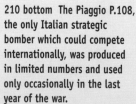

210 bottom The Piaggio P.108, the only Italian strategic bomber which could compete internationally, was produced in limited numbers and used only occasionally in the last year of the war.

211 bottom The twin-engined English Handley Page Hampden used in the first bombing raids against Germany.

France rapidly disappeared from the scene of the conflict due to its occupation so there was no opportunity for significant development in the bomber sector. However, on the eve of hostilities, the Armée de l'Air clearly displayed its antiquated approach, seeing that it still had in service obsolete bombers such as the Amiot 143 and the Bloch 200 and 210. Moreover, the development plans interrupted by German occupation did not provide for the introduction of strategic bombers: the types being prepared were light or medium twin-engined aircraft such as the Potez 630, the LeO 451, and the Amiot 351 and 354.

The Soviet air force's approach also remained mainly tactical, despite its great tradition in producing large multi-engined bombers: the Tupolev TB-3 was still in service in 1939 but by then had been superseded for front-line duties, while the more modern four-engined strategic Petlyakov Pe-8 never proved to be up to the tasks required of it. In addition to the twin-engined Tupolev SB-2, whose excellent performance had made such an impression in Spain, the structure of the armed force continued to be based on other models of light or medium bombers, such as the Ilyushin Il-4, the Tupolev Tu-2, and the Petlyakov Pe-2.

A completely different course was followed by the two main allies against the Axis, Great Britain and the United States. In 1939 England's RAF bombing force was still composed of machines whose design concept dated back to the beginning of the decade. The main types in service were the single-engined Vickers Wellesley and Fairey Battle, and the twin-engined Armstrong Whitworth Whitley, Bristol Blenheim, Handley Page Hampden, and Vickers Wellington. But recovery was not long in coming. In 1936, assessing with great farsightedness the fundamental role of the bomber as an instrument of strategic attack, the Air Chiefs of Staff had started a program for the production of heavy four-engined bombers. The new machines were the Short Stirling, the Handley Page Halifax, and the Avro Lancaster. While entering service at an advanced stage of the war, they performed a crucial role as operations in Europe started to evolve in 1941 after the Battle of Britain, with the air force playing a major role in the second turning point in the war. It was in this period that the Allies started a series of massive raids on enemy territory, which continued until the last days of the conflict.

Avro Lancaster

GREAT BRITAIN

After the Short Stirling and the Handley Page Halifax, the Lancaster was the last heavy bomber deployed by the RAF during the war.

Although it entered service almost a year and a half after its two predecessors, the four-engined Avro proved itself to be the best of them all. The production figures are impressive: from the end of 1941 to the beginning of 1946, 7377 Lancasters were built in three basic versions.

The first prototype of the design, which was an improved version of the twin-engined Manchester, made its maiden flight on January 9, 1941. Immediately afterwards, production started on the first variant, the Mk.I, (3425 built), which entered service early the following year.

Due to the high production rates, there was a problem with the lack of Rolls-Royce Merlin engines. This led to the production of a second version of the bomber, fitted with an alternative engine, the Bristol Hercules radial.

The new prototype was taken into the air for the first time on November 26,1941, and together with two other experimental versions, was subjected to an intense round of trials

which continued until early the following year.

The results were satisfying and production began immediately under the name of Lancaster Mk.II. The new bombers entered active service in March 1943, and gradually re-equipped a number of units of Bomber Command. Despite their good specifications, the Lancaster Mk.IIs were never as good as those fitted with Rolls-Royce engines, and production was stopped after 301 had been built. The arrival in Great Britain of the first Merlins built in the United States under licence by Packard quelled fears of a lack of these engines. Consequently, the Mk.III version (of which 3039 were completed) returned to the original engine, and was fitted with those built in America. In the drawings: A Lancaster Mk.I.

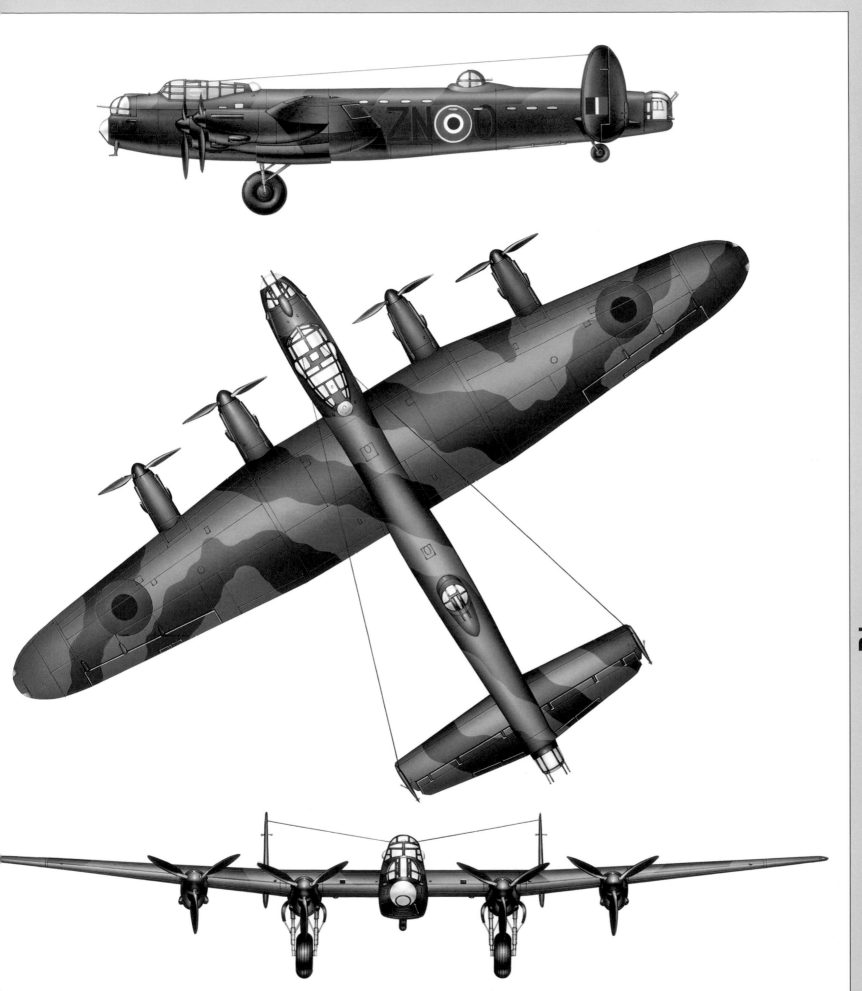

214 top The four-engined Short Stirling was the RAF's first strategic bomber. It entered service in 1940.

The impressive industrial programs were given absolute priority: 2371 Short Stirlings were completed; 6176 of the Handley Page Halifax; and 7377 of the Avro Lancaster. For the Stirling, the debut in combat operations took place on February 10 –11, 1941, with a raid on Rotterdam. This mission was the first in a long series of bombing raids performed by the Short bomber, first during both day and night, then exclusively at night, until there was an adequate supply of the better Halifax and Lancaster bombers.

The Halifax came into service only three months after the Stirling and on March 11, 1941 performed its first bombing mission (on Le Havre). From this date until April 25,1945, the four-engined Handley Page bombers performed 75,532 combat missions and dropped over 227,000 tons of bombs on targets in Europe. Its career was overshadowed only by that of its direct successor, the incomparable Avro Lancaster, which completed 156,000 missions during the war and dropped a total of 608,612 tons of bombs. Apart

214

214 bottom The Vickers Wellington made the first RAF attacks on German cities.

215 top A Handley Page Halifax bomber. These aircraft were used for a long time in operations over Germany and were fitted both with in-line Rolls-Royce Merlins and Bristol Hercules radial engines.

215 bottom The RAF's most important bomber, the Avro Lancaster.

from its excellent flying characteristics and overall performance, the Lancaster's success was also due to its great payload capacity, which allowed it to use bombs of increasing size and weight. There was even a 21,953 lb (9979 kg) "Grand Slam", the heaviest bomb ever carried by an airplane during the war, which was dropped for the first time on March 14, 1945.

The cost of these operations was shared by Great Britain and the United States. In the years immediately leading up to the war, the Americans had managed to fill the existing gap and build an entirely new generation of bombers, whose evolution, apart from crucially conditioning the course of the conflict,

led the way for the rest of the world. This development not only affected the category of light and medium bombers (with the excellent twin-engined Douglas, North American, and Martin planes), but also that of the large four-engined aircraft. The very first two produced, the immortal Boeing B-17 Flying Fortress and the Consolidated B-24 Liberator, were, alongside the British Avro Lancaster and Handley Page Halifax, the great protagonists of the battles in the bloody skies over Europe.

218 top and 219 1941 saw the debut of one of the most famous four-engined American bombers, the B-17 Flying Fortress.

Together with the B-24 Liberator, the Flying Fortress played a predominant role in strategic operations. Thousands were built in a wide range of variants.

The B-17, in particular, was the airplane that perhaps more than any other contributed to the destruction of the Third Reich and the end of hostilities in Europe. Designed in summer 1934, 12,731 were built overall and its most intense and deadly use is embodied in two dates: August 17, 1942, with the commencement of daytime bombing over Europe, and January 27, 1943, with the beginning of similar missions over German territory.

The Consolidated B-24 Liberator designed in 1939, never achieved the popularity of its companion-rival, but this large four-engined bomber made a great contribution to the course of the war. It was also produced in huge quantities, more than any other American Second World War combat aircraft: in all, 18,188 came off the assembly lines. The B-24 entered service in June 1942, and most of its initial activity was concentrated in the Middle East and the Pacific.

It was in the fight against Japan that the best strategic bomber of the conflict, the Boeing B-29, was deployed. This modern, powerful four-engined bomber designed in 1940, represented the first world-class weapon in history, and also the last of the war. Some 3970 were built, 2000 of which were delivered between 1943 and 1945. Its realization engaged the US aeronautical industry in the most massive and complex program of the war years, with thousands of companies involved in the production of components and systems to keep the assembly lines running. The first prototype made its maiden flight on September 21,

218 bottom The Consolidated B-24 Liberators, photographed while launching small caliber bombs, were used operationally on all fronts, but chiefly in the Middle East and the Pacific. In 1944–45 they played a major role in the massive bombing raids on Germany.

1942, and the first unit destined to receive the B-29, the 58 Very Heavy Bombardment Wing, was organized and set up in 1943. Toward the end of the year it was decided to use the new airplanes in the Pacific, as part of 20 Bomber Command, which had bases in India and China.

The first combat operation took place on June 5, 1944; 10 days later the first raid on Japan was performed and, from November 24 onward, these missions took off from the airports of the Marianne Islands. From the first mission against Tokyo until the historic day of August 6, 1945, an increasingly intense and devastating crescendo of attacks were carried out by the B-29. This aircraft specialized in attacks with incendiary bombs, first by day and then by night, at low altitudes, avoiding the enemy defences. The activity culminated with the dropping of two nuclear bombs on Hiroshima and Nagasaki, on August 6 and 9, 1945.

Japan deserves a separate mention. While the war was raging in Europe, on the other side of the world, Japan was still preparing its forces. Bombers were developed in a similar way to Germany, with the main types in the army and navy still represented by medium twin-engined aircraft. Despite displaying excellent general performance and long range, they clearly began to show their limits as the war progressed.

North American P-51 Mustang

UNITED STATES

The US Aeronautics industry provided the cell, the British the engine. The combination of these two technologies resulted in the North American P-51 Mustang, the best fighter of the Second World War. Of the 15,367 P-51s built, most survived the war and remained in active service until the Korean War, well into the jet age.

Work on the project began in April 1940, on the basis of a request from the British Purchasing Commission in search of efficient aircraft.

The prototype flew on October 26, 1940. The airplane, given the name Mustang Mk.I, entered service in spring 1942 as a reconnaissance aircraft. The Mustang was not yet an optimal machine due to the insufficient performance of its Allison engine. The final result was obtained with the Rolls-Royce Merlin built under licence by Packard. Production began in spring 1943 with the P-51B (1988 built) and P-51C (1750) versions. The P-51Bs of the USAAF reached Britain in November 1943, where they were stationed with the 8th Air Force. The development of the project led in 1944 to a new version, the D, which was the most widely produced (shown in the drawings).

The main characteristic of these aircraft (of which 7956 were built) was the drastic revision of the fuselage, made necessary to overcome problems of pilot visibility, and the adoption of a drop cowling system. These structural modifications, together with a more powerful engine, and increased armaments, resulted in the optimum configuration of the Mustang, which would remain unchanged for the rest of its production life. Together with the P-51DS, 1500 P-51Ks were built, fitted with a different type of propeller. Test flights of some more lightweight prototypes led to the design of the last version, the P-51H which, at 470 mph (784 km/h), proved to be the fastest of the entire family. Only 555 of this version of the Mustang were built before the end of the war, and few of them took part in the final operations against Japan. In Europe alone, during the war, the P-51s of the USAAF performed a staggering 213,873 missions, for a total of over 1.12 million hours of flight, and destroyed 4950 enemy planes, 4131 of these on the ground, representing 48.9 percent of total enemy losses.

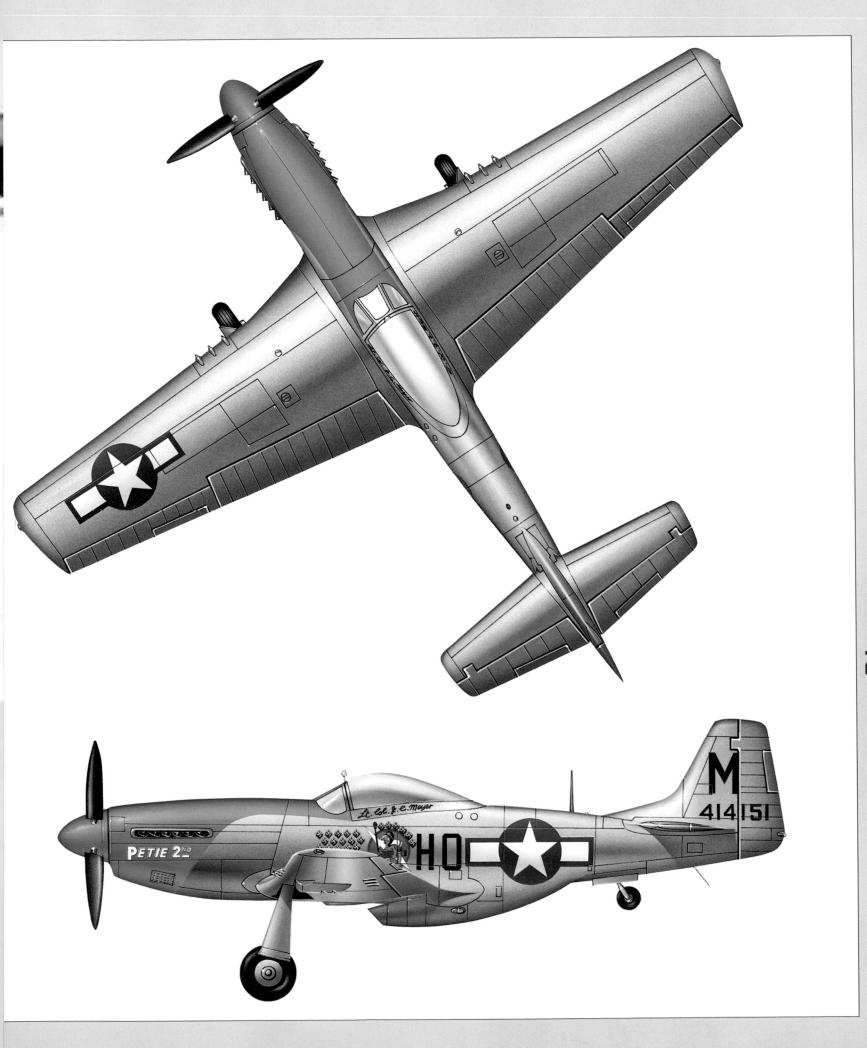

and fast. However, they had disadvantages, mainly due to the vulnerability of their cooling systems, in the form of long pipes and radiators, which were often housed in the wings. If these vital components were broken as a result of enemy fire, engine function was inevitably compromised, despite the engine itself not having been directly hit.

In the case of radial engines, the problems were the exact opposite: less vulnerability and greater reliability, but significant size and increased weight. These limitations, however, were rapidly overcome as engine power increased, and these engines soon began to be widely used in all categories of airplanes. In Europe, the most significant example was the Focke Wulf Fw.190, one of the best fighters in the war, which owed much of its fame to its radial engine, the large BMW 801.

Thanks to careful design work, this engine had been perfectly combined with the aircraft's relatively small and compact cell. The range of power of these engines—the first high-performance versions in their cat-

224 top A German solution to obtain better performance was the Dornier Do.335 of 1943 (top) with two engines fitted in the fuselage, one with a tractor propeller and another with a pusher propeller in the tail. But the fighter was never mass-produced.

224 bottom A Focke Wulf Fw.190D. In this fighter, the original radial engine was replaced by a V-12 engine fitted with an annular radiator.

225 top The engine of the Kawasaki Ki.61 Hien: this was a version of the German Daimler-Benz DB 601 A built under licence.

225 bottom The N version of the P-47 Thunderbolt, designed for the war in the Pacific.

egory developed by German industry after the beginning of the war—went from an initial 1600 hp to almost 2300 hp in the last series.

In Great Britain, radials developed alongside liquid-cooled engines, with excellent results, especially in the design series produced by Bristol. Among the many types, the large and reliable Hercules of 1939 (double-row, 14 cylinders, 1800 hp) was without doubt the best known and most widespread, since it equipped famous airplanes such as the Handley Page Halifax, the Short Stirling, the Bristol Beaufighter, and, to a lesser extent, the Avro Lancaster.

It was in the United States that this type of engine became most widely used and perfected, dominating aircraft production of the period. There were few types of American combat aircraft fitted with in-line engines, and the North American P-51 Mustang, one of the best fighters in the war, owed its success to the adoption of the English Rolls-Royce Merlin.

This particular situation had originated in the 1920s, a period in which, despite the great experience acquired in major international competitions, the development of liquid-cooled engines had been neglected, as industry preferred to focus on the more promising line of radial engines. Nevertheless, the level and quality of the products more than compensated for this failing and, in addition to all bombers, most fighter planes were also fitted with radial engines, especially in the Navy.

Republic P-47 Thunderbolt

UNITED STATES

This was not only the largest and heaviest single-seat single-engine aircraft built during the Second World War, but also served as an exceptional combat machine in the roles of bomber escort and ground attack. 15,683 P-47s left the assembly lines between 1942 and the end of the war in 1945, making it the most widely produced American fighter of the conflict. A great many of these airplanes remained in service after the war in the military air forces of around 15 countries. The prototype flew for the first time on May 6, 1941, and in test flights the Thunderbolt fully proved its power, flying at 379 mph (633 km/h) and climbing to an altitude of 14,630 ft (4572 meters) in only five minutes, despite its high takeoff weight.

In March 1942, aircraft of the initial series, the P-47B (in all, 170) began to leave the assembly lines and were followed in August by the first of 602 P-47Bs. The new fighter became operational in early 1943, with the units of the 8th Air Force based in Great Britain. But the major production variant (12,602 built in total) was the P-47D, which entered service in 1943. This version of the Thunderbolt (in the drawings) fitted with an engine providing more power at altitude and in emergency situations, was able to carry more bombs; it also featured a drop cowling providing total visibility.

The P-47Ds were the first to serve in the Pacific in the units of the USAAF and were also distributed to the Allies: the USSR, Great Britain, Brazil, Mexico, and units of Free France.

After an order for 130 P-47Ms (with a more powerful engine), which began delivery in December 1944, the final production series focused on the N variant, optimized for the particular needs of the war in the Pacific, of which 1816 were built. These last Thunderbolts, in particular, were fitted with a new wing and had a maximum range of 2100 miles (3500 km).

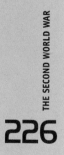

BLOOM'S TOMB

Chance Vought F4U Corsair

UNITED STATES

The Chance Vought F4U Corsair went down in history as one of the best fighters of the Second World War. Together with the Grumman F6F Hellcat, it was used as an on-board combat aircraft in the last two years of the conflict against Japan. In the course of 64,051 missions (54,470 from bases on land and 9581 from aircraft carriers) completed by the pilots of the US Navy and the US Marine Corps, the F4Us destroyed 2140 enemy planes in combat, while suffering only 189 losses.

Production continued constantly for over 10 years up until December 1952. A total of 12,571 were built, and the aircraft continued to provide front-line service in the units of the US Navy until

December 1954. It had a longer career in the French navy, which continued to use the F4U until October 1964.

The prototype made its maiden flight on May 29, 1940. The initial version, the F4U-1 numbered 688, and were followed on the assembly lines by 2066 F4U-1As with a modified engine, undercarriage, and cockpit. The main variants were the F4U-1C (armed with four 20-mm cannons) and the F4U-1D of 1944, with a more powerful engine and armament (in the drawings). Toward the end of 1944, the first F4U-4s made their appearance, in which the already excellent performance of the fighter was further improved. The new Corsairs were only ready in time to take part in the last battles against Japan. Another war was

imminent, however, in Korea, and the last versions of the F4U had a chance to demonstrate their great worth as combat machines. The F4U-4 (2357 built up to August 1947) was followed by new variant (the F4U-5) whose prototype had flown

on April 4, 1946.

The final evolution of the Corsair was completed in 1951 with the F4U-6, which appeared under the name of AU-1 in January the following year. The aircraft had been optimized for ground attack and tactical

support. The AU-1 served as the basis for the last variant, the F4U-7, of which 94 were built for the French Aéronavale, who wanted a multi-purpose tactical aircraft for operations in Indochina. Production ended in December 1952.

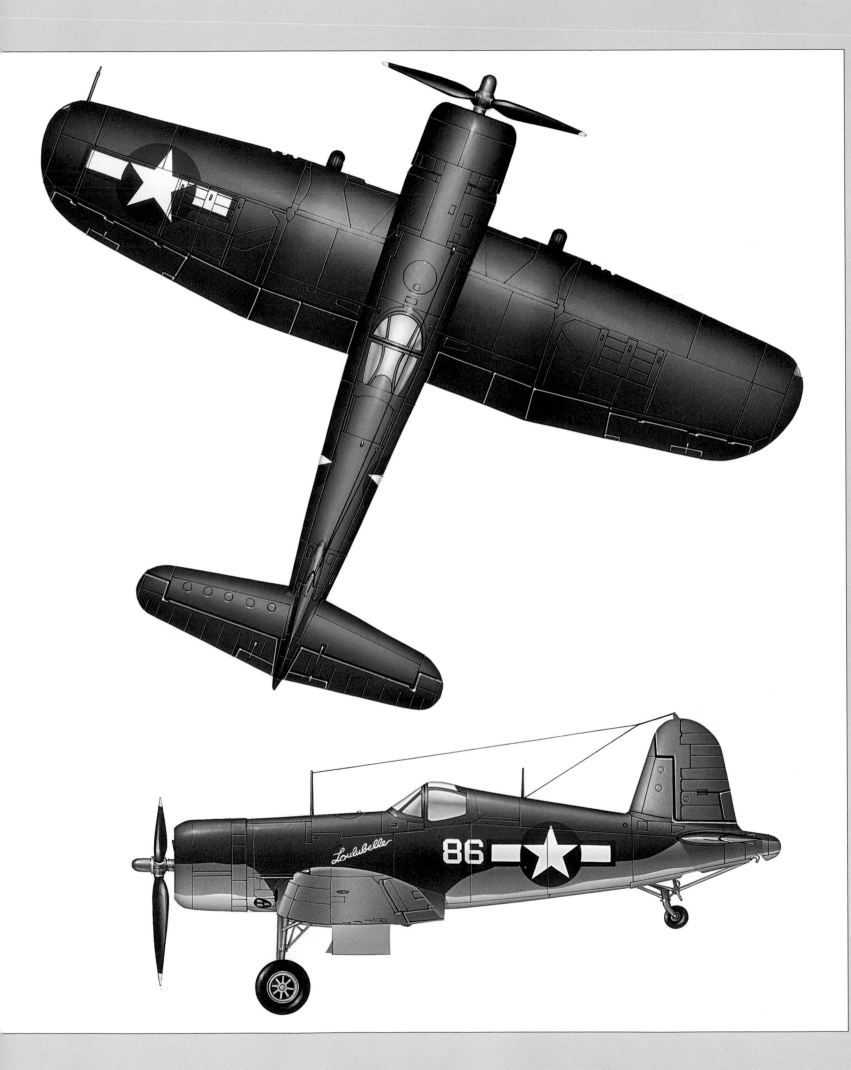

THE JET FIGHTER

The jet era began on August 27, 1939, on the eve of the outbreak of Second World War. On that day, at the Heinkel airfield in Marienehe, the first airplane in history to be driven by a jet engine successfully made its maiden flight. The machine was a Heinkel He.178, a small high-wing experimental monoplane built specifically to accommodate a turbo jet engine (a He.S3b with 836 lb/380 kg thrust, designed by Hans Joachim Pabst von Ohain) whose development had been funded three years earlier by Ernst Heinkel himself. The pilot was Flight-captain Erich Warsitz.

232 top The single-seat fighter version built in Czechoslovakia after the war.

232 center and bottom The Messerschmitt Me.262 Schwalbe in the version with a radar, made its operational debut in July 1944 as an interceptor fighter. It took part in memorable dog fights with Allied aircraft, but the jet failed to save the Luftwaffe and Germany from collapse.

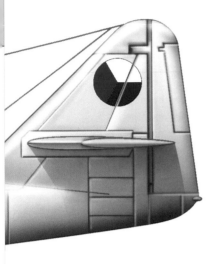

This event gave first advantage to Germany in the race to develop the jet engine. This contest had started in the 1930s and continued with growing ferocity throughout the war, pitting the German and British aeronautical industries against each other in a head-to-head confrontation. The Heinkel He.178 remained at the prototype stage, but still made a precious contribution to the development and production of powerful new machines and first-generation turbine engines, allowing Germany to beat its great rival in the next challenge: the deployment of a combat aircraft fitted with the revolutionary new engines. This was the Messerschmitt Me.262, which made history as the first jet in the world to see active service.

Appearing as a prototype on July 18,1942, and entering service in autumn 1944, the Me.262 proved to be a formidable weapon, thanks to its exceptional speed, which was greater than that of any other aircraft existing at the time. But luckily for the Allies, the enormous potential of this machine was only minimally exploited by Germany.

Some historians have speculated that if the Messerschmitt Me.262 had been available earlier and if it had been used immediately in the role to which it was best suited (as a pure fighter), the course of the Second World War would very probably have been different.

The Germans, however, were also pioneers in other fields: while the Messerschmitt Me.262 was the first jet fighter in the world, the Arado Ar.234 was the first bomber in the history of aviation to be fitted with this revolutionary form of engine.

Together, these two exceptional combat aircraft were the best weapons deployed by the Luftwaffe in the last year of the conflict, even if their operational use did not manage to change the course of the war. In particular, only a couple of hundred of the Arado Ar.234 (christened Blitz, "Lightning", which appeared as a prototype on June 15, 1943) were built, and its combat activity was extremely limited.

233 The Gloster Meteor was the first English jet to enter service, but did not do so until summer 1944, and was not actually used in operations. Its flight performance was inferior to that of the German twin-engined jet.

Messerschmitt Me.262 Schwalbe

GERMANY

This elegant, powerful combat aircraft marked the end of an era in aviation and the beginning of a new age.

With the Messerschmitt, the jet engine made its brilliant debut on a scene that had been dominated by traditional alternative engines. The results were incredible: thanks to its exceptional performance in terms of speed, and its heavy armament, the Me.262 proved to be a formidable threat from the moment it entered service in autumn 1944. However, the manufacturing drive lost momentum, as a series of variants was introduced which attempted to adapt the airplane to a variety of roles—as a bomber, then a night-fighter. The consequence was that the 1430 built overall in the last months of the conflict entered service too late and in too low a quantity to affect the course of the war. The project, which had been launched in late 1938, was delayed by the lack of reliable turbines and the first of the 23 pre-series Me.262 A-0s did not appear until 1944.

The initial version was the A-1a fighter, armed with four 30-mm cannons (in the drawings). These were followed by the A-2a bombers, able to carry up to 2200 lb (1000 kg) of bombs and, in October 1944, the first night-fighter version, the B-1a/U1, derived from the Me.262B-1a training variant was launched. Very few aircraft of this type were delivered in 1945, while the definitive B-2a model did not go beyond the prototype phase.

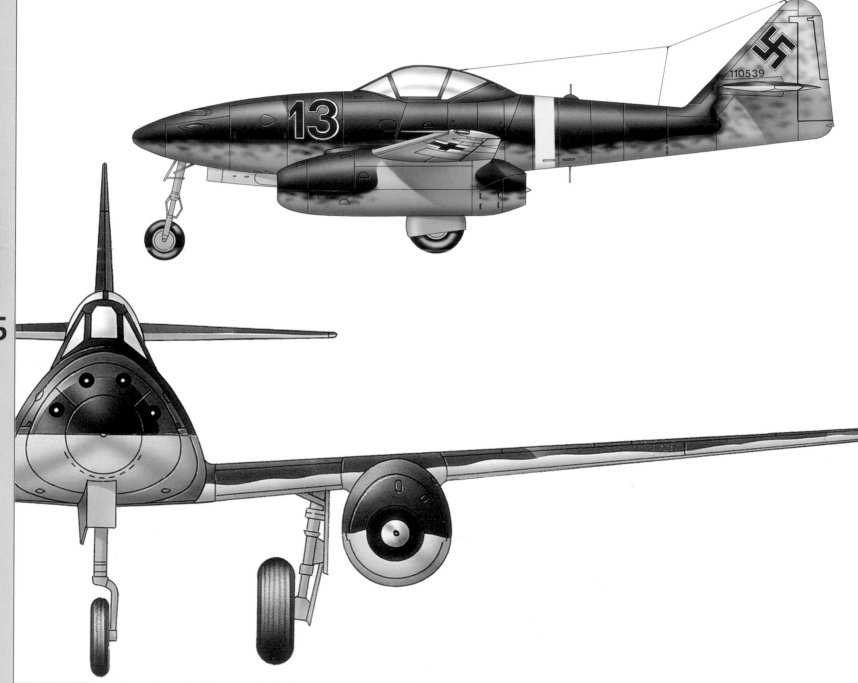

There was a third, equally revolutionary aircraft, the Heinkel He.162 Sala-mander, whose prototype flew on December 6, 1944, having been built in only three months. The project was aimed at developing an interceptor similar to the Me.262, but cheaper and simpler to produce. The production schedules of 4000 per month remained hypothetical, and only a very small number of Salamanders managed to enter service.

Great Britain was not far behind and the technological results they achieved were of an equally high level. Less than two years after the Heinkel He.178's maiden flight, the Gloster E.28/39 experimental prototype made its debut, powered by a Whittle W.1 engine with 858 lb (390 kg) thrust on May 15,1941 from the base at Cranwell in Lincolnshire.

This engine had been designed by Frank Whittle, who in 1930 had been the first in the world to patent research on a gas turbine, which would be tested for the first time on April 12,1937. The Gloster E.28/39 also remained one of a kind, but served as the basis for development of the first British jet to become operational, which was also the only Allied airplane of the new generation to enter service before the end of the war: the Gloster Meteor.

Work on the program started in August 1940 and the first flight had been completed in the fifth prototype on March 5, 1943. The engine of the initial production run of Meteors (Mk.I) was one of the turbo jets derived from the Whittle W.1, the W.2B/23 model with 1700 lb (770 kg) thrust, perfected and built by Rolls-Royce and given the name of Welland. Apart from its limited use in the last months of the war in Europe, the Meteor marked the beginning of a phase which would witness rapid growth immediately after the war and ensure Great Britain world leadership in the field.

British experiences also paved the way for the United States, where the jet era began later than in Europe. The first jet aircraft produced by North American industry (the Bell P-59 Airacomet) was designed on the basis of engines developed by General Electric and derived directly from the English Whittle W.2B, for which the construction plans had been purchased in 1941.

The P-59 (which took its maiden flight on October 1, 1942) was nevertheless a transitional machine and was never used in combat. Used in training and for operational assessment, it laid the foundations for the

entry into service of the first "real" jet fighter in the American air force, the Lockheed P-80 Shooting Star.

The progress made during the war by Japan in the field of jet propulsion deserves a mention. On August 7, 1945, the *Nakajima Kikka* (Orange Blossom) made its maiden flight.

This was Japan's first jet combat aircraft, produced directly under the influence of its German ally. While very similar to the Messerschmitt Me.262, this twin-engined jet for attack and high-speed bombing roles was an entirely original design. But the end of the war put a definitive end to the program.

238 bottom The Messerschmitt Me.262.

239 top The Messerschmitt Me.163, the fighter without a tail, with an arrow wing and rocket engine, (left) designed by Alexander Lippisch, had high climbing speed but extremely limited range.

239 center The Heinkel He.162 Volksjaeger, the first light jet fighter in history, was partially built of wood and armed with two 20-mm cannons.

239 bottom The first American rocket aircraft, the Bell P-59 Airacomet, made its maiden flight on October 1, 1942.

Messerschmitt Me.163 Komet

GERMANY

At the cutting edge of international aeronautical production of the time, the Messerschmitt Me.163 Komet was the first aircraft in the world driven by a rocket engine, although the delay with which it arrived on the scene of the conflict prevented its potential from being fully exploited.

An original feature of this small and very fast aircraft was the absence of a traditional undercarriage: take-off took place using a detachable wheel structure; landing by means of a skid housed in the belly of the aircraft. The first mission took place on May 13, 1944, over the skies of Bad Zwischenahn, the base of

Erprobungskommando 16, the first unit of the Luftwaffe set up to test the Komet in operational conditions. The mission, performed by a pre-series aircraft painted red, marked the beginning of intense activity which would continue for the whole of the last year of the war. In all, just over 300 Me.163s were completed, mostly of the B-1a version (279 built), the only one to see active combat service (in the drawings). The first encounter with Allied bombers took place on July 28 in the area of Merseburg, when five Komets of the 1/JG 400 attacked a formation of Boeing B-17s. Its use highlighted a wide range of defects, including severe limitations in

attack, seeing that the extremely high speed with which the Me.163s approached the bombers gave them only three seconds to fire, in addition

to problems of engine control (it could only run for 7 1/2 minutes, meaning that it had to be turned off and restarted during flight, often

creating serious difficulties). Production of Me.163 B-1s ended in February 1945, before the airplane could be perfected.

Bell P-59 Airacomet

UNITED STATES

The jet era came to the United States later than to in Britain and and Germany. The airplane which typified the beginning of this real revolution was the P-59 Airacomet, a transition machine that never saw combat and was mostly used for training and assessment of the new form of propulsion. ,In all, just under 70 aircraft (prototypes included) of two versions of the P-59 left the assembly lines between 1944 and 1945. The first of the three XP-59A prototypes was designed in spring 1942, and the plane was taken on its maiden flight on October 1. The Airacomet never proved to be an exceptional machine, due to its limited power and difficult handling at low speeds.

Most of the P-59s were assigned to the 412nd Fighter Group, a specially set up experimental unit within the 4th Air Force, which became a vital training center for the pilots and ground staff who would be working with future models of jet aircraft.

Some Airacomets were modified for target dragging duties, with the installation of a second cockpit in the nose, in front of the pilot. In the drawings, a P-59A.

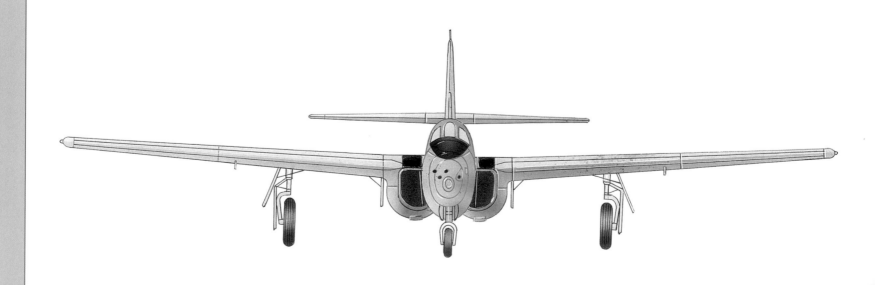

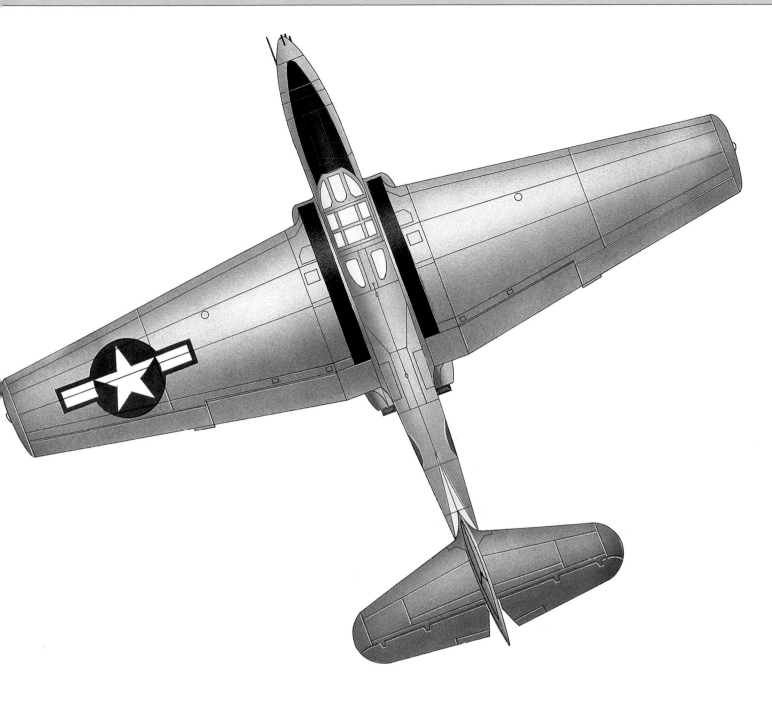

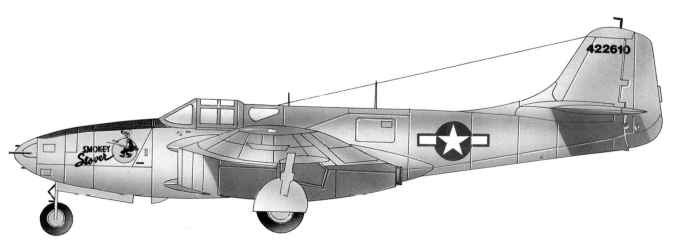

Brewster F2A Buffalo

UNITED STATES

The Buffalo, the first monoplane fighter to enter service in the US Navy, in practice showed itself to be completely unsuitable for the difficult role for which it was designed. Its operational use in the units of the US Navy and the US Marine Corps only lasted a few months, after which the small, stumpy Brewster fighter began to be replaced by the better Grumman F4F Wildcat. Work on the project began in 1936, and the first prototype flew in late 1937. At the end of the cycle of tests on June 11, 1938, an initial series of 54 airplanes was ordered.

Deliveries started exactly one year later, but the US Navy only deployed 11 of the aircraft ordered.

The remaining 43 were sent to Finland, at the time engaged in battle with the Soviet Union. In the meantime, orders were made for another 43 aircraft of the second version (the F2A-2, delivered in August), having a more powerful engine. These machines (one is shown in the drawings) were also destined for the export market.

In the meantime, its use in the US Navy had highlighted the airplane's limitations and, in particular, the flimsiness of the undercarriage and

insufficient armour.

On January 21, 1941, 108 of the third version, the F2A-3, were ordered, but the problems remained. The only American unit to use the Buffalo in combat was the VMF-221 of the Marines, on June 15, 1942 at Midway, with disastrous results: in the course of the battle, only 7 out of 25 aircraft managed to return to base, the other 18 were shot down by Japanese Zeros. 507 of the Brewster F2As were built up to March 1942.

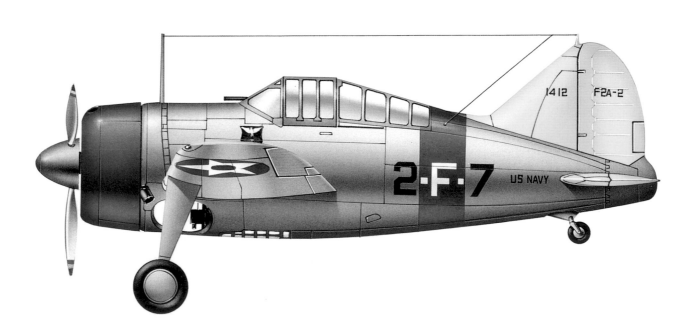

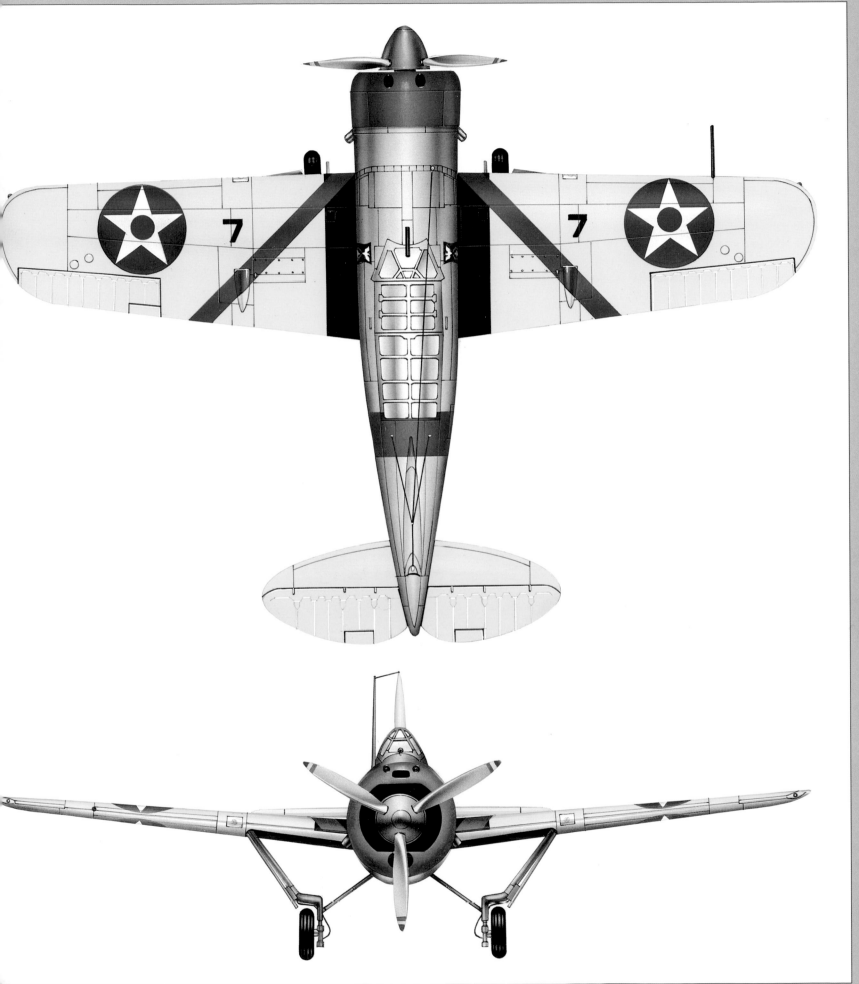

Curtiss SB2C Helldiver

UNITED STATES

This large, powerful on-board single-engined bomber was the last combat aircraft produced by Curtiss for the US Navy and the Marines. Around 7200 were produced in a variety of versions, and from November 1943 onward, it was deployed alongside the older Douglas SBD Dauntless as a dive bomber, taking part in all the naval air operations until the end of hostilities. The SB2C had a lone and intense career: many aircraft of the later production variants remained in active service until the 1950s. The first SB2C-1 left the factory in June 1942, and deliveries to the units started in December. Full operational activity was achieved in the second half of the following year.

The Helldiver made its combat debut on November 11, 1943 over Rabaul. In 1944, the second main production version appeared (the SB2C-3, of which 1112 were built), fitted with a more powerful engine driving a four-bladed propeller and characterized by other minor improvements (in the drawings).

The most important variant was the SB2C-4, whose offensive flexibility was improved with the installation of four under-wing battens to hold four 127-mm rockets or 500 lb (227 kg) bombs. This version of the Helldiver was produced in great quantities: Curtiss alone built over 2000.

The final version was the SB2C-5, which appeared in early 1945 with increased-capacity fuel tanks. 970 of these were built.

These aircraft were also fitted with radar and were able to perform night missions.

252 top The twin-engined English Bristol Beaufort was also used as a torpedo-bomber.

252-253 The Fairey Swordfish was a famous seaplane deployed by the British Fleet Air Arm. Although antiquated, it made an important contribution to the operations of English aircraft carriers in the first year of the war. It played a major role in the attack on the Italian naval base at Taranto in 1940.

252 bottom The Douglas TBD Devastator torpedo-bombers, also used by the US Marines in the battle of Midway.

And in many cases, "naval" airplanes proved to be superior to their land-based counterparts. A perfect example of this is the Japanese Mitsubishi A6M Reisen fighter, the famous Zero, the very symbol of Japanese air power.

The conflict in the Pacific fully demonstrated just how much on-board airplanes had changed naval warfare. From Pearl Harbor onward, aircraft carriers played a decisive role, revolutionizing the very concept of the traditional naval battle, and replacing battleships at the top of the fleet hierarchy. Tactical and strategic objectives were no longer achieved by means of direct cannon hits, but by using aircraft with an operating range 10 times higher than that of ballistic firepower. The airplane thus became the real protagonist. From the Battle of the Coral Sea in May 1942 (the first naval battle whose outcome was decided exclusively by airplanes) to Midway, and all subsequent operations, sea power would never again be separated from air power.

253 top The Grumman F4F Wildcat on-board fighter was used in the early stages of the conflict in the Pacific, stationed on smaller, so-called escort aircraft carriers.

253 bottom The Wildcat was also produced in a seaplane version, but only in limited quantities.

This lesson became clear to everyone, both victors and defeated, even if some of them, such as Germany and Italy, never had the opportunity to put it into practice. In Germany, the only aircraft carrier fitted out was the *Graf Zeppelin* which, despite being launched in 1938, never entered service. In Italy, it was only in July 1941, after defeat in the sea battle at Capo Matapan, that the decision was taken to build an aircraft carrier, the *Aquila*. This was to be followed by a second ship (the *Sparviero*), but the course of the conflict made these desperate attempts useless. As for France, its *Béarn* was a victim of the Occupation.

253

Grumman TBF Avenger

UNITED STATES

Destined to replace the TBD Devastator in the role of on-board torpedo-bomber, the Grumman TBF Avenger made its combat debut in the same circumstances in which the old Douglas monoplane dramatically left the scene—in June 1942 during the battle of Midway. It was anything but a happy start: of the six Avengers that took part in the mission, five failed to return to the aircraft carrier Hornet and, in addition, no hits were successfully made in the attacks against the Japanese navy. However, this initial failure was fully compensated for in the following mission: this heavy Grumman torpedo-bomber revealed itself to be one of the Navy's most effective weapons in the last three years of the war. In all, 9836 in a wide range of versions left the assembly lines by 1945 and, after intense operational activity in the Atlantic and the Pacific, many remained in front-line service until 1954. The Avengers did not only fight under American insignia, but also under those of the British Fleet Air Arm (who deployed 958 of them), and of New Zealand. After the war, they also entered service in Canada, France, Holland, and Japan.

Work on the project started on April 8, 1940 and the first flight took place on August 1 the following year. The initial version, the TBF-1, was followed by the second major production series, the TBF-3, which was more powerful and could carry a larger bomb load (in the drawings). These aircraft, of which 4644 were built, entered service in April 1944. 222 went to the British Royal Navy, which used them to equip the units stationed on the aircraft carriers *Formidable, Illustrious, Indefatigable,* and *Victorious.*

Grumman F6F Hellcat

UNITED STATES

The balance of air superiority, which had rested with the Japanese since Pearl Harbor, shifted in favour of the Americans during 1943. The Grumman F6F Hellcat was the machine that together with the Vought F4U Corsair, contributed to this decisive change in the status quo. Powerful, fast, well-armed, and protected, the Hellcat was the pride of America's on-board air force in the last two years of the war. In all, 12,275 left the assembly lines. In combat, they accounted for an exceptional number of victories: out of a total of 6477 enemy aircraft destroyed by Navy pilots, 4947 were victims of Hellcats; this figure rises to 5156 if we include the victories clocked up by the

F6F of the land-based units and those stationed with the US Marine Corps.

The project was developed in 1941, and the first experimental prototype (XF6F-1) made its maiden flight one year later, on June 26, 1942. This machine, named the XF6F-3, served as the basis for the first mass-produced version which, ordered in huge numbers by the US Navy from May onwards, started to come off the production lines in early October. The first delivery was made on January 16, 1943 to the aircraft carrier *Essex*. On August 31, the F6F-3s had their baptism of fire during an attack on Marcus Island, operating from the *Essex*, the *Yorktown*, and the *Independence*. Meanwhile, the rate of production was maintained at a high level: in 1943, 2545 F6F-

3s were delivered, 252 of which went to the British Fleet Air Arm, who assigned them the name of Hellcat Mk.I and started to deploy them in July. In all, 4403 aircraft of the first version left the assembly lines. Of these, 205 were equipped for night-fighter roles: the F6F-3E and F6F-3N

variants were characterized by a starboard under-wing fairing which contained the radar apparatus. April 4,1944 saw the maiden flight of the first Hellcat of the F6F-5 variant, the most widely produced (7870, of which 932 went to the Royal Navy). It differed from the previous

version in its engine and greater firepower, which now allowed a maximum of 1995 lb (907 kg) in bombs to be loaded.

This version (in the drawings) served as the basis for a series of night-fighters (F6F-5N) of which 1434 were built. Production ended on November 16, 1945.

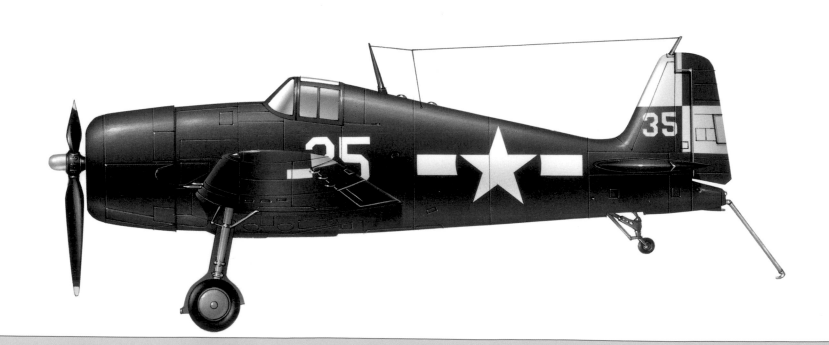

Camouflage

After two decades of peace, war once again changed the appearance of military aircraft and the rules of camouflage changed them into grim machines of war. The basic need to make the aircraft as indistinguishable from its background, the land and the sky, was combined with the need to break up its lines and profile, in order to make it more difficult to be sighted and identified by the enemy. Many military air forces—including the Royal Air Force—studied pre-established color combinations to obtain the maximum camouflage.

The British took an extremely rational approach. In a series of directives issued at the beginning of the war, the RAF camouflage was standardized according to a basic formula, variable only in function for the type of airplane and the zone of operations. The upper surface was always painted in two colors, and the combination of light and dark patches followed six fundamental patterns, depending on whether the aircraft was a single-engined monoplane, a twin-engined monoplane with a wingspan of no more than 70 ft (21.3 meters), a twin-engined monoplane

with a wingspan of over 70 ft (21.3 meters), a four-engined monoplane; single-engined biplane; or twin-engined biplane. The colors were chosen on the basis of the zone of operations.

There were three main color schemes: *Temperate Land Scheme* with dark green and dark brown; *Temperate Sea Scheme* with dark green and dark gray; and *Middle East Scheme* with dark brown and sand.

High-altitude reconnaissance aircraft, meanwhile, were painted all over in various shades of sky-blue. From September 1941 onward, for the fighters based in Great Britain, the colors of the *Temperate Land Scheme* were changed to dark green and dark gray. The approach adopted for the lower surfaces was more complex.

The half-black and half-light-gray color scheme (the borderline was along the middle of the aircraft) of 1939–40 was changed to light sky-blue, very light green, and then light gray. Night bombers had their lower surfaces painted black, similar to those of night fighters. For aircraft operating in the Middle East the color of the lower surfaces was generally a deep blue. The machines of Coastal Command and

seaplanes, meanwhile, generally had lower parts and side sections painted white. For trainers the color was yellow, for aircraft used to drag targets, yellow and black with diagonal stripes. The national insignia were in six positions, integrated with a rectangle with red-white-blue stripes on both sides of the fin.

The cockades changed a number of times, but from 1942 to 1945 their use became standardized: blue and red on the upper wing surfaces; blue, white, and red on the lower surfaces, with the same emblem bordered in yellow on the sides of the fuselage. The only exception were the units of the South East Asia Command, where the use of red was avoided in insignia to avoid confusion with those of Japanese aircraft.

In France the solution chosen by the Armée de l'Air was similar, with rules established in 1939. Before the Occupation the upper parts of the aircraft were painted in extremely irregular patches in three colors: dark green, dark brown, and medium gray, arranged without any apparent order and without a fixed borderline with the lower section, which was generally in light gray.

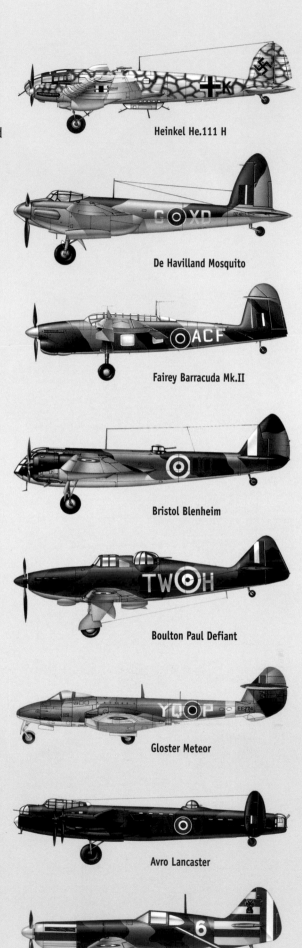

Heinkel He.111 H

De Havilland Mosquito

Fairey Barracuda Mk.II

Bristol Blenheim

Boulton Paul Defiant

Gloster Meteor

Avro Lancaster

Dewoitine D.520

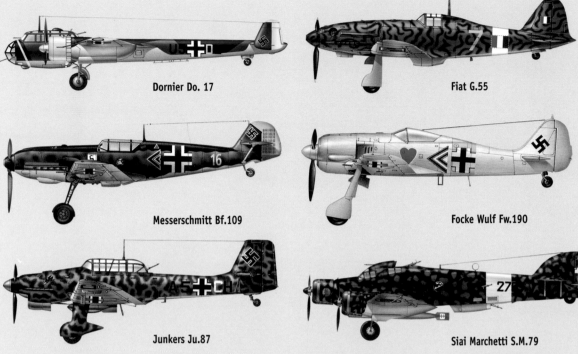

Dornier Do. 17

Fiat G.55

Messerschmitt Bf.109

Focke Wulf Fw.190

Junkers Ju.87

Siai Marchetti S.M.79

The national insignia were in six positions, with the national colors of red, white, and blue painted on the rudder.

In principle, the German Luftwaffe followed the same approach, but in practice the camouflage schemes adopted during the war by the various units and in the various theaters of operation were completely different from each other and impossible to classify.

The basic rules defined for all types of aircraft established combinations of dark green and light green for the upper surfaces, with the colors arranged in rigid geometrical forms with broken and angular lines; for the lower surfaces a uniform shade of light sky-blue was used. The upper color scheme, however, also had a variant, designed for the theater of the African desert: a uniform sand color. This basic camouflage remained standard in the first years of the war and in particular in multi-engined aircraft in service with the bombing and transport units. Those that quickly abandoned the official color schemes were the fighter units.

In the course of the Battle of Britain, the Messerschmitt Bf.109s began to adopt showy individual color schemes and subsequently, with the expansion of the conflict to the theaters of Africa and Russia, the phenomenon became uncontrollable and changeable, and was adapted according to needs. The integration of the standard livery was simplified by the introduction of special washable paints, which were applied to the base color to create temporary camouflage effects responding to specific environmental situations. Especially in Africa and in Russia, bombers and fighters with incredible color schemes were seen: patches and stripes in various shades of green applied roughly over sand-colored bases or rudimental sprays of white on green and sky-blue backgrounds.

This extreme personalization reached its peak in the last years of the war, when another type of basic camouflage began to spread, with the combination of two different shades of very light gray, together with closely set dark patches on a lighter background. This scheme was adopted above all by night fighters, in which there was another variant with the partial or total coloring of the lower surfaces black.

Separate mention should be made of the national insignia, which, while standardized with the black cross with a white border applied to both sides of the fuselage and to the upper and lower wing tips and with the runic cross painted on the fin, gradually ended up losing the white background, thus becoming less visible.

We should also remember another particular color scheme, adopted to identify the main theaters of operation: for the Eastern front the airplanes were characterized by lower wing tips painted yellow and a stripe of the same color on the fuselage; for the African front, meanwhile, the same scheme was adapted, but using white.

The camouflage adopted by the Regia Aeronautica was simpler.

There were two basic schemes: Continental and desert. The former was based on a uniform dark green shade on the sides and top of the airplanes, without making any distinction between multi-engine or single-engined aircraft. In the latter, the upper coloring was a sand-colored base onto which were applied green patches or fine, closely packed irregular lines (a color scheme the British ironically referred to as "sand and spinach"). Often, when aircraft with the continental-style camouflage were used in particular areas, such as the desert or

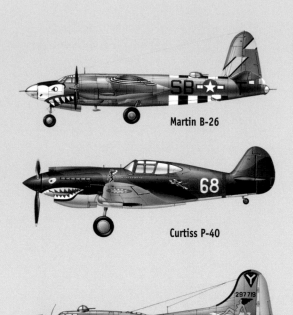

Martin B-26

Curtiss P-40

Boeing B-17

Grumman F6f

Brewster F2A

Macchi M.C.202

mountains, the inverse color scheme was applied to them: ochre or sand-colored patches on a dark green background. The lower surfaces were generally light gray or very light sand. In autumn 1940, a white band was added to the fuselage (yellow on the Russian front). The airplanes of the Social Republic generally followed the continental color scheme. Exceptions could be found in fighters, which were painted according to unusual color schemes, with a variety of shades of green, with combinations of green and light brown, or even with various shades of gray.

As far national insignia, the standard symbol was a white cockade edged in black with three stylized fasces, positioned on the four wing surfaces.

The colors were sometimes inverted on the lower surfaces. To these was added the insignia of the regime at the center of the fuselage (the fasces on a sky-blue background) and the cross of the House of Savoy (the Italian Royal Family) on the rudder.

For the air force of the Italian Social Republic, the wing cockades became square, while a small tricolor rectangle with a yellow border was applied to the sides of the fuselage and the fin.

In the United States the practice of camouflage had been basically abandoned in the period between the two wars. The airplanes of the USAAC and of the US Navy flew resplendent in brilliant colors, among which yellow dominated, and covered with insignia, decorations, and bright patches of color.

In the Navy, they went so far as to associate the distinctive function of the various unit components with their color: yellow, red, blue, black, or white segments painted on the engine fairing indicated the elements of an operational unit on sight.

Very often, especially in the years leading up to the war, the airplanes were left to shine with their natural color of polished aluminium. In Clark Field, in the Philippines, some time before the Japanese attack, a pilot reported that the reflection of the sun on the surfaces of a B-17 could be seen at a distance of over 66 miles (110 km).

The outbreak of war rapidly changed this situation, even if there were delays while waiting for industry to produce the matte paints necessary to camouflage the airplanes in sufficiently large quantities. In the US Army air service, the rules were standardized according to an extremely simple color scheme. After a brief period in which a formula similar to that of Britain was adopted (irregular green and brown patches on the upper surfaces, light sky-blue or light gray on the lower surfaces), there was a move towards a combination of *olive drab* and *neutral gray*. The strict respect of this livery, however, did not last long. In 1943, airplanes resplendent in unpainted metal once more appeared on the battlefield.

Among the first were the B-26s used in the Pacific, which soon became known as the "Silver Fleet". This departure from the rules was initially justified by the fact that the elimination of the matte paint allowed a slight increase in speed. It was subsequently argued that air supremacy had been achieved, a condition which removed the need to hide from the enemy. In the last year of the war, both in Europe and in the Pacific, aircraft without camouflage grew in number, and were covered with colorful unit emblems and unusual decorations, which have often been quoted as real examples of Pop Art.

In the US Navy, meanwhile, there was greater respect for the rules. Until mid-1941, they adopted a uniform light gray color scheme. Subsequently, gray was only used on the

Nakajima Ki-43

Mitsubishi J2M

Mitsubishi Ki-67

Ilyushin Il-2

Lavochkin La-5

number of times. Up until August 18, 1942, they maintained the classic white five-pointed star on a blue background with a red circle in the center, accompanied (until March 1941 for the USAAC and from 1941 to 1942 for the US Navy) by 13 alternating white and red stripes on the rudder. Then, until July 1943, the red center of the star was abolished, since many thought it looked too much like a target for enemy pilots.

From this date up to September, they adopted an emblem which added two white rectangles to the sides of the blue circle, with a red border, which was subsequently replaced by a blue border. These insignia remained standard until 1947 in four positions: on the sides of the fuselage, on the upper surface of the port wing, and on the lower surface of the starboard wing.

In Japan, camouflage was subject to fairly precise rules, but in practice was extremely complicated and often confused.

They repeated the approach adopted by the Luftwaffe, with an infinite range of individual variations, and those deriving from the needs of the

theaters of operation.

Since the war against China, the Army had adopted a color scheme based on olive green and brown patches, separated by thin white or sky-blue stripes on the upper surfaces, with the lower surfaces painted light gray.

At the outbreak of the war there were two basic tendencies: dark olive green and light gray, or green patches or stripes applied to the unpainted metal surface of the airplane.

The lower sections were often left in unpainted metal. In practice there were a large number of variations, with coloring performed directly in the field or with additions suggested by the pilots. In the last two years of the war, however, a white stripe was used on the rear section of the fuselage, which made it easier to identify airplanes in combat.

The national insignia was the red circle of the Rising Sun painted in six positions, normally surrounded by a white stripe when used on dark surfaces. In many units stationed for defence of the homeland, the red circle was inserted in a white triangle.

In the Navy, at the

outbreak of war, many aircraft were painted gray, with the engine cowling painted black.

The bombers also adopted a color scheme with brown, dark green, and light gray patches on the lower surfaces. Subsequently, the camouflaging was changed to dark green and gray (or sky-blue and a natural color) on the upper and lower surfaces. Also for on-board aircraft, in 1943 the combination of dark green and light gray became standard. There were, however, exceptions for land-based units, which often adopted color schemes similar to those of the Army.

The Soviet Union adopted perhaps the simplest color scheme. There were two basic schemes: olive green-light gray and olive green and brown patches on a light gray background. The national insignia (the red star could be underlined with a white or yellow stripe) was normally placed in six positions, with two on the fin-rudder section. Exceptions to these schemes were represented only by the application of white paint in the winter months and for operations in snow-covered areas.

lower surfaces, while the other surfaces were painted in a shade of *sea green*. For onboard airplanes, this color was also extended to the lower surfaces of the wing which, once folded, faced upwards. In 1943, a three-color scheme was adopted, with dark blue on the upper surfaces shading into gray-sky-blue on the sides and then into off-white on

the lower sections. At the beginning of the following year, for all on-board airplanes, the coloring was changed to an eggshell *midnight-blue,* a scheme which remained in use until the mid-1950s. The only exceptions were unit emblems, generally white in geometric symbols.

The Army and the Navy changed the national insignia a

GREAT AIR BATTLES

THE BLITZKRIEG AND THE STUKA

September 1, 1939, 4.45 am. The Second World War begins. The Polish border was breached in various places by 53 German divisions, supported by an overall air force of 1000 bombers and 1500 fighters. This avalanche literally swept aside everything it found in its path, and in the space of a few hours would demonstrate to the entire world the effectiveness of the *Blitzkrieg*, the "lightning-war" on which Hitler's military strategies and those of his high command were based.

September 1, 1939, 4.26 am. Exactly 90 minutes before zero hour, three German bombers took off into the fog and headed at extremely low altitude towards a bridge over the Vistola. It was the first military operation of the conflict. The three Junkers Ju.87 Stukas of the 1st Stukageschwader had an objective of extreme importance for the progress of operations. The job was to strike, in a precision attack, the controls of the system of mines set up by the Polish to destroy the bridge itself, and thus keep this important passing point intact. This was crucial for the successful meeting of the two main German attack forces, the northern armies commanded by General von Bock, and the southern armies led by General von Rundestd. The mission was completed successfully at exactly 4.35. The first blitzkrieg began 10 minutes later.

262 and 263 After its debut in
Spain, the Junkers Ju.87 Stuka
was one of the great
protagonists of the Second World
War. This dive bomber was used

throughout the European front,
in Russia and North Africa. It
was used to equip a large
number of units in the Regia
Aeronautica (see photo left).

The campaign in Poland lasted about a month. In the course of the 27 days which it took Germany to wear down Polish resistance, the effectiveness of close collaboration between air and land forces was clearly shown, and was fully exploited for the first time by the German high command. And in this context, the most important role was played by attack aircraft rather than by high-altitude traditional bombers. While the twin-engined Dornier Do.17s and Heinkel He.111s hammered the targets situated more deeply in Polish territory, destroying factories, airports, and cities (Warsaw first of all), wearing down the population, on the battlefield the real protagonists were the Stukas, the dive bombers designed especially for this specific role and used in great quantities. Incessantly, implacably, the Junkers Ju.87s were launched to clear the way for the armoured units of the Wehrmacht, and had exceptional success, made easier by the relative absence of enemy anti-aircraft defences. They acted as a form of flying artillery, and were perfectly co-ordinated by the officers of the Luftwaffe assigned to the individual land units with liaison duties. The Stukas demonstrated that they were able to destroy any target with absolute precision, sowing terror among the enemy with the characteristic wail accompanying their dive towards the target, which varied from troops, artillery, and cavalry formations, to vehicles, tanks, depots, and road and rail junctions. In September 1939, then, the Junkers Ju.87 became a symbol of the Blitzkrieg and of Germany's air power.

Designed in 1933, and produced until 1944 (over 5700 were built in about 10 versions), the Stuka (abbreviation of *Sturzkampfflugzeug*, or 'dive -bomber', the word used to indicate all aircraft of this type in Germany) went down in history as one of the most widely used combat aircraft in the German arsenal.

Since its establishment, the Luftwaffe firmly believed in the strategic function of the air force. Particularly convinced was its first Chief of Staff General Walther Wever, a staunch supporter of the theories of the Italian Giulio Dohuet. This situation underwent a sudden change in 1936, after the death of Wever during a flying accident. His successors, from the army and without any particular aviation experience, did not intend to follow the original strategy.

Consequently, under the direction of General Ernst Udet, who had been a fighter pilot in the First World War, the Luftwaffe began to focus on the tactical aspect of its forces to the disadvantage of strategic considerations. This approach led to a series of decisions which would crucially affect the outcome of the conflict, including the blind belief in the medium day-time bomber as the optimal strategic weapon and in the ground-attack aircraft as the best tactical means. Consequently, the Luftwaffe concentrated all its efforts and planning on cooperation with the Army (based on the political view that the future conflict would be a lightning war exclusively).

In this context, Udet was the most convinced supporter of dive bombing. And it was in this climate that the Junkers Ju.87 was born. Udet firmly supported the production of the Stuka after having witnessed the exhibitions of American Curtiss Helldiver biplanes, and his total faith in this type of machine remained unaltered even after a serious accident which nearly cost him his life. When flying one of these very aircraft during a show at Tempelholf in Berlin, he was forced to jump out with a parachute as his airplane failed to respond to his attempts to pull it up out of its dive. The Stuka had strong points and weaknesses. Exceptionally robust and accurate, it was, however, slow and vulnerable. These negative aspects went unobserved during its first combat experiences in Spain. In an operational theater characterized by relatively poor anti-aircraft defences, the Junkers Ju.87 proved itself to be an excellent weapon—precise, effective and deadly—and contributed to convincing the heads of the Luftwaffe that they had made the right choice.

266 The Stuka could carry a 2200 lb (1000 kg) bomb under the fuselage and other smaller bombs under its wings. It was undoubtedly a precision weapon, but was slow and vulnerable to fighter attacks. The second member of the crew had a 7.9-mm machine-gun at his disposal (above).

Poland was the next testing ground for the theories of Ernst Udet. And here also the Luftwaffe achieved brilliant success. The association between Stuka and Blitzkrieg continued on May 10,1940, when Germany attacked Belgium, Holland, and Luxembourg, and on June 5, when it moved the offensive towards France. The first defeat was just round the corner. During the Battle of Britain, the Ju.87 fully displayed its limits, and its legendary status gradually disappeared.

The Battle of Britain marked the end of the blitzkrieg concept. This did not mean the end of the role played by attack aircraft or by the Stuka in particular. This aircraft remained basically irreplaceable in the arsenal of the Luftwaffe, to the point that the German aeronautical industry did not manage to replace it with another, equally effective, model.

THE BATTLE OF BRITAIN

The Battle of Britain was the first great air battle of the Second World War. Apart from purely military objectives, the confrontation between the Royal Air Force and the Luftwaffe was also a battle over the role of modern combat aircraft, as conceived by these two nations. The winners and losers in this long and bloody fight were not just men, machines, and organizations, but also the different theories of air war. And those that lost were the theories that had guided the formation and growth of the German Luftwaffe. Germany learned this lesson to its cost, but paradoxically never managed to act in the light of this new-found awareness. For the rest of the war, its air force continued to lack effective strategic potential, despite its massive commitment in theaters of operation spread all over the world, against adversaries who were constantly strengthening their equipment and resources.

267 The great defenders of English skies in 1940-41. A replica of the Hurricane and, to the bottom, a unit with Gladiators and Hurricanes at a British base in December 1939 during a visit by King George V.

Hawker Hurricane

GREAT BRITAIN

The Hawker Hurricane was the RAF's first fighter monoplane.

Apart from the Battle of Britain, the Hurricane made its mark in history for many other reasons: it was the first British interceptor armed with eight machine-guns; the first to exceed 300 mph (480 km/h); and the most widely used fighter by the Allies in the first two years of the war. It also had an enviable operational career (which continued from late 1937 until the end of the war, on practically all fronts), and impressive production figures, with 14,233 built in three basic versions between 1936 and 1944.

The prototype first flew on November 6, 1935, and the Hurricane Mk.I (in the

drawings) reached units in December the following year.

In September 1940, the first aircraft of the second major variant, the Mk.II, was introduced with a more powerful engine and improved weaponry. Around 7300 were built.

The first definitive version was the Mk.IIB armed with 12 machine-guns; the second was the Mk.IIC equipped with four cannons. These airplanes equipped 96 units of the RAF between 1941 and 1944, and were used widely on all fronts, especially in North Africa and the Far East. More powerful armament also characterized the last variant of the Mk.II series, the D, which made its appearance in 1942, and of which around 800 were built. On March 4, 1943

the prototype of the third major production variant, the Mk.IV, with even more powerful weaponry, made its maiden flight. Thanks to the adoption of a "universal wing", in addition to two 7.7-mm

machine-guns, it was possible to install two 40-mm anti-tank cannons and two 500 lb (227 kg) bombs or, alternatively, additional detachable fuel tanks or eight 60 lb (27 kg) rockets. With the

adoption of this deadly weaponry, the Hurricane became the first Allied aircraft to use air-to-land missiles, allowing its operational activity to be significantly extended. 524 Mk.IVs were built.

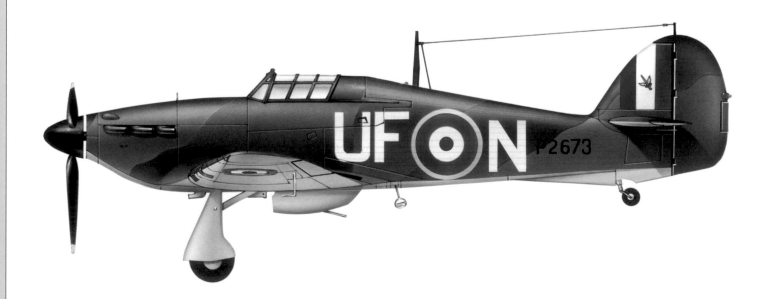

The basic attack strategy drawn up by Hitler and the German high command was relatively simple: annihilate the RAF, then destroy the aeronautical industry, and all of Great Britain's supply lines, thus forcing the government to surrender. According to General Alfred Jodl, Chief of Staff of the Wehrmacht, the invasion by ground troops would take place once air supremacy had been achieved. "The army," he wrote, "would land only to give the *coup de grâce*, if this was still necessary, with Britain economically paralyzed and deprived of its air power. Final victory is only a matter of time". He forecast surrender by the end of August or early September.

But events were to prove Jodl and the other German strategists dramatically wrong. The Battle of Britain, conceived as a swift summer military campaign, was transformed into a long, bloody, and gruelling test-

270 top A Hurricane.

270 bottom One of three Spitfires converted into seaplanes. The airplane was a Mk. VB and flew for the first time on October 12, 1942. The project provided for the deployment of these fighters in the Pacific, but in the event was not followed up.

ing ground which fully engaged the adversaries well beyond the German forecast period. It lasted until May 1941, when Hitler finally admitted defeat and turned his attention to another, although no less powerful antagonist, Russia. This was the first great turning point in the course of the war.

Even if the beginning and end of operations are generally set at August 13 and October 31, 1940 respectively, historians today agree in subdividing the development of the operations into five phases. The period between July 10 and August 7, 1940 is considered a preparatory phase, during which the Luftwaffe operated mainly against sea traffic in the Channel, with the intention of drawing British fighters into combat and wearing them down.

The first phase proper began August 8 and ended exactly 10 days later; it was aimed at destroying the RAF's fighter potential. The first large-scale daytime attack against airports, radar stations, and installations located along the south and southeast coast of England was performed on August,13, and this day is remembered as the official beginning of the battle, going down in history under the name of *Adlertag*, the Day of the Eagle. 1485 airplanes were used, coming wave after wave, in massive formations. Two days earlier, on August 11, according to Winston Churchill's *Memoirs*, the ratio of forces was dramatically to Britain's disadvantage: the RAF had 704 operational fighters, of which 620 were Hurricanes and Spitfires, and 350 bombers. The Luftwaffe, meanwhile, had 933 Messerschmitt Bf.109 fighters, 375 twin-engined Messerschmitt Bf.110 fighter-bombers, 346 Junkers Ju.87 Stuka dive bombers, and 1015 Dornier, Heinkel and Junkers twin-engined bombers, for a total of 2669 airplanes.

271 top The Fairey Battle.

271 bottom Pilots and technicians prepare a Bf.109 for take-off before a mission escorting German bombers.

Messerschmitt Bf.109

GERMANY

Between 1936 and 1945, at least 35,000 Messerschmitt Bf.109s were built in a number of variants. In the course of its long and intense career on all fronts, this small, agile combat aircraft achieved a position of importance that went well beyond its mere production figures (which were the highest of the war), earning itself an important place in the history of aviation. Work on the Bf.109 began in summer 1934, in response to official specifications for a monoplane interceptor to replace the Heinkel He.51 and Arado Ar.68 biplanes. The airplane was completed in September 1935, and the first aircraft of the initial production series, the Bf.109B, appeared in

February 1937. The B variant was followed by the C, with more powerful weaponry, and then by the D, fitted with a Daimler-Benz DB 600 engine. This marked the transition towards the first mass-produced version, the Bf.109 E (in the drawings), characterized by the use of the more powerful and reliable Daimler-Benz DB 601.

The first Bf.109 E-1s were completed in early 1939 and in the space of a year overall production of the various sub-series had reached levels of 1540. After this variant, the great protagonist of the Battle of Britain, aircraft of the significantly improved F version began to enter service in January 1941. These were considered by many to be the best of the entire family. Production was

massive, and the Bf.109 Fs had a brilliant operational career, especially in the first months of use, when in certain cases the fighter proved to be superior even to the RAF's Mk. V Spitfire.

It was due to the need to consolidate this superiority that the next

in the series, the H, was brought out in 1942. This version had the highest production figures. Christened the Gustav, this airplane entered service in late summer 1942.

The Bf.109 K was the last operational variant and one of the best. In

November 1944, deliveries began of the first production series, the K-2 and K-4. These airplanes entered service in early 1945. The final series, the K-6, was characterized by its more powerful weaponry, which had been optimized for attacks against bombers.

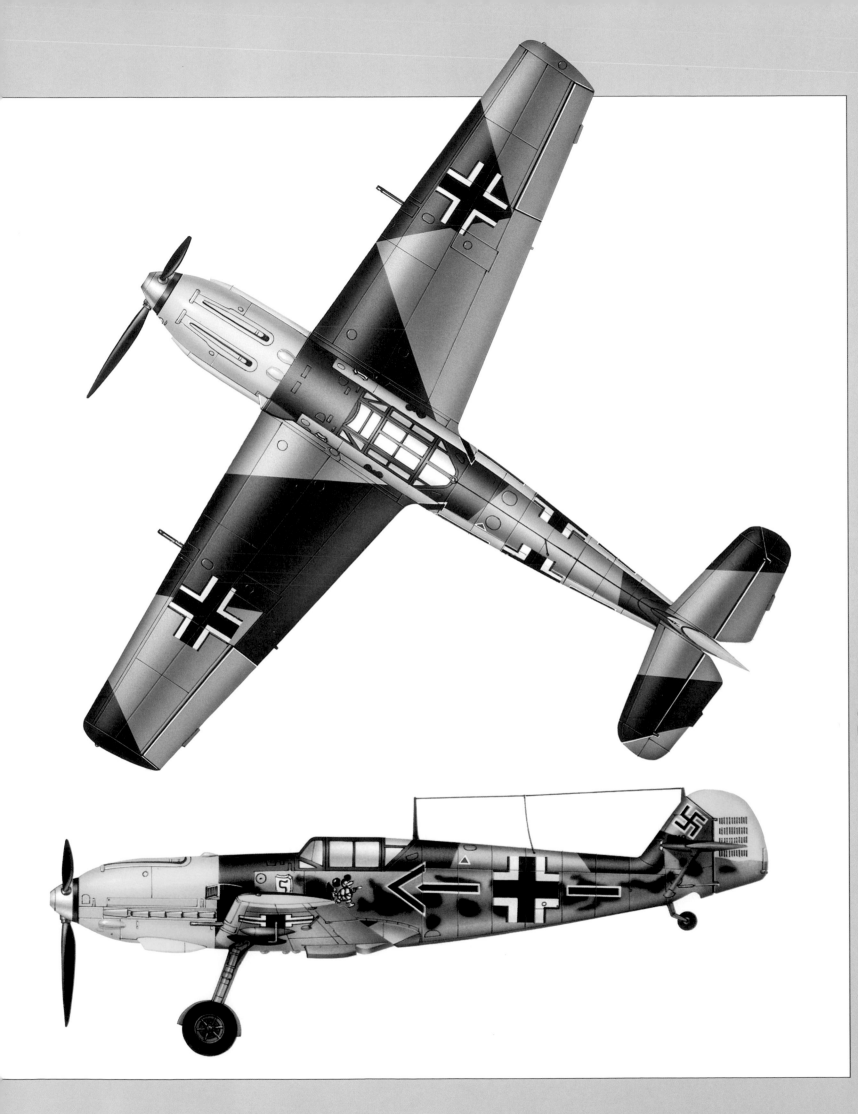

The raids continued without interruption for days on end. The most violent was on August 15, with the intervention of three German Luftflotte against British airports, but these efforts failed to bring the hoped-for results. By August 18, the Luftwaffe had lost 363 aircraft, against Britain's 211. Above all, the German air force had not achieved the aim of wearing down the enemy fighters. The British pilots, in fact, had received orders to give priority to attacking bombers and not to get drawn into combat with German interceptors. It was in this period that the strategic limitations of the Luftwaffe's aircraft became strikingly clear. This set off a chain reaction of consequences. The Heinkel He.111 and Dornier Do.17 bombers, penalized by their limited range and lack of effective defence, had to be continuously protected, before, during, and after the missions. This task was given to the Messerschmitt Bf.109 fighters, which were thus limited in their movements and forced to abandon their main role as interceptors. Nor were better results achieved by the aircraft which Göring had given such positive propaganda, such as the Junkers Ju.87 and the Messerschmitt Bf.110, which were slow and vulnerable. The Stukas, in particular, were withdrawn from operations on August 18, after suffering heavy losses. Adolf Galland, Commander of the 3rd Group of Jagdge-schwader 26, commented on the basic failure of the bomber escort missions and attacks aimed at destroying the enemy fighters as follows: "The range of the Messerschmitt Bf.109s was too low and the Stukas, which had swept aside everything in their path in Poland and France, suffered catastrophic losses. They attracted the Hurricanes and Spitfires like honey attracts bees".

During those weeks there were peaks of combat activity. In the words of Peter Townsend, at the time a Hurricane pilot, in his book *Duel of Eagles:* "In the 48 hours of 15–16 August, the RAF responded to the incredible number of 3500 Luftwaffe missions with 1750 missions of its own fighters, and inflicted on the enemy

274 top and 275 top A Spitfire modified after the war and still flying in Europe. In effect, the British fighter was only used in the single-seater version.

274 bottom The Bf.110 initially proved itself a good fighter but its limitations in terms of manouvrability and speed soon became evident.

the heaviest losses it ever suffered: 120 aircraft down, against 55 of ours. On 18 August, there was furious dog-fighting, with 950 Luftwaffe raids and 760 missions performed by our fighters. Losses: 71 German aircraft, 29 English fighters. On 30 and 31 August the Luftwaffe made a supreme effort against the airports defending London, unleashing upon them a whirlwind of 2800 raids. Our losses were extremely heavy: 65 fighters were downed. The blackest day of the whole battle was however the 31st, with 39 airplanes failing to return to base". His conclusion is particularly bitter: "The human losses on the English side were catastrophic: an average of 115 pilots killed and injured per week. This was almost double the number of young men who came out of flying school in the same period of time. And the situation was even worse than it seemed, because the young men who filled the empty places didn't have the same experience as the pilots who had died. And the massacre continued...".

The second phase of the Battle of Britain from August 19 to September 6,

275 bottom Initially developed as a civil transport aircraft, the Focke Wulf Fw.200 Condor was armed and used for troop transport and as a reconnaissance plane, and more sporadically as a bomber.

1940 saw the Luftwaffe changing strategy and tactics. The targets became the airports, above all, and industrial installations, while the massive formations were abandoned in favor of small groups of high-ly protected and escorted aircraft, in order to limit the reaction of enemy fighters. But not even this approach worked. Nevertheless, on September 3 a secret order was issued which indicated the 20th as the earliest date for the departure of the invasion fleet.

The third phase started with this premise and was characterized by a new change in strategy. It began on September 7, with the first mass attack on London performed by 300 bombers. Two days previously, Hitler had ordered "raids against the civilians and air defences of the major British cities" and Hermann Göring, who had personally assumed control of the offensive, planned a deadly series of attacks against the British capital. The aim was not only to cause panic among the population, but also to disperse the defence fighters, by means of isolat-ed raids in all the areas which could be reached. On the evening of September 7, more than 1200 airplanes were involved in one of the largest air duels of the conflict, which lasted just over half an hour. The German attack involved 300 bombers escorted by 600 fighters, and dropped 337 tons of bombs. The culmination of this phase was reached on September 15, with an extremely violent daytime raid on London, and continued to the 26th.

Subsequently, and up to 5 October, German pressure began to ease off. Hitler, who up until September 17 waited for the air victory promised by Göring, had to postpone the invasion indefinitely. It was clear that the Luftwaffe had not managed to perform the task it had been given. And this was not only due to serious losses, but above all due to the desperate British defence, which had used its potential to the full, achieving a balance which was extremely difficult to maintain, upset as it was by massacres of pilots. and a lack of aircraft. Between September 7 and 30, 247 fighters were shot down, compared to 433 German airplanes.

276 top British fighter ace, Group Captain Douglas Bader.

276 bottom Formation of Heinkel He.111s in flight in the skies over England.

277 bottom A Junkers Ju.88.

On October 6, 1940, the fourth phase began, in which the Germans suspended daytime attacks and concentrated all their operations on night-time bombing missions, in order to try and reduce losses. Formations of bombers operated with the assistance of excellent radar apparatus, but the British reaction continued to be efficient and deadly. On October 31 Hitler convinced himself that it was not possible to destroy the British fighter force. Since August 13, the Royal Air Force had lost 915 airplanes, compared with Germany's 1733. Combat, however, continued, even if the original objectives of the invasion plan had been definitively abandoned.

On November 1, 1940 there was another change in tactics, with the beginning of the fifth and last phase of the Battle of Britain, which continued until 10 May 1941. This involved strategic attacks, almost exclusively at night, aimed at industrial centers, with the aim of paralyzing production. The largest and most devastating raid was that of November 14 on Coventry. London also suffered attacks almost every night. The last were performed on the night of May 10, 1941, with over 500 bombers. But in the end, this effort proved fruitless. Germany abandoned the duel with its most direct adversary and turned to other fronts.

PEARL HARBOR

Just over an hour—that was how long the Japanese attack on Pearl Harbor on December 7, 1941 lasted. In this short time, 353 airplanes, which had taken off from six aircraft carriers 250 miles away, inflicted a most crushing defeat on the armed forces of the United States: 178 airplanes destroyed, another 159 damaged,18 ships sunk or seriously damaged, 2403 dead, and 1178 injured. On a strategic level the result was even more spectacular; with its force of battleships basically annihilated, the American Pacific fleet was deprived of one of its most important components precisely at the moment of greatest need. This situation continued for some months and further slowed down the full launch of operations to combat the power of an enemy which appeared increasingly invincible.

Much has been said and written on Pearl Harbor, its political and military background, and its implications within the scenario of the Second World War. It is, nevertheless, worth looking briefly at the salient points of the event, even if only to highlight the fundamental role played by the air force, and in particular by on-board aircraft. Both sides had an opportunity to test the great potential of the modern airplane and the enormous strategic and tactical importance of the air weapon in a theater of operations that was predominantly sea-based. And while the Japanese victory at Pearl Harbor served as a confirmation of military theories put into practice since the phase of rearmament and preparation for war, for the United States this first defeat provided the motivation to continue the process of modernizing aviation (not only aircraft, but also organizational and tactical aspects), and for accelerating the growth of its strictly military potential.

The United States had recognized for some time the excellent position of the natural port at Pearl Harbor on the island of Oahu in Hawaii. Since the beginning of the century it had been a naval base, whose importance continued to grow. It was precisely this advance post in the middle of the Pacific which the Japanese Admiral Isoroku Yamamoto had chosen as the target for the first strike of the war. The fundamental

premise for success in the vast aeronaval and amphibious operations planned against Malaya, Siam, the Philippines, and Hong Kong was that of neutralizing the American fleet. Yamamoto's plan, presented to the Navy Joint Chiefs of Staff in summer 1941 was accepted, albeit after great resistance.

Preparation was intense and exacting, not only for the men who would take part in the action, but also for the equipment and weaponry. In consideration of the shallow water of Pearl Harbor, for example, the normal torpedos were modified with the addition of special wooden fins, while high potential armor-piercing bombs were made from 356-mm grenades used by Navy cannons. Particular care was given to training the crews of the attack force. The large naval formation took to the seas in early November, from various ports and following different courses, with the aim of making the massive concentration of forces pass unobserved. It was composed of 31 ships, concentrated around six aircraft carriers (*Akagi, Kaga, Hiryu, Soryu, Zuikaku,* and *Shokaku*) with 392 aircraft on board, including Mitsubishi A6M2 fighters, Aichi D3A1 dive-bombers, and Nakajima B5N2 torpedo-bombers. Command was given to Admiral Chuichi Nagumo.

On November 22 the fleet met in the Bay of Tankan, in the remote Curili Islands. On the 25th the order to depart was made and the following day the Japanese fleet set sail for Hawaii. On December 2, Admiral Yamamoto gave the final go-ahead for the operation (with a message in code that said "Climb Mount Niitaka") and five days later, at 3 am on December 7, the naval force reached its position 250 miles (400 km) away from Oahu.

278 and 279 top In the tragic hours of Pearl Harbor, the USAAF only had a few trainers, the old Curtiss P-36 Hawks (profile), and a few P-40Bs (in the left-hand photo, pilots of a P-40 unit scrambling) in Hawaii.

279 bottom A P-40.

Curtiss P-40

UNITED STATES

Even if it was mediocre, the Curtiss P-40 was paradoxically the most important American fighter in the first two years of the war. Its strength lay in two factors that were fundamental at a time when all the resources available had to be used by the Allies to react to the offensive in Europe and the Far East: immediate availability and availability in large quantities. In fact, starting from 1939, 13,738 P-40s left the Curtiss assembly lines, a number which, in the end, placed the production figures for this fighter in third place overall, second only to much better machines, such as the Republic P-47 and the North American P-51.

Equally vast was its operational use, which covered all fronts, from Europe and Africa, to the Pacific and Russia, under the insignia of almost all the Allied countries.

The design of the P-40 dated back to March 1937, and was based on the cell of the previous model, the Curtiss P-36A, replacing the original radial engine with a liquid-cooled V-12 Allison V-1710. The first prototype made its maiden flight on October 14, 1938, and two years later, on April 4, 1940, the first mass-produced P-40A appeared. By October around 200 airplanes had been delivered to the units of the American air force. At the same time, another 140 of these aircraft, originally ordered by France, were taken by Great Britain, who called them Tomahawks and used them for training. The second variant was the P-40B (Tomahawk II in the RAF) of 1941, with more powerful weaponry and armour, and self-sealing fuel tanks. This was the

first to see combat, in Africa under British insignia and with America in Pearl Harbor and China, where they also bore the insignia of the famous American Volunteer Group, General Claire Chennault's Flying Tigers (in the drawings). The first significant modifications appeared in the P-40D (maiden flight May 22, 1941, of which 582 were built, almost all going to the RAF who named it the Kittyhawk I) and in the subsequent P-40E, which started delivery in August

1941 with a different engine and weaponry, and a modified and shortened fuselage, and undercarriage. In particular, the P-40E (2320 built) was the first to serve in the units of the USAAF in Europe, in the Mediterranean theater. Despite the evident limitations of the machine, which became increasingly used as an attack aircraft and increasingly less as an interceptor, Curtiss continued to try to improve it. In 1942, the P-40F version (1311 built)

appeared, equipped with a 1300 hp Rolls-Royce/Packard Merlin V-1650-1, which was followed in the same year by the P-40K and in 1943 by the variants L, M, and N. In these versions, there was an attempt to lighten the cell in various ways and to increase the engine power. The P-40Ns (deliveries started in March 1943) were also the last to serve with the USAAF, and their production run (5220 built) was the last off the assembly lines, on November 30, 1944.

282 top and 283 top The fixed-undercarriage Aichi Val was one of the protagonists in the attack on the American base at Pearl Harbor, together with the more modern Zero.

At exactly 6 am the first airplane of the assault wave, led by the frigate Commander Mitsuo Fuchida, took off from the *Akagi*. Fifteen minutes later, another 182 aircraft followed: the first formation was composed of 49 B5N2s armed with bombs, another 40 torpedo bombers, 51 dive-bombers, and 43 escort fighters. At 7.15 a second wave followed, with 170 airplanes (54 bombers, 80 dive-bombers and 36 fighters), commanded by the corvette Captain Shigekazu Shimakazi. The target of the torpedo bombers was the ships at anchor in the main port of Pearl Harbor. The other airplanes, meanwhile, planned to attack the airports of Wheeler, Hickam, Ewa, Kenehoe, and Fort Island.

At 7.02 am the first Japanese formation was detected by the radar of the US Army installed at Opana, but for a number of reasons the alarm was not received in time. At 7.48 Commander Fuchida launched the first positive signal ("To, To, To", a Japanese term meaning 'Fight'), and some minutes later the message of attack ("Tora! Tora! Tora"). At 7.55 am the first bombs fell on Pearl Harbor with devastiating effects, taking the Americans completely by surprise. The torpedoes hit the battleships *West Virginia*, *Arizona*, *Oklahoma*, *Nevada*, and *Utah*, and the cruisers *Helena* and *Raleigh*, while the battleships *California*, *Maryland*, *Tennessee*, and the support ship Vestal were struck by bombers.

The bombers also inflicted damage on the battleship *Pennsylvania*, the cruiser *Honolulu*, and the destroyers *Cassin*, *Downes*, and *Shaw*. Fuchida's airplanes also unleashed their fury against the aircraft on the various airfields, and their work was completed by the second attack wave, which performed its task with dead-

282 bottom At least two Mitsubishi A6M fighter-bombers captured by the Allies in the Pacific islands were tested in flight to assess their characteristics.

283 bottom Japanese bombs raining down on the American battleships *Arizona*, *West Virginia,* and *Oklahoma* at anchor in Pearl Harbor.

ly ferocity. At 9.30 the operation was over and the formations returned to their respective aircraft carriers, which had meanwhile cruised to 190 miles (300 km) from Oahu. In all, the Japanese had lost only 29 aircraft (some during deck landing manouvres) and five mini-subs, a total of 64 men killed or lost in action, plus one prisoner, an insignificant amount compared to the serious damage inflicted on the enemy.

The final American losses were heavy: the *Oklahoma*, the *Arizona*, the *Utah*, and the mine-layer *Oglala* had been sunk; seriously damaged were the *California*, the *West Virginia*, the *Pennsylvania*, the *Tennessee*, the *Maryland*, the *Nevada*, the cruisers *Helena, Raleigh, Honolulu*, the destroyers Cassin, Downes, and Shaw and the support ships *Vestal* and *Curtiss*.

Yamamoto had thus achieved a crushing victory. Due to a series of entirely fortuitous coincidences, two of the three aircraft carriers in service with the US Pacific Fleet, the *Lexington* and the *Enterprise*, managed to avoid the Japanese attack, since they happened to be at sea, the former at Midway, the latter heading for Wake Island. Together with the *Saratoga*, these ships represented the only advance point for many long months; they formed the nucleus of an air–naval power which would grow during the war.

The kamikazes

Kamikaze, Divine Wind. In autumn 1944, this word (used by the Japanese to refer to the typhoons with which the protective gods had destroyed the Mongol invasion fleets of Kubla Khan in the waters of Kyushu in the 13th century) became synonymous with death and destruction. Glorious death, in the purist tradition of the Bushido (the code of honor of the warrior, whose origins date back to the Middle Ages), for the pilots who chose to crash their planes into enemy ships; destruction for the allies, who, in the few months between October 1944 and the end of the war, suffered great losses in men and means, because of the activity of Japan's suicide pilots. In summer 1944, after the massive American offensive against the Marianne Islands, Japan was no longer able to halt the Allied advance. There was nothing left but a last desperate strategy: kamikazes, the Divine Wind. The idea of setting up special units for suicide attacks against the enemy naval forces came to Admiral Takijiro Onishi, commander of the first Air Fleet based in the Philippines. On October 19 he

proposed that his officers use fighters armed with a 550 lb (250 kg) bomb for this purpose. The proposal was accepted and the 201st Flight was transformed into a special attack corps. It had 26 Mitsubishi A6M Zeros at its disposal; half were destined for suicide missions, the other half for escort duties.

The first kamikaze operation took place on October 25, on the occasion of the Battle of Leyte Gulf. Five A6M5s armed with bombs, escorted by another four fighters, crashed into the escort aircraft carriers *Kalinin Bay, Kiktun Bay, White Plains,* and *St. Lô,* seriously damaging the first three and sinking the last. In the cold and brutal logic of war, for the price of five fighters and the lives of the same number of pilots, greater military results had been obtained than those achieved by the over 250 airplanes which had attacked the American fleet using traditional methods.

It was precisely this consideration that drove the activity of suicide units, in a crescendo that would be stopped only with the end of the war. The role of kamikaze aircraft became increasingly important, and the number of volunteers

multiplied.

There was practically no limit to the type of aircraft that could be used—from the best models of fighters and bombers to machines which had been superseded for conventional combat, but which were considered suitable for missions as flying bombs. The attack techniques were also established, in a set of rules that provided for two assault procedures: at altitude, with the approach performed at around 22,400 ft (7000 meters), selection of the target, descent to about 3200 ft (1000 meters), and then a final dive bomb against the target; and at low altitude, with an approach just above the surface of the sea (to reduce the possibility of being detected) and a climb up to about 1280 ft (400 meters) before impact with the enemy ship. Their main targets were aircraft carriers.

This great determination also led to the introduction of an aircraft specially designed for suicide missions, the Yokosuka MXY7 Ohka ('Cherry Blossom') rocket plane. Ohka's operational concept was simple and effective: the flying bomb was transported by a mother aircraft and, once released, glided as far as possible towards the target.

In the final approach phase, speed was increased to over 540 mph (900 km/h), thanks to the thrust of three rocket engines, until it crashed into the target.

The study and construction of a prototype without an engine saw rapid progress and in late September 1944 10 MXY7 Ohka 11s, the initial version of this type of aircraft, had already been completed. These were able to transport a load of 2640 lb (1200 kg) of explosives in the nose. Without waiting for the results of the tests, the Navy started to produce the airplane and 775 Ohka 11s (the only ones used in combat) were completed by the end of March the following year. However, another three improved versions were designed, taking the total built to 852.

The new suicide weapon made its operational debut on March 21, 1945, although the mission was a failure, since the 16 twin-engined Mitsubishi G4M2es carrying the flying bombs were all intercepted by enemy fighters and forced to drop their bombs much earlier than intended. But success was not long in coming. On April 1, 1945, the American battleship *West Virginia* was damaged, and 11 days later, the

destroyer *Mannert L. Abele* was sunk off the coast of Okinawa. In April 1945, with the American landing on Okinawa, saw kamikaze activity peak. One of the most massive missions was performed on April 6, when a wave of 355 suicide airplanes was launched against the enemy fleet in an attempt to stop the invasion. 248 of them were shot down, but the damage to the Allied ships was vast. In the following weeks, up to June 21, the date which marked the end of the campaign, kamikaze operations involved over 1800 airplanes.

These airplanes managed to sink or put out of action 39 ships and damage another 368. The number of suicide attacks then reduced in intensity and became infrequent. The last kamikaze mission was completed on August 15, 1945 by Vice-Admiral Matome Ugaki, commander of the Fifth Air Fleet, who flew towards death accompanied by seven other pilots.

The next day, Admiral Takijiro Onishi, the most enthusiastic supporter of the suicide attacks, took his own life. In his will he addressed himself to the families of the dead volunteers, declaring that he could not survive those who had made such a glorious sacrifice.

THE ATOMIC BOMB

August 6, 1945 marks the beginning of the atomic era. On this day on board a four-engined Boeing B-29 bomber christened *Enola Gay* and commanded by Colonel Paul W. Tibbets, Major Thomas F. Ferebee activated the switch that released the first nuclear bomb ever used in warfare. At that moment, the B-29 was flying at an altitude of 30,820 ft (9630 meters) and at a speed of 316 mph (528 km/h). The bomb (christened *Little Boy*) was cylindrical, 10 ¹/² ft (3.27 meters) long and 2 ft, 7 in (80 cm) in diameter; it weighed 8980 lb (4082 kg). It contained two blocks of Uranium 235, which would "fire" against each other, triggering off a nuclear reaction. *Little Boy* exploded around 780 ft (244 meters) above the city of Hiroshima, destroying 80 percent of the city's buildings and killing around 70,000 people in just a few seconds.

Three days later, on August 9, another B-29 christened *Bock's Car*, piloted by Major Charles W. Sweeney, dropped another atomic bomb on Nagasaki. *Fat Boy* (as this second bomb was nicknamed) was based

Boeing B-29 Superfortress

UNITED STATES

The dropping of two nuclear bombs on Hiroshima and Nagasaki on August 6 and 9, 1945 brought an end to the war and marked the beginning of the atomic age. The airplane that will always be associated with these two dates is the Boeing B-29 Superfortress, the largest and most powerful bomber of the conflict, the first strategic weapon on a world level.

The production of this machine, in technical and technological terms, perfectly embodied the enormous contribution given by the conflict to the development of bombers. This is shown by the fact that, apart from their use in the war against Japan, many of the 3970 B-29s built played an active role in the Korean War and remained in service until well into the 1950s. The first prototype flew on September 21, 1942 and the first pre-series YB-29 made its maiden flight on June 26, 1943. In the meantime an ambitious production plan had already been drawn up: Boeing's two assembly lines in Renton and Wichita were to be supported by those of Bell in Marietta and of Martin in Omaha.

It was no simple task to perfect this great bomber, and in particular, the engines and propellers presented a number of problems. In the first 175 aircraft produced, 9900 defects of various kinds had to be eliminated.

The B-29 was an extremely complex machine: a high-wing monoplane of great length with a front tricycle undercarriage, whose circular-section fuselage was entirely pressurized (with the exception of the bomb compartment, which was connected to the front and rear sections by means of a narrow tunnel). The engines were four turbos-upercharged Wright R-3350 Cyclone radials. Defensive armament consisted of 10–12 12.7-mm machine-guns in four turrets remote-controlled from central stations and of a tail turret, which also housed a 20-mm cannon. Offensive weaponry comprised 9 tons of bombs.

In addition to the basic version, there were two main variants of the B-29 introduced during the war: the A, with a slightly larger wing, increased fuel capacity and changes to the armament (of which 1222 were built), and the B (311 built), with defensive armament removed except for the rear machine guns.

The drawings show an example of the photo-reconnaissance variant, the F-13A.

224877

DOUBLE EXPOSURE

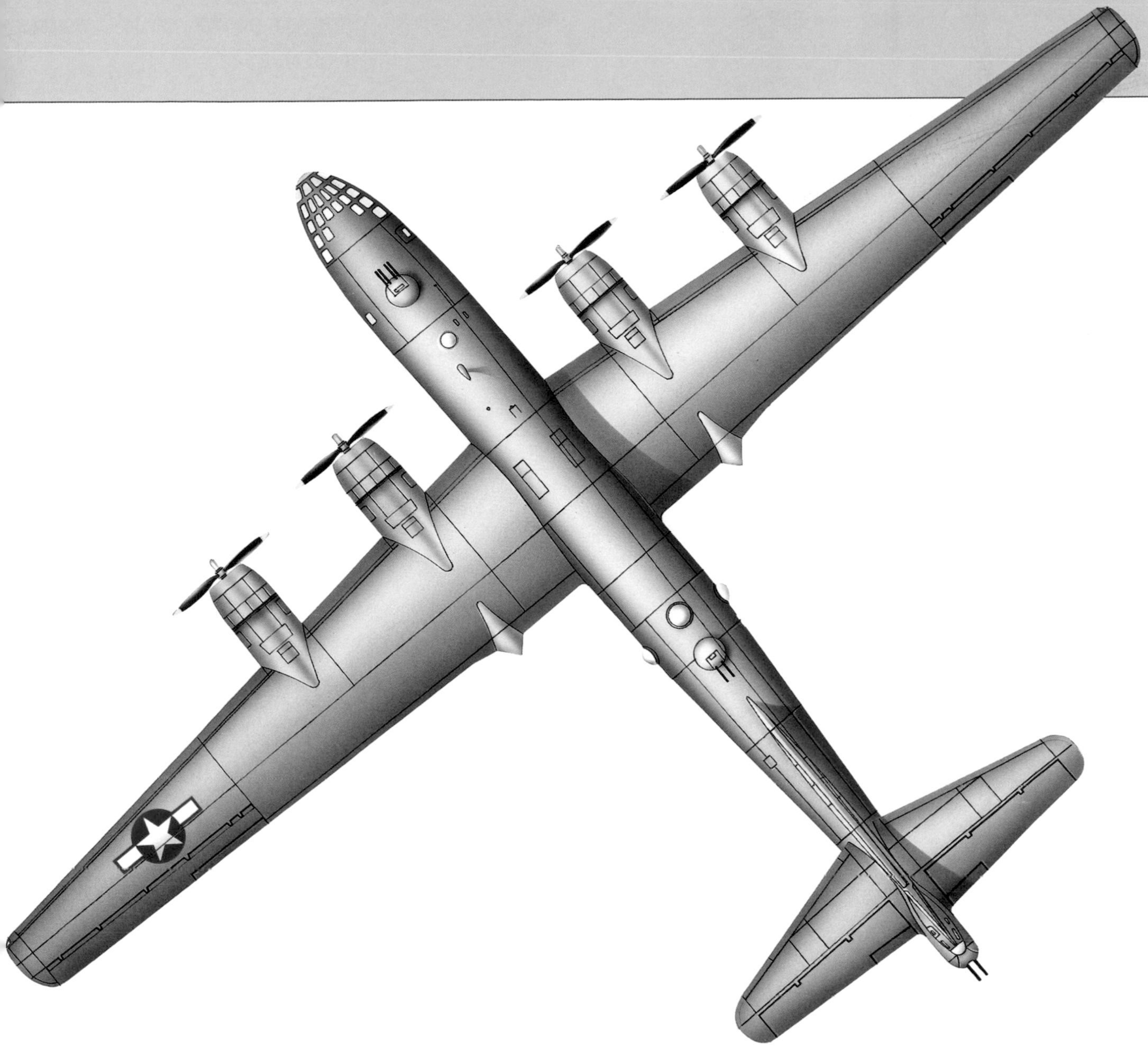

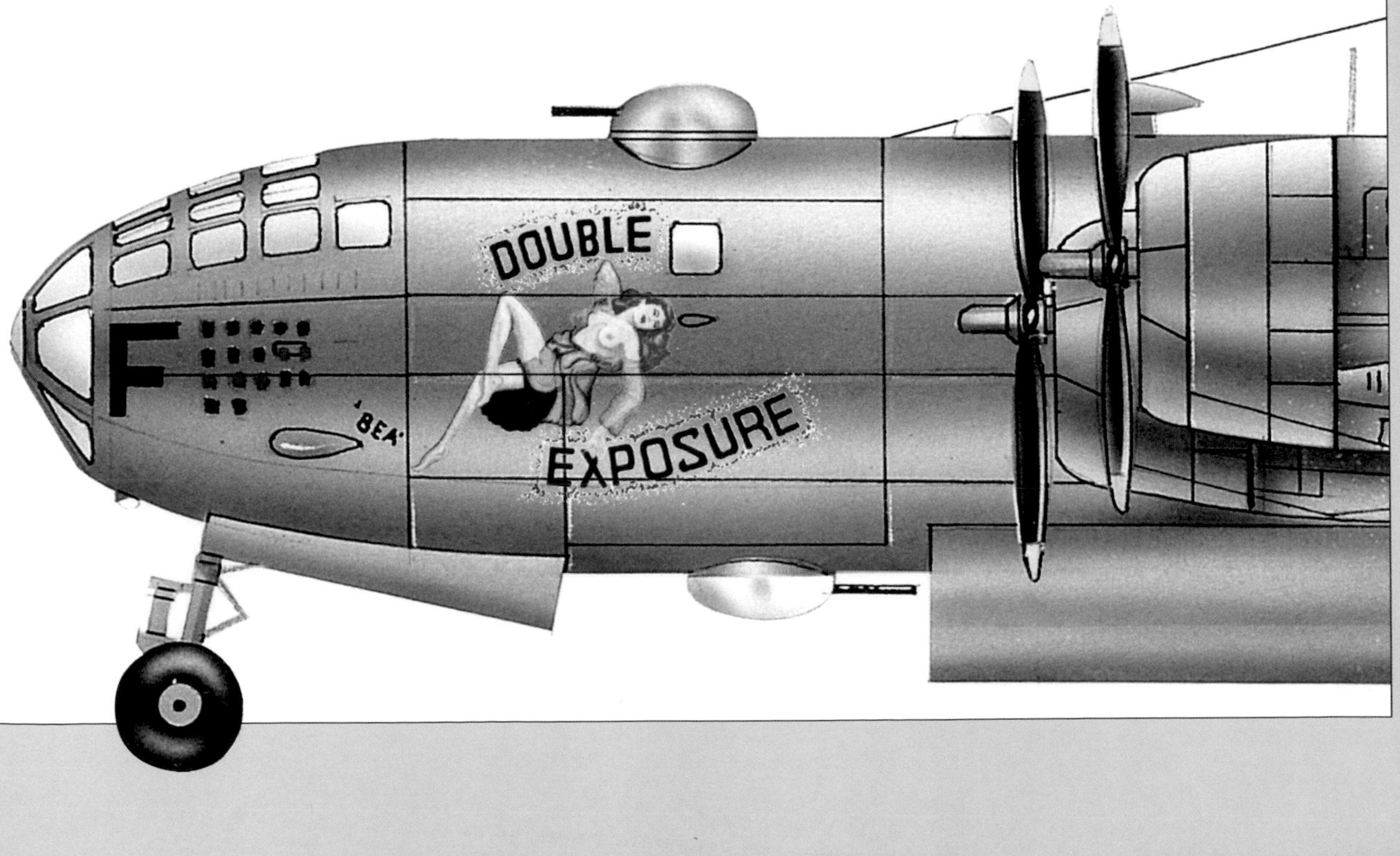

DOUBLE

F

'BEA'

EXPOSURE

The airplane that would carry the deadly new weapon, the four-engined Boeing B-29, was also ready, and at the base of North Field, on Tinian, in the Marianne Islands, the unit chosen for the mission—the 509th Composite Group, commanded by Colonel Paul W. Tibbets—had been waiting since April.

They did not have to wait long. On July 26, the Allies sent the Japanese an ultimatum requesting its unconditional surrender. The Japanese refusal led to the decision to use nuclear weapons if other, heavy conventional attacks proved to be useless. On July 27, many Japanese cities were warned of the imminent raids and the next day six of them were bombed. There followed other warnings, on July 31 and August 5, but in vain. The targets originally chosen for the first atomic bomb were Kyoto, Hiroshima, Yokohama, and Kokura. The first and the third in the list were replaced by Niigata and Nagasaki. Hiroshima was chosen as a primary target. The rest is history.

290 top Liberators in flight over an island in the Pacific after the end of the Second World War.

290 bottom B-29s in flight drop their payload of bombs.

291 A B-29 assembly-line.

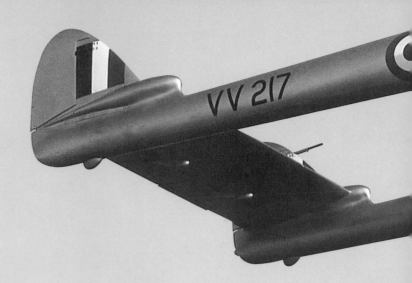

292 top The double-tail plane of the British de Havilland Vampire.

292 bottom Only after the arrival of the Russian MiG-15 fighter in Korea were the Americans forced to deploy the North American F-86A Sabre, their first jet fighter with a swept wing.

293 The Douglas AD Skyraider attack aircraft.

Korea: the last piston-engine fighter planes and the first jets

The first act of the Cold War opened in Berlin in June 1948. Germany, devastated by the Second World War, had been divided by the Allies into four zones of influence, and the fate of the German capital became the bone of contention between the former allies. On one side was the United States, Great Britain, and France, with their will to rebuild Europe; on the other was the USSR, with expansionist goals. Stalin wanted to encompass Berlin within the Soviet zone and thus take the first step toward the annexation of the whole of Germany. The blockade of the city and all its roads was the first attempt to wrest it from the allies. It was a moment of high tension, remembered in those years as the moment when the Third World War was closest to breaking out. The breaking point came on June 27, when

the West decided to accept the challenge and to respond with one of the most dramatic and spectacular military operations ever performed in peacetime—the historic airlift aimed at supplying the German capital and its 2.5 million inhabitants with food, fuel, basic necessities, and anything else that was necessary for survival. It was an immense effort, a real trial of strength performed under the gaze of the Soviet armies which were waiting to intervene at the first sign of failure. The continuous and unstoppable flow of American, British, Canadian, Australian, New Zealand, and South African transport planes supplied Berlin from the sky, and on May 11, 1949, when it became clear that the operation could have continued indefinitely, the blockade on the city was finally lifted. The airlift, however, did not slow down. The last of 277,278 flights was completed on September 30 by a four-engined Douglas C-47. In all, over 2,326,000 tons of supplies had been transported, with a record daily peak of 12,480 tons achieved on April 16.

Despite being divided in two, Berlin started to live again, but the Cold War, this new specter, was only just beginning.

The confrontation between East and West became increasingly bitter and its escalation ended up conditioning the alliances and policies of the entire world, which was divided on the basis of the two blocs of influence. This period of history was led by the United States and the Soviet Union, the great antagonists, and was characterized by an extremely delicate balance of power, always unstable, and always ready to degenerate into armed warfare. The effects of this perverse mechanism, a real "balance of terror", were incredible. Starting from 1950s, the arms race never let up and saw unprecedented progress, fuelled by the need to maintain the ratio of the forces in the field and to constantly confront the adversary with more powerful and effective weapons. The air forces underwent the most drastic developments.

294 The Douglas C-47 Dakota was used to transport troops and supplies by the Allies and the South Koreans.

294-295 The American twin-engined fighter, the Grumman F7F Tigercat.

295 center A fighter of the Royal Navy, the Hawker Sea Fury.
295 bottom The Cessna Bird Dog.

296 top The most advanced fighter of the USAF in the skies of Korea—the Republic F-84G Thunderjet.

296 bottom The Lockheed P-80 Shooting Star, which arrived too late to take part in Second World War, saw its first active service in the Korean War. It was quite fast but insufficiently armed.

With the move from propellers to jet engines, the end of the Second World War brought to a close a whole era in the history of the airplane. The potential of the jet had already been evaluated in the final phase of the war and the technology to exploit it was basically ready. What was missing was the construction and debugging of more powerful and reliable jet engines. In this field Britain clearly led the way in the West, but the United States, thanks to the contribution in terms of experience and technology provided by its ally, soon made up for lost time. It was thus, in the immediate post-war period, that a new generation of combat aircraft began to be created by designers. The time-scale of this process, however, was not the same in the two opposite camps. In the West they suffered the effects of slowed military aircraft production and the cuts to the armed forces which characterized the first years of peace. In the Eastern bloc, with the Soviet Union aiming to consolidate its role as a major player, things were entirely different. The already impressive aeronautical industry had been developed to the full and production had achieved heights which passed practically unobserved from the outside world.

After the non-violent confrontation in Berlin, it was a mere nine months before the first armed

KOREA: THE LAST PISTON-ENGINE FIGHTER PLANES AND THE FIRST JETS

clash between the idiologically opposed combatants. With the outbreak of the Korean War on June 25, 1950, the Cold War brought the jet age to maturity. In this southeast Asian country half-way around the world, the United States and its allies had the opportunity to test in combat not only its forces, but also the validity of the respective military theories and tactics, not to mention the most suitable strategies for exploiting the potential of the new aircraft. And these aircraft were the real protagonists of the three-year war.

The initial phases of the conflict were fought with propeller-driven aircraft of the last generation such as the North American P-51 Mustang and Chance Vought F4U Corsair American fighters, or the British Hawker Sea Fury, and attack aircraft such as the Douglas AD Skyraider, and the Boeing B-29 bomber. These machines had reached their maximum potential, incorporating the best aeronautical technology generated by the war that had just finished; in many cases these were still extremely effective craft.

298 top An entire unit of Douglas Skyraider AD-4 assault planes operated in Korea (seen here, an airplane of the French Armée de L'Air). These single-engined aircraft were particularly robust and could carry a large payload.

298 bottom The Skyraiders proved to be particularly effective in tactical roles. Their active service came to an end during the Vietnam War.

But in this unusual mixture of old and new, the lead was soon to be taken by jet aircraft.

The first dogfight between jets took place on November 8, 1950 in the area of the Yalu River between a US Lockheed F-80, piloted by Lieutenant Russell J. Brown, and a Soviet MiG-15. The latter was shot down and the victory went down in the annals of American aviation. But things did not always go this well. The small, agile, and well-armed MiG-15, unknown in the West, proved to be the greatest adversary of Allied fighters, and its excessive power tipped the balance of air supremacy for a long time.

The shock was similar to that caused in 1941 by the appearance on the Pacific front of the Mitsubishi A6M, Japan's famous Zero, and only the arrival of a competitive machine (in this case the North American F-86 Sabre), and the greater experience of the American pilots managed to reduce the enemy advantage and bring the situation back under control. Paradoxically, despite great technological progress, air battles were fought in exactly the same way as in the skies of the Second World War, with interception taking place after visual identification of the enemy, and then pursuit until he was in range of the machine-guns or cannons, with victory invariably being won by the better pilot. The only differences were that the duels took place at an altitude of almost 48,000 ft (15000 meters) and at speeds of around 600 mph (1000 km/h). In the end, figures confirmed the overall superiority of Allied air power: from December 1950 (when the Sabre entered service) until July 27,

1953 (the date of the surrender), no fewer than 792 Chinese and North Korean MiG-15s were shot down, with a ratio of 12 to 1 in favor of the American fighters. In the history of the airplane, confrontation between these two aircraft was reminiscent of that which, 10 years earlier, had seen the RAF's Spitfire pitted against the Luftwaffe's Messerschmitt Bf.109. The skies over Korea witnessed the last "traditional" dogfights, those in which man and machine were in perfect symbiosis, in a direct close-quarter challenge with the enemy, and in which skill and courage almost always proved to be determining factors. And the aces of that war (the leading American was Captain Joseph McConnell, credited with 16 victories) were also the last representatives of a class that died with them: in the following years the concept of fighters would be radically transformed by electronics and missiles.

The lesson learnt in the Korean War were terribly important for both sides, and clearly demonstrated that the new era of aviation was suspended between the past and future. But this phase of transition did not last long. The West, which had seen the measure of Soviet air power in the field for the first time, immediately put its operational experience into practice with new research on engines and structures, producing new aircraft designs, and increasingly sophisticated and devastating weapons. The effects in the Communist bloc were similar, with the war in Korea further stimulating the arms race. While the first generation of jets went through its short life cycle, the second generation was already being developed. The challenge was on all fronts: absolute supremacy was at stake.

299 top A North American P-51D of a South African unit.

299 bottom The fourth prototype of the Douglas XBT2D-1, the only one to be equipped with a massive air-inlet hub. This solution was abandoned in industrial production.

Lockheed P-80 Shooting Star

UNITED STATES

The Lockheed P-80 was the first jet fighter to see service with the US Air Force. Its development in the last years of the Second World War embodied the effort of American industry to make up for lost time compared with the British and Germans in the development of a new generation of combat aircraft. The design of the Bell P-59 Airacomet in 1942 was a transition machine, difficult to debug, and with unimpressive performance; in May 1943 the technical department of the USAAF decided to exploit this experience and produce a new, more powerful and effective fighter.

The project was given to Lockheed, who managed to produce a flying prototype in less than six months, before the deadline laid down under the strict terms of the contract.

Between June 24, 1943 and January 8, 1944, the date of its maiden flight, work was frenetic, but the results exceeded all expectations. Despite being fitted with a relatively low-powered engine, the prototype managed to fly at over 480 mph (800 km/h) and in the course of the long cycle of test flights, the adoption of more

advanced engines further increased this already excellent performance.

The end of the war saw a reduction in the massive production programs, which had foreseen the construction of 500 of these fighters, and the aircraft of the initial P-80A version did not reach the front-line units until December 1945. 917 were

built of this variant and the subsequent B version, while 798 of the final C version of 1948 (in the drawings) left the assembly lines. The development of this version was stimulated by a record-breaking flight made by Colonel Albert

Boyd on June 19, 1947 in a modified P-80A, which achieved the world speed record at 623.608 mph (1003.811 km/h). The P-80, already christened *Shooting Star*, and whose name was changed to the F-80 in 1948, had its baptism of fire in Korea. In the first four months of

use these airplanes performed over 15,000 missions and then, replaced by the better North America F-86 Sabre, were used as tactical fighter-bombers for the entire duration of the war. The shortness of this operational career was made up for by the "second life" that the Lockheed fighters

experienced as trainers, bearing the identification code T-33. The production of this twin-seater variant continued until 1959. In the United States alone, where it became the basic training machine, 5691 were built. It was exported to around 30 countries, and was built under licence in Canada (656) and Japan (210).

"EVIL EYE FLEAGLE"

THE FOUR
AIR POWERS

One of the effects of the end of the Second World War was that of concentrating and limiting development of the aeronautical industry to those countries that had resources and the political and economic strength to use them. The direct rivalry between the United States and the USSR became the points of reference. In addition to developing increasingly advanced machines, armaments, and systems for their own armies, the two superpowers provided their allies with the means to maintain the equilibrium of forces in the field. In the face of this effective monopoly on the market of international armaments, very little space was left for anyone else. From the early 1950s onwards, the nations of the Warsaw Pact were seriously compromised by their dependence on the USSR. In the West, meanwhile, the situation was more flexible. Apart from some original projects realized in Holland and Canada, the immediate post-war period saw the aeronautical tradition of Sweden forcefully re-emerge. In this Scandinavian country, the need to maintain its historic role of independence, especially considering its closeness to the USSR, had taken industry to particularly high levels. However, Sweden remained an isolated and self-con-

302 top Successor to the Vampire, with a more powerful engine and a new wing structure, hundreds of the de Havilland D.H.112 Venom were built, 250 in Switzerland alone.

302 bottom The Grumman F9F-8 Cougar of 1951, the swept-wing evolution of the Panther.

tained phenomenon, since the excellent combat airplanes developed by Saab were used exclusively by Sweden itself for self-defence. For decades the growth of world aviation was influenced by the evolution of the combat airplane in the two major powers. Great Britain and France were the only two exceptions to this rule. The former because it did not want to abandon its dominant role in Europe. The latter, meanwhile, because it fully intended to re-conquer it.

303 top A Lockheed P-80, the first jet fighter to see active service with the USAF.

303 bottom The North American F-86D, the all-weather fighter version of the Sabre. The aircraft was armed with rockets alone.

303

North American F-86 Sabre

304

UNITED STATES

MiG Killer. Among the many nicknames applied to the North American F-86 Sabre, this more than any other conveys the idea of the success it achieved as a combat machine. The Sabre, the first jet of the USAF with a swept wing, was also the last classic fighter. Easy to handle, powerful, and fast, it was ideal for close combat. The long operational career of this airplane followed two parallel paths, seeing that the same basic project was also used to develop naval variants.

The first project worked on by North American was the design of a jet fighter for the US Navy. In 1944 the company also decided to develop a version for the USAF, but the project did not come to anything until after the war. On June 20, 1946, three prototypes were ordered, the first of which made its maiden flight on October 1 the following year. Deliveries of the initial variant (of which 554 were

built) began in February 1949, and the main subsequent series were the E in 1951 (333 built) and the F in 1952 (2239). In autumn 1952, these Sabres had their baptism of fire in Korea. The final variant was the H, which appeared as a prototype on April 30, 1953. 477 were built, and were received by the USAF between January 1954 and August 1955.

The Sabre's long story did not end with the day-fighter versions. The development of the F-86 line also saw the introduction of versions equipped with radar for all-weather interception. The first variant, the D, characterized by its conspicuous nose section which housed the avionics and was the origin of its

curious nickname of *Sabre-dog*, commenced delivery in March 1951. 2504 were built, and large quantities were also supplied to the NATO countries. It was due to a request from NATO that the K version was developed in 1954. The prototype made its maiden flight on July 15. 221 out of the 341 built were produced in Italy by Fiat, and of these, 63 went to

the *Aeronautica Militare Italiana* (Italian Military Air Corps), while the others were exported to France, West Germany, Holland, and Norway. In particular, from 1956 onwards, the AMI also brought into service 180 Sabre Es built under licence by Canadair. The Canadian industry was the main licensee of the design and from 1949 to October 1958 completed 1814 in a range of versions. The second major manufacturer under licence was the

Japanese company of Mitsubishi, which built 300 F-86Fs, while Australia's Commonwealth Aircraft Corporation produced another 112. The Sabre entered service bearing the insignia of at least 26 countries, in some of which it remained active until the 1990s.

In all, over 8670 were built.

In the drawings, an F-86E.

Douglas AD Skyraider

STATI UNITI

"The best tactical support airplane in the world". This phrase sums up the great qualities of the Douglas AD Skyraider, the last single-seater combat aircraft to use a piston engine. Production of this large powerful airplane, which was designed in 1944, started after the war. Its baptism of fire was in Korea, and it also played a major role in the Vietnam War, in which it proved much more efficient than many of the more sophisticated jets of the time. The Skyraider's career lasted almost 20 years and its production history was

particularly rich and complex. Between 1945 and 1957, 3180 were built in seven variants. The great versatility of the machine was exploited in various series optimized for specific duties: reconnaissance, counter-measures, night and all-weather attack, and anti-submarine missions. In all these roles, the Skyraider proved so effective that in 1966 the American military authorities seriously considered the possibility of recommencing production.

The program was launched in June 1944.

The US Navy had requested a torpedo-bomber and dive bomber

to replace the old SBD Dauntless, and the proposal by Douglas, initially refused, was accepted after significant revision.

The XBT2D-1 Destroyer II prototype made its maiden flight on March 18, 1945, and immediately showed peaks of speed which could compete with those of the best on-board fighters, the F6F Hellcat and the F4U Corsair. On May 5, the BTD-2 was declared winner of the contract and orders were made. This marked the beginning of the airplane's long history of development. In February 1946, it received the official

designation of AD Skyraider.

After the four basic variants, in the AD-5 version of 1951 the single-seater setup was abandoned in favor of the two-seater. In the subsequent AD-6 and AD-7 attack versions, the airplane once more became a single-seater. The long career of the Skyraider ended in the US Navy on April 10, 1968. But the airplane also served with the Fleet Air Arm and the Armée de l'Air, in addition to the USAF and the air force of South Vietnam, where it entered service in 1961.

In the complex designation of the

Skyraider, the roles of night-attack and all-weather, radar patrol, and electronic counter-measures were identified by different suffixes, respectively N, W, and Q. In 1962 however, with a new US inter-force system, the AD code changed to A-1, as did the codes for the different versions: the AD-4N became A-1D, while the AD-5, the AD-6, and the AD-7 were changed to A-1E, A-1H (in the drawing), and A-1J. This apparent confusion was simplified by the pilots in the field, who preferred to identify the airplane with two simple and effective names which went down in history— *Able Dog* and *Spad*.

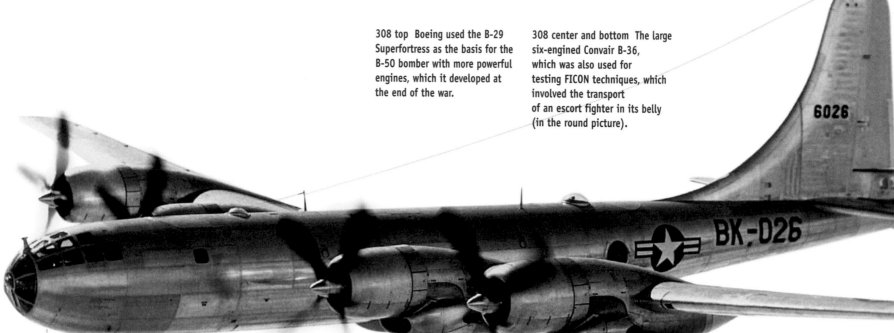

308 top Boeing used the B-29 Superfortress as the basis for the B-50 bomber with more powerful engines, which it developed at the end of the war.

308 center and bottom The large six-engined Convair B-36, which was also used for testing FICON techniques, which involved the transport of an escort fighter in its belly (in the round picture).

UNITED STATES

In the new world order resulting from the war, the United States had emerged as the leading Western power. The commitment in the struggle against its old adversaries Germany and Japan, and the resources of a formidable industrial system had allowed aeronautical technological and production to achieve extremely high rates of growth. And, despite the drastic cuts in military orders and the abandonment of many development programs which followed the end of the conflict, this enormous potential was once more exploited to the full to react to the threat of the former Soviet ally. The pause was brief.

The jet engine was the new undisputed protagonist and American industry had lost a significant amount of time in the long race between England and Germany which had led to the creation and use of the first jets in history. All its efforts were thus concentrated in this sector, with

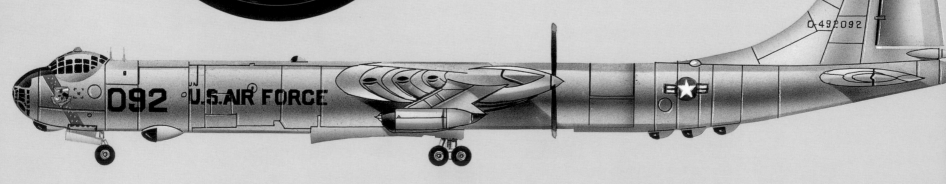

the aim of making up lost ground in terms of technology and re-acquiring design independence.

Just how great America's initial dependence was on Britain is shown by the birth of the Bell P-59 Airacomet, the first American jet airplane. This fighter had been designed in great secret in 1941, after General Henry H. Arnold, Chief of Staff of the USAAF, had seen the prototype of the Gloster E.28/39 in Britain and had managed to obtain from the British the construction plans for the Whittle W.2B turbojet, the new engine at the time being produced by Rolls-Royce. The task of developing an initial series of jet engines was given to General Electric, while the Bell Aircraft Corporation was chosen (September 4, 1941) for construction of the cell. The Airacomet, which was structurally conventional and not particularly competitive, served to test out engines and to activate an initial production line in American factories, in addition to training pilots and ground staff.

These experiences, however, were fundamental to the development of the new technology. A few months after the end of the war, the units began to receive the first valid jet aircraft produced by American industry, the Lockheed F-80 Shooting Star, a machine that finally came of age and served as the basis for the rearmament programs of the air force. The Lockheed fighter was also the first of an entire generation of combat aircraft that left a deep impression on Western production in the period. The modernization of aircraft was accompanied by a real revolution in the armed forces on an organizational and operational level.

309 top Specialists at work on a Republic F-84 fighter. The aircraft was simple to maintain because the upper part of the fuselage could be entirely dismantled to allow easy access to the turbo-jet engine.

309 bottom The RF-84F Thunderflash reconnaissance aircraft replaced the older piston-engine photo-reconnaissance airplanes.

310 top The Vought (Chance Vought) F7U Cutlass was an efficient on-board fighter without a horizontal tail plane and with a double fin. It was the first plane of the US Navy to use turbo-jets with an afterburner.

On September 18, 1947, the USAAF was released from its historical subjection to the Army, which dated back 1920, and made independent. Its new acronym became the visible sign of its independence: USAF, United States Air Force. The Navy, its old rival, launched a similar development and rearmament program, taking an active role in the development of new machines suitable for its specific uses. The era of the on-board jet was marked by the McDonnell FH Phantom, a transition fighter, which in its brief operational life, was the first jet airplane to land on a US Navy aircraft carrier on July 21, 1946. The Grumman F9 Panther and Cougar and the McDonnell F2H Banshee subsequently added to and completed the first generation.

The move from propellers to jet engines was slower in the sector of strategic bombers. The transition phase was long, above all because the Boeing B-29, which had come out of the war as the best strategic weapon of all, was still unsurpassed.

To extend the operational life of this immortal four-engined plane, the United States developed

310 bottom The all-weather Northrop F-89D Scorpion interceptor had a straight wing and two turbo-jets joined at the root of the wing. It did not have fixed weaponry but was fitted with two rocket-launching pods at the wing tips.

311 bottom A typical product of the Soviet aeronautical industry in the 1950s was the Ilyushin Il-28 bomber, characterized by its extremely simple construction.

an improved variant, the B-50, that came into service in 1949, in which range, general performance, and bomb capacity were significantly increased. The last representative of the "old" technology was the Convair B-36, a giant hybrid designed in the war period as a weapon able to strike occupied Europe from bases in the American continent. It remained a symbol of US air power for over 10 years, and acted as the first nuclear deterrent in the equilibrium between East and West. And this was despite the appearance in 1951 of the initial versions of the USAF's first efficient jet bomber, the Boeing B-47.

SOVIET UNION

The process of expansion in the post-war years that allowed the Soviet Union to share supremacy with the United States in the aeronautical field, dated back to the final years of the Second World War.

Mikoyan-Gurevich MiG-15

SOVIET UNION

Remaining in the history of aviation as the first symbol of Soviet air power, the MiG-15 was designed after the end of the Second World War by the work group headed by Artem Mikoyan and Mikhail Gurevich. With the availability of the first turbo-jets derived from the British Rolls-Royce Nene, development progressed quickly and the airplane immediately looked promising. Particularly advanced for the period was its configuration with swept wings and tail plane, a technical solution based on the research and experience of German scientists during the war. By its maiden flight, on December 30, 1947, the prototype displayed excellent handling and speed, and in March 1948 mass-production was started. Toward the end of the year the new fighter began to re-equip the units of the VVS. At the outbreak of the Korean War in June 1950, over a thousand had already been delivered, and the combat debut of the MiG-15 in Chinese hands, in November of the same year, was a real shock for the high commands of the West.

The fighter (which in NATO code was assigned the name FAGOT) was superior to the Lockheed F-80 and more agile, and displayed better climbing speed and a higher ceiling than the more advanced North American F-86 Sabre. Its armament, with two 23-mm cannons, was also particularly powerful. The needs of the war in Korea boosted production to the limit, and also led to the creation of many more powerful variants.

The production lines remained active in the USSR until 1953. In Poland, Czechoslovakia, and China, however, development under licence still continued for a number of years. It is estimated that over 8000 of these fighters were built (the drawings show the MiG-15 UTI two-seater training version). The development of the basic design continued during the production of the MiG-15 and the optimum evolution of the cell was achieved with the MiG-17, which was completed in 1949. While similar to its predecessor, the new fighter was fitted with a new 45° swept wing, a more advanced profile, and more efficient control surfaces, not to mention a more powerful engine equipped with an afterburner. The defects which still afflicted the MiG-15 in flight were thus overcome and the new machine was put into production in August 1951. Deliveries to the units started early the following year. The MiG-17 (FRESCO in NATO code) was also built in great quantities and numerous variants, the last of which were armed with missiles.

Over 6000 were built up to 1958. About another 3000 were built under licence in Poland, Czechoslovakia, and China. It entered service in all the countries of the Warsaw Pact and in around 30 other nations.

The MiG-17 did not arrive in time to intervene in Korea, but played a major role in the long and bloody war in Vietnam.

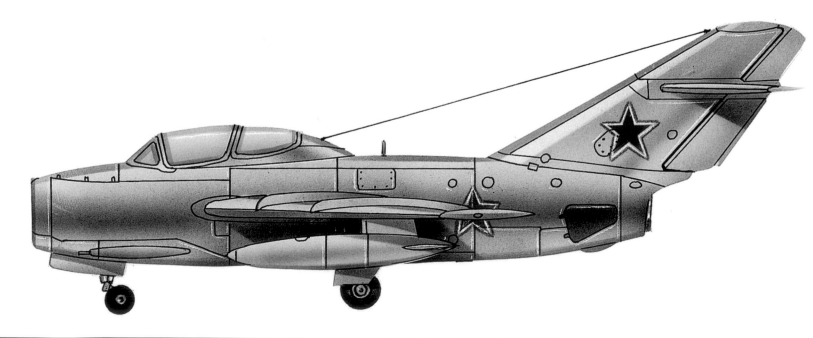

This contribution to development had been provided by the former Allied powers: first with the enormous quantity of means, materials, and machinery sent during the war to modernize the industrial system; then with the supply of the most advanced technology—jet engines. It came as a big shock to American pilots in Korea when they realized that the first-generation Soviet fighter MiG-15 they were up against was a precise copy of the British Rolls-Royce Nene turbo-jet. The development of this machine, which embodied the independence achieved by industry behind the Iron Curtain, marked the start of apparently unstoppable progress. The MiGs epitomized the air power of the Soviet bloc to the West.

However, before achieving this result, Soviet technicians and designers had had to overcome immense problems; in 1945 the VVS (the military air corps) was still a long way from having a valid jet combat aircraft comparable to those of the West.

In Germany, during the final phase of the war, the Red Army had plundered documents, materials, and technicians from the German laboratories and research centers. The booty was impressive: the Heinkel factory in Vienna, where the Heinkel He.162 had been produced; the BMW plants in Eisenach; the whole of Junkers; and the Luftwaffe's experimental center in Reichlin. In particular, they captured many engineers involved in the design and experimentation of BMW and Junkers turbine engines, the same engines that

had equipped the last combat airplanes of the Reich. The aim was to use these significant technical and human resources to build a technological base upon which design independence in the engine field could be developed, but efforts had not been successful. Industry had only managed to produce copies of German turbines, without managing to develop them further. Evidence of this is evidenced by the fact that the dozens and dozens of prototypes were produced in this period but remained at the initial development phases, with only a few of them managing to achieve temporary operational deployment.

In this cycle of frenetic activity, all the major aircraft designers were involved. And when in 1946 there arrived the unexpected British "present", the many workgroups led by Mikoyan and Gurevich, Tupolev, Ilyushin, Yakovlev, and Sukhoi put all of their great experience to use and wasted no time. The MiG-15, designed and finalized in a few months, represented their first success. And it was precisely this formidable group of technicians who, starting in the 1950s, guided the growth of Soviet air power.

In the first generation of military jets, evolution was not limited to the sector of fighters, but also affected that of medium bombers and tactical aircraft. In these categories of machines the production of the USSR surpassed that of the West, especially with the Ilyushin Il-28, a versatile workhorse that saw long and widespread use in the air forces of Eastern Bloc countries.

314 and 315 One of the most widespread fighters of the USSR in the 1950s, the MiG-17. The fighter, derived from the MiG-15, was used in Vietnam and was provided to almost all the air forces of the Warsaw Pact countries. Top right: A two-seater trainer bearing the insignia of Pakistan. Bottom right : A detail of the aircraft viewed from the front. Bottom left: One of the MiG-17s of the Cuban Air Force captured by the Americans during the crisis in the area.

Hawker Sea Fury

GREAT BRITAIN

The last in the line of a famous family of fighters designed by Sydney Camm, the "father" of the Hurricane, the Sea Fury was the last combat aircraft to use a piston engine in the Fleet Air Arm and one of the best in its class.

Although designed during the Second World War and originally destined for the RAF and for the Royal Navy Air Corps, this fast and powerful single-seater entered service only after the war was over and only as an on-board fighter. However, well into the jet age, the Sea Fury still managed to hold its own: the Royal Navy kept it in front-line service from 1947 to 1954, a period of seven years, and purchased 615 out of an overall

production of 860.

Its baptism of fire was the Korean War, in which the Sea Fury took an active part with the units on board the aircraft carriers *Ocean*, *Theseus*, *Glory*, and *Sydney*.

On many occasions it proved to be superior even to the enemy's more modern jet fighters, especially in ground-attack missions, where the better handling at lower altitudes

of this propeller-driven airplane compared with jets was a great advantage. There were a number of victories against the MiG-15: the first was recorded on August 9, 1952, by a pilot of 802 Squadron on board the *Ocean*, Lieutenant Peter Carmichael.

Work on the project had begun in 1943, at the request of the two armed forces, and was originally aimed at producing a lighter version of the Tempest fighter fitted with

a radial engine. The optimal configuration was achieved by installing a large and powerful Bristol Centaurus engine in a cell characterized by a sleek fuselage and a wing structure similar to that of the Tempest, but shorter and lighter.

The prototype made its maiden flight on September 1, 1944, but the end of the war led to the cancelling of RAF orders.

This left the Royal Navy, and in 1945 Hawker perfected the naval

version of its airplane, which was accepted and put into production the following year. The Sea Fury was produced in two basic versions, the F.10 and the FB.11 (in the drawings), and a trainer version, the T.20. In addition to its use in the units of the Fleet Air Arm, it was also successfully exported, serving in Canada, Australia, Egypt, Holland, Pakistan, Morocco, Iraq, West Germany, Burma, and Cuba.

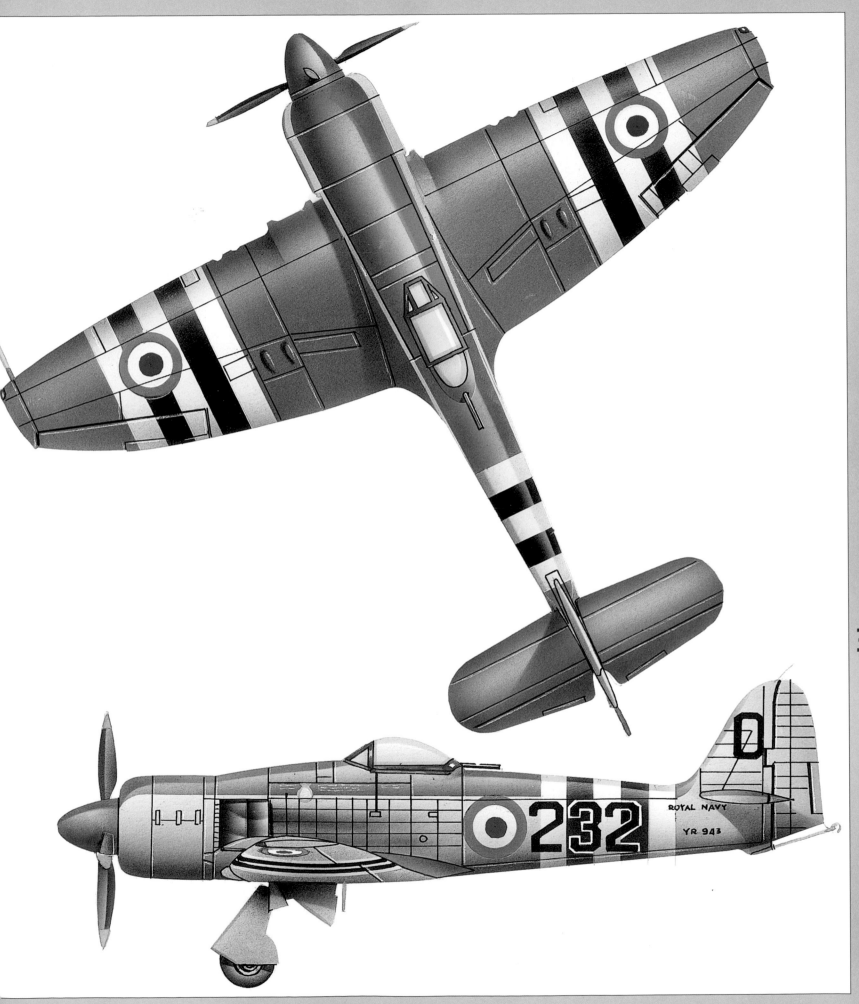

GREAT BRITAIN

Exhausted by the war, Britain faced the first years of peace with the need to reconstruct its economic, social, and industrial system which had been thrown into chaos by the long conflict. The most profound effect of this austerity was the drastic slowing down of military production, a direct consequence of the freeze on orders. Even the glorious RAF, which in 1945 was considered one of the most powerful air forces in the world, suffered the effects of demobilization and, in the three following years, was reduced to a little over a thousand combat aircraft and 38,000 men.

The budget cuts had important consequences for the quality of equipment as well: the Royal Air Force, the only Allied military air force to have used a jet airplane during the war, had to wait until 1950 before its day fighter units were entirely converted to machines of this type and until 1952 to complete the modernization process of night and all-weather fighter units. In this transition phase, alongside the new Gloster Meteors and de Havilland Vampires, first-generation jets, propeller-driven combat aircraft continued to operate in the front line for many years. These were the last of that family of machines which originated in the

318 top Of the many versions of the Meteor twin jet, this model is the N.F.11 night-fighter, equipped with radar.

318 bottom A Vampire bearing the insignia of the Mexican Air Force.

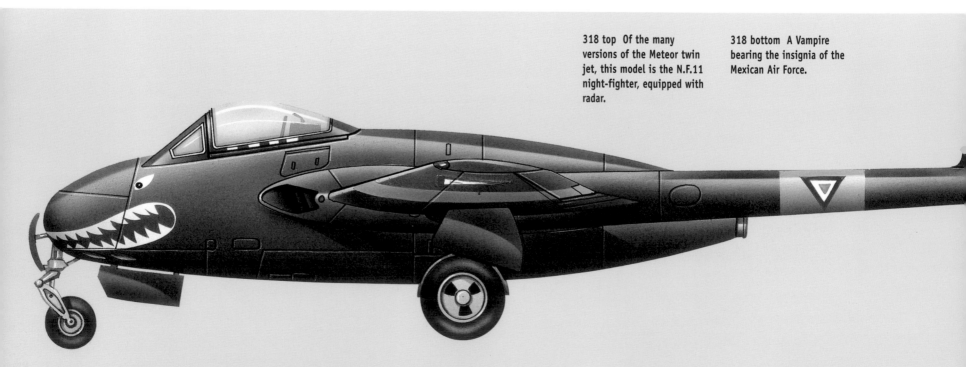

319 top The Vampire was in service in the 1950s in dozens of air forces around the world.

319 bottom A squadron of RAF Vampires scrambling.

years of the conflict: the de Havilland Hornet, the Hawker Sea Fury, and the Bristol Brigand, successors of the Beaufighter.

The phenomenon was even more evident in Bomber Command: until the arrival in 1951 of the first British Electric Canberra twin-jet aircraft, the bomber units of the RAF continued to use the aging Avro Lincoln and even the American Boeing B-29.

This period of relative stasis lasted until the first signs of the Cold War, when British strategists realized that from a position at the international forefront in the aeronautical field, the nation had fallen into the background, surpassed by the economic and military power of the American and Soviet giants. With the blockade of Berlin and the appearance of the first alarming signs of the growing tension between the two blocs, the armament policy was re-implemented. The outbreak of the Korean War gave the second definitive boost and led to implementation of the first program of RAF development in the post-war years. In March

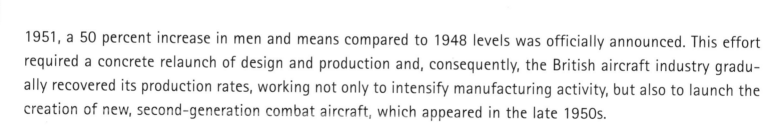

320 The first English Electric Canberra bombers were delivered to the RAF in 1951. The twin-jet obtained great success in the ranks of many air forces, performing tasks of bombing, reconnaissance, training, and electronic warfare. It was also mass-produced in the United States by Martin as the B-57.

1951, a 50 percent increase in men and means compared to 1948 levels was officially announced. This effort required a concrete relaunch of design and production and, consequently, the British aircraft industry gradually recovered its production rates, working not only to intensify manufacturing activity, but also to launch the creation of new, second-generation combat aircraft, which appeared in the late 1950s.

321 top The Ouragan, built by Dassault.

321 bottom Line-up of French Dassault Mystère II fighters of the Armée de l'Air.

FRANCE

It was the great desire for recovery which drove France to once more develop its aircraft industry, that had died under German occupation. Subsequently, the political choices of the government opened the way for a strategy of expansion and independence which has remained unchanged until the present day. The name that remains indissolubly linked with the rebirth of French military aviation is that of Marcel Bloch, the great constructor who during the conflict, joined the Résistance, was captured by the Nazis, and imprisoned in Buchenwald. In 1946 Marcel Bloch returned to his old factories, intending to recommence his activity and thus give a new lease of life to French aircraft production. The first thing he did was to change the name of the company to Dassault, the name he had adopted as a partisan. Then, firmly convinced that France had to produce its own combat jet in order not to be dependent on British and American supplies, he threw himself into the development of a jet fighter. Work took place on the project in the total absence of official support, and success was only achieved at the end, after the brilliant performance of the prototypes.

But the appearance of the Ouragan (the name given to the airplane which equipped the reborn Armée de l'Air in 1950) was only the first step. The fighter had originally used a Rolls-Royce Nene turbo-jet built

322 top The Israeli Air Force, besides the Ouragan, is also equipped with Mystère B-2 planes.

322 bottom A Super Mystère B-2 during landing and slowed down by its parachute

323 A patrol of Vampire Trainers in acrobatic flight. The two-seater British jet was widely used in the 1950s.

under licence by Hispano-Suiza and thus still did not represent the complete technological independence so sought-after by Marcel Dassault. This was achieved soon after with the construction of the first entirely French-produced jet engines made by Snecma. In 1945, this state industry had taken over the historic Gnome-Rhône and three years later had launched its first turbo-jet, the Atar. It was precisely with this engine that Dassault managed to achieve the second, important step: the development of a supersonic airplane. The Mystère and the Super Mystère of the early 1950s opened the way to a successful design series and was followed by even more significant results. The most prestigious was that of the Mirage, the combat airplane which, thanks to its excellent performance and success on the international market, managed to earn France a place once more in the exclusive club of major military powers.

324 top This twin-engined tactical support aircraft, developed in the 1970s as an anti-tank weapon, proved to be irreplaceable in its class.

324 bottom The pilot of a Fairchild A-10 Thunderbolt II ready for take-off.

325 bottom The Bell X-1, the first aircraft in the world to break the sound barrier in horizontal flight. Propulsion was provided by a single rocket engine with two propellants.

Vietnam and the Cold War

"**H**ey Ridley, listen, there's something wrong with this machmeter, it's gone completely off the scale!". This short, excited radio communication announced the arrival of the supersonic era in American aviation. It was October 14, 1947, and the experimental Bell X-1 aircraft was flying at over 38,400 ft (12,000 meters), after having been released from a B-29 bomber which had taken off from the Muroc Air Force base in the Californian desert. The pilot, Captain Charles E. "Chuck" Yeager, had just given full power to the rocket engine and enclosed in his cramped cockpit, had to rely on his instruments for information on the flight. In reality, the speedometer was not broken, but had simply not been calibrated to record speeds of over Mach 1. "Great; if it is, we'll mend it, but you just go ahead and break it if you want!", was how Captain Jackie L. Ridley, the engineer

responsible for the program, replied to Yeager's worried message. The fact that his X-1 had just reached a new milestone in the history of the airplane was confirmed on the ground: for the first time the sound barrier had been broken, with a speed of 646 mph (1078 km/h) in horizontal flight at an altitude of 40,960 ft (12,800 meters).

This date and this result were just the beginning of a long series of successes, which made Chuck Yeager one of the most famous pioneers in modern aviation. In 1953, with an improved version of this airplane (the X-1A), performance increased with astounding progress: on November 21 a speed of Mach 1.3 was achieved, and on December 2 and 8, Mach1.5 and 1.9 respectively. On December 12, 1953 Yeager achieved Mach 2.44 (2655 km/h), almost 2 1/2 times the speed of sound, and achieved the world record for an aircraft without a swept wing. That day, however, the flight was dramatic and risked ending in tragedy.

At the peak of the thrust, at over 73,600 ft (23,000 meters) in altitude, the airplane suddenly became uncontrollable and dived 9 miles (15 km) in less than a minute. It was only at the last minute that the pilot managed to regain control and bring the aircraft back to base. "You know, if I'd had an ejector seat you wouldn't have found me still in here... I think I broke the roof with my head." This was how Yeager explained his terrifying experience to colleagues on the ground.

The story of the Bell X-1 and its most famous test pilot epitomizes the atmosphere in the field of military aircraft development in United States in the early 1950s. This new phase was triggered by the enormous technological thrust generated by the Second World War, and opened up prospects previously unimaginable. With the latest protagonist in aviation, the jet engine, still at the beginning of its life, speed was the most

326 top and bottom right The improved, X-1A version of the first American supersonic airplane flew at over 1650 mph (2655 km/h) in December 1953.

326 bottom left Chuck Yeager, the first supersonic pilot in the world.

important challenge and this was closely linked to the experimentation with innovative materials and structural solutions aimed at making the airplanes even more efficient.

Behind the enthusiasm of the pilots, reminiscent of the great excitement surrounding the discovery of the airplane's potential in previous decades, there was a different and much more worrying reality. What was really at stake, once again, was the search for supremacy. The Cold War had fuelled the incessant race arms race between the two opposing blocs, and the confrontation had been transformed into a global nightmare. In the Korean War in which the air forces had been the main protagonists, with the new jet aircraft trialed for the first time after the Second World War, the United States had tested the modernity of its new Soviet adversary's weaponry in the field. It realized that the supposed margins of superiority of the Western arsenal were extreme-

ly narrow and that the overall ratio of forces had to be changed to their advantage. This was an important lesson, and operational experience had been rapidly translated into significant investment in research, above all in the field of engines and structures, and in industry, with the primary objective to produce new and more advanced combat aircraft. It is no coincidence that the record flight by Yeager on December 2, 1953 was only a few months after the end of the Korean War, demonstrating how strongly the United States desired to react and needed to make up lost ground.

327 top The Douglas X-3 Stiletto was not fully developed due to the insurmountable difficulties with its engines.

327 bottom Another experimental aircraft produced by Bell, the X-2. Its flying life ended in September 1956 in an accident that saw the loss of plane and pilot, but it nevertheless established an unofficial world speed record of 2094 mph (3370 km/h).

328 top The North American X-15 just after being released by the mother plane (in the left photo attached under a B-52) at the moment when the rockets are being turned on.

In the context of this intense activity, a vital role was played by a formidable aerospace research project, the Experimental Research Aircraft Program, of which the X-1 was the first significant result. Created in far-off 1942, in the darkest period of the Second World War, this program proved to be fundamental for the development of military aviation. Tests using experimental aircraft (the famous "X planes") performed in the 1950s and 60s explored all the frontiers of flight, and proved to be an irreplaceable source of experience and technological contribution at the highest level. They were the first to fly at speeds above the speed of sound and to use variable geometry wings; the first to reach and exceed 320,000 ft (100,000 meters) in altitude and to achieve speeds of over Mach 6; the first to test sophisticated metals, rocket engines, and revolutionary aerodynamic solutions.

This enormous technological resource was transferred directly to industry, and the results were not long in coming. The second generation of American combat jets was launched in 1950s thanks to the boost provided by research, marking the beginning of total design independence and triggering off progress which put the United States firmly in a position to lead the West in the aeronautical field.

The sound barrier

The speed of sound is the speed at which sound waves move through the atmosphere. This varies with altitude and temperature: for example, the speed of sound is 740 mph (1234.8 km/h) at sea level and 640 mph (1066 km/h) at 35,2000 ft (11,000 meters). For years, the speed of sound represented a real obstacle (hence the term "the sound barrier") for pilots who tried to break it: airplanes began to vibrate and became unstable, finally resulting in loss of control. Compressibility phenomena, encountered and studied for the first time in the post-war period, caused a great number of accidents before their causes were established.

Sound waves are propagated through air by means of concentric spherical surfaces which cause variations in pressure. If an airplane is traveling at a speed lower than the speed of sound, it remains 'inside' the sound waves it causes and flight proceeds normally. However, when its speed reaches that of sound, the aircraft "catches up with" the sound waves and is faced with strong resistance and disturbance. Once the barrier has been breached (on the ground a characteristic "bang" can be heard, similar to an explosion), everything returns to normal. To break the sound barrier, an airplane must have particularly well-designed aerodynamic features, but above all, the necessary power.

X planes

In order to understand the enormous evolution in American military aviation during the first half of the Cold War, we need to look at the most significant phases of the Experimental Research Aircraft Program and the excellent results achieved by X planes in the 1950s and 60s.

The X-1, the first of the family, and the first American aircraft with a rocket engine, was designed in 1946 to study the problems of supersonic flight. Its story is linked to that of Charles E. Yeager; apart from his records, the achievements of this airplane also include an altitude record of 70,176 ft (21,930 meters) achieved by Frank Everest on August 8, 1949.

The X-1 was developed in another three improved versions, designated X-1A, X-1B, and X-1D. Six months after the record of December 12, 1953, on June 4, 1954 the first aircraft reached an altitude of 87,792 ft (27,435 meters) piloted by Arthur Murray. The X-1 programme continued until 1958, and the total number of flights was 231.

The study of the features and aerodynamic performance of the swept wing at altitude and at even higher speeds led to the production of the subsequent experimental aircraft, the X-2, from Bell. Of the two aircraft ordered in 1946, only one was developed after an accident destroyed the second prototype on May 12, 1953. The main goals achieved by the X-2 were an altitude record of 117,238 ft (36,637 meters) on September 7, 1956, piloted by Iven Kincheloe; and a speed record of 2022 mph (3370 km/h) on September 27. The second of the two flights had a tragic end: as had happened to Yeager's X-1A three years earlier, the airplane went out of control soon after exceeding the speed of Mach 3 and crashed to the ground killing the pilot Captain Milburn Apt.

The analysis of the aerodynamic and structural behavior in prolonged flights at supersonic speed was at the root of the development of the X-3 by Douglas.

Having abandoned rocket engines, two Westinghouse turbojets were chosen for propulsion. But it was precisely the lack of engines with sufficient thrust that led to the discontinuation of the program. The only one built flew for the first time on October 20,1952 and remained in service for three years, even if it did not achieve the pre-established goals. More than for its performance, the X-3 was remembered for the elegance of its lines, characterized by slender forms and a small wing, which earned it the unusual nickname of *Stiletto*.

The failure of the experimental Douglas aircraft was made up for in following years by the North American X-15, a machine which surpassed all previous achievements and reached the maximum limits of stratospheric flight. The specifications for the X-15 were issued by NACA on June 24, 1952 in a period in which the USAF was finishing work on the X-1 program and starting that of the X-2. The requests were for the production of an aircraft with rocket propulsion able to reach altitudes of 10–48 miles (18–80 km) and speeds of 4–10 times the speed of sound.

The program was handed over to industries toward the end of 1954 and the winning design was produced by North American, who signed the contract on June 11, 1956, with an order for three aircraft. There were various problems to be faced and overcome. There were structural problems, issues with the surfaces of the airplane, which had to withstand extremely high temperatures, as well as problems regarding the fine-tuning of an efficient rocket engine.

The first prototype, the X-15, left the factory on October 15,1958 and on March 10 the following year was taken up under the wing of a specially modified B-52 bomber. Three months later, on June 8, the first free descent was successfully performed and on September 17 there was the first flight with the engine running. The tests continued for a long period, due to the lack of the definitive XLR-99-type engine, whose development had undergone significant delays.

The first of the 199 missions was not performed until November 15, 1960. Up until October 24, 1968, the sequence of records was incredible: the most significant were obtained on November 9,1961 by Bob White, with 3951 mph (6586 km/h); and on April 30, 1962 by Joe Walker, who reached an altitude of 259,001 ft (80,938 meters).

On 22 August 1963 the same pilot flew to 345,472 ft (107,960 meters).

Significant changes to the second aircraft sent to the factory for repair after a forced landing on November 9, 1962, led to the single example of the X-15 A-2. This airplane proved to be the fastest of them all: on October 3, 1967 piloted by William Knight, it reached a speed of 4363 mph (7273 km/h). This record flight also represented the swansong of this machine which, after another emergency landing, was irreparably damaged.

The loss of the third aircraft, on November 15,1967, marked the end of the program.
The only surviving X-15 made its last flight on October 24, 1968.

Lockheed F-104 Starfighter

UNITED STATES

Leaving the scene in 2004, some 50 years after its maiden flight, the Lockheed F-104 Starfighter earned a place among the immortals of aviation. This was the first fighter to fly at over Mach 2 in service with the USAF, and characterized an entire age in the air forces of the West, achieving success above all in Europe, Canada, and Japan, where over 70 percent of the 2578 built were produced under licence.

The Starfighter was launched in 1952 on the basis of the experiences in the Korean War, when the USAF decided to introduce a day interceptor characterized by bisonic speed to replace the North American F-100. On March 12,1953 Lockheed was awarded the contract for the program and the first of two prototypes designated XF-104 flew one year later, on March 4,1954.

Production commenced on the basis of orders for 153 F-104As and 26 two-seater F-104B trainers. Deliveries to the units began on January 26,1958, but in operational use the aircraft displayed general inadequacy compared to predicted performance.

Orders were drastically reduced and despite changes and increased power, the subsequent version, the C (in the drawings), only had a production run of 77, of which 22 were two-seaters (F-104D). These aircraft, transformed into fighter-bombers, were used in Vietnam until July 1967, with little success. The F-104Cs, moreover, were the first to be exported to Germany (20 designated F-104DJ) and Japan (30 F-104Fs).

It was export considerations and the need to give the allies a valid common combat airplane which led to the second phase of the Starfighter's career, since its future in the USAF seemed uncertain. In 1958 Lockheed developed a version specially designed for the German Luftwaffe. This was the F-104G, which appeared as a prototype on June 7,1960. In the same year, the airplane was also chosen by Canada, Holland, Belgium, Japan, and Italy. These countries launched a massive combined industrial program which, apart from 101 aircraft of the single-seater version and 200 of the two-seater TF-104G produced by Lockheed, completed the rest of the massive production-run under licence. The Starfighter entered service with the air forces of Germany, Italy, Japan, Holland, Belgium, Canada, Turkey, Greece, Nationalist China, Denmark, and Norway. The Aeronautica Militare Italiana initially received 125 F-104Gs and 28 two-seater TF-104Gs, and it was precisely Italy which took the development of the F-104 to the limit, producing the last version of the fighter, the F-104S, with Lockheed in 1966.

The first production aircraft entered service in 1969. The Aeronautica Militare received 205, and another 40 were ordered in 1974 by Turkey. In 1980 and 1997 the Italian airplanes were subjected to two important updates in weapons systems and avionics. The last F-104s left active service in May 2004.

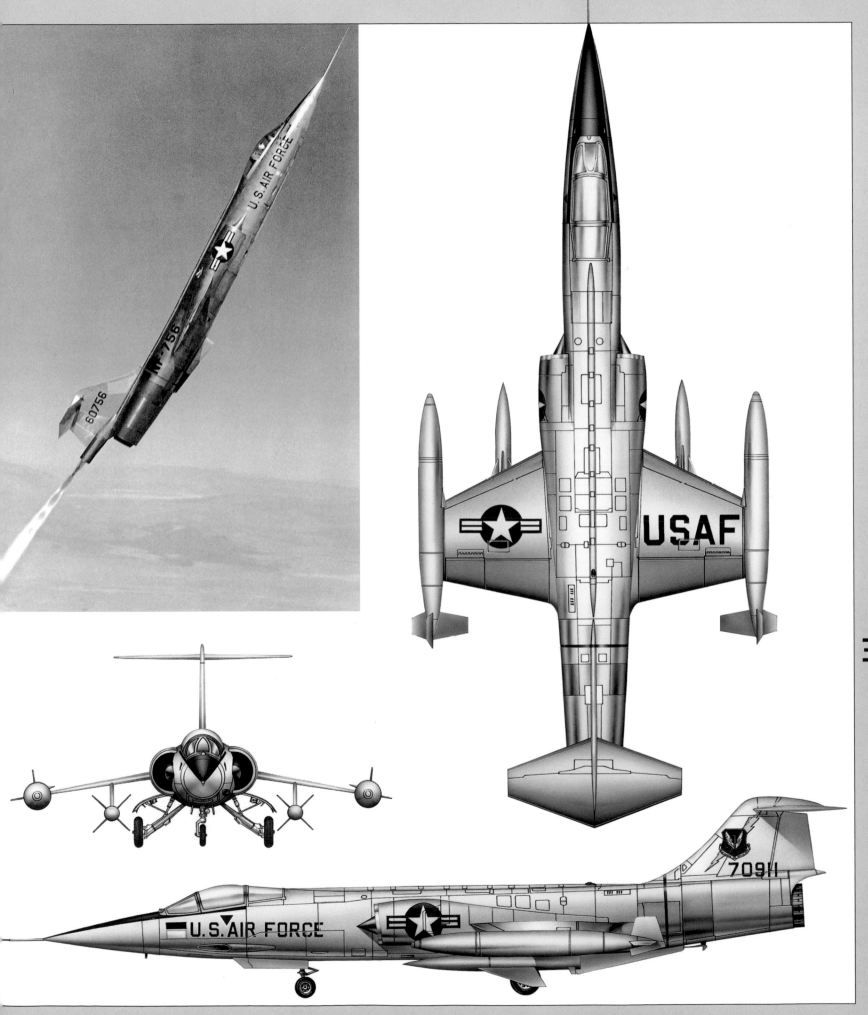

334 top and center Another famous fighter-bomber was the McDonnell F-4 Phantom. Over 5000 were built and served for years in many units of the US Navy, US Marine Corps, USAF and 12 other foreign air forces. It was successfully deployed in air operations in Vietnam.

The competition between the United States and the Soviet Union in this field was particularly heated. It was perhaps the main element in the search for supremacy, considering that electronics not only benefited the machines, but made it possible to create an entire communications network able to manage all the aspects of modern warfare, of which airplanes were only one of the many components.

It is sufficient to think of the enormous importance of surveillance radar, of reconnaissance devices, of the sophisticated battlefield control systems installed on board the flying command centers, the by now famous AWACS, to have an idea of what exactly was at stake.

334 bottom Boeing E-3A Sentry, the best known of the western AWACS (Airborne Warning and Control System) aircraft.

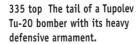

335 top The tail of a Tupolev Tu-20 bomber with its heavy defensive armament.

335 bottom Sukhoi Su-7, a large single-engine swept-wing aircraft designed for attack duties. A derivate was the Su-17, with greater weapon capability.

At the beginning of the 1950s, the United States were decidedly at the forefront in military electronics and the Korean War had reinforced this conviction. But their supremacy did not last long. The backwardness of their adversary in this sector, whose origins dated back to the Second World War, was soon to disappear.

In 1945, after the end of hostilities, the USSR had entirely made up the gap in the engine field which separated it from the Allies with whom it had shared the war effort. But it remained far behind in the development of other military technologies such as radar, with which it had been supplied by its allies during the conflict, but whose development and latest advances were jealously guarded by the British and Americans. Consequently, in the new world order, alongside the design and production of efficient combat jet aircraft, maximum priority was given to the implementation of these systems, in the attempt to make good the disadvantage. The greatest efforts were initially concentrated on the production of a valid land-based surveillance radar, to be used for air defence systems, and an airborne interception radar. This was a particularly complex task, but in the end was crowned with success. In the frenetic climate of rearmament, in which the Soviet Union basically ignored the civil economy, and channeled the majority of its economic resources into military needs, it made up lost ground in those major areas of technology in which it had lagged. And, as had happened in the aeronautical field during the Korean War, the West was surprised to discover that it no longer possessed the superiority it was convinced it held, even in the sector of avionics.

The first Soviet land-based surveillance radar appeared in 1951. Two years later, at the end of the Korean War, the USSR announced the existence of the first type of airborne interception radar. The significance of these innovations was extremely important and went well beyond simple operational use: it clearly indicated the concrete signs of achieved independence. Having made up for their initial disadvantage, the USSR displayed unstoppable growth in the development of these systems, increasingly integrating them with the avionics of the aircraft, above all with the advent of missiles. Complete operational equality was achieved with the United States in the early 1960s, also thanks to the great technological fallout deriving from research carried out on space programs.

336 top The Lockheed U-2, the famous American spy-plane, basically a motorized glider specifically designed for high-altitude reconnaissance flights. One of these aircraft was shot down in the Soviet Union during a spying mission. The pilot, Gary Powers, went on trial in Moscow.

336

336 center The Grumman E-2 Hawkeye, a US Navy aircraft for long-range reconnaissance duties. The radar antenna is mounted in an elevated position on the back of the fuselage.

336 bottom Soviet pilots at the end of a training exercise with the Sukhoi Su-17.

337 top In 1953 the US Navy chose the Vought F-8 Crusader as a supersonic carrier-based fighter. It was characterized by a high variable incidence wing to facilitate deck take-off and landing.

337 bottom The Lockheed P-3 Orion marine patrol aircraft and, in the round picture, one of its large turbo-prop engines.

The concrete effects of this process were manifested directly in the aircraft production of the two main adversaries. And the fighter, the combat aircraft *par excellence*, was the category to benefit most from these innovations.

Second-generation American jets represented US air power for two decades. These were powerfully armed airplanes able to operate at twice the speed of sound, and based on the most sophisticated materials technologies.

Vought-LTV F-8 Crusader

UNITED STATES

One of the most widespread carrier-based supersonic fighters of the 1960s,

The Crusader remained in production for ten years, from 1955 to 1965, during which time 1261 were built. It had an extremely long service life: until 1986 in the units of the US Navy and even up to December 1999 in those of the French Aéronavale. Moreover, this airplane was also the last designed by the glorious Chance Vought before its merger into the LTV group in August 1961.

The project was launched on the basis of a set of specifications from the US Navy, issued in September 1952, which requested the creation of a carrier-based air superiority fighter able to fly at Mach 1.2 at altitude. Chance Vought

won the contract for the production of two prototypes, designated XF8U-1, the first of which made its maiden flight on May 25,1955. The most original characteristic of the airplane was its variable incidence wing, designed to reduce speed and improve stability in landing, while also allowing the pilot excellent visibility during the delicate phase of approach to the aircraft

carrier. Right from the first flights, the prototypes proved the great potential of the machine and the development phase was fairly rapid: production was started in late 1955, and on December 20 the following year, the US Navy declared the first unit operational. This was equipped with the initial F8U-1 version (subsequently renamed F-8A), of which 318 were built. There followed 130 F8U-1Es (F-8B) with limited all-weather performance and, in December 1957, the first of 144 F8U-1P (RF-8A) reconnaissance aircraft.

In this role, which they performed until 1986, the Crusaders were called "the eyes of the fleet". The evolution of the family

continued with air superiority versions. The F8U-2 (F-8C) of 1959, of which 197 were built, thanks to its more powerful engine and a series of structural changes, had a maximum speed of almost Mach 2.

The all-weather fighter version underwent similar improvements and the first F8U-2N (F-8D) flew in February 1960; deliveries of the 152 completed started in June. The final variant was the F8U-2NE (F-8E), also an all-weather fighter, which appeared in mid-1961, and of which 286 were built. In 1965 a vast modernization program was set up aimed at extending the operational life of the Crusader.

Over three years, 446

airplanes of all the versions were updated in terms of avionics, wings, and various other structural components.

The fact that these were very different machines from the previous ones was demonstrated by a new change in name: the aircraft of the versions D, E, C, and B were reclassified as F-8H, F-8J (in the drawings), F-8K, and F-8L.

The Crusaders had their baptism of fire in Vietnam. The second largest user after the US Navy was the French Aéronavale, who bought 42 in a specially designed version, the F-8E(FN), which they put into service in late 1965 on the *Foch* and *Clemenceau* aircraft carriers.

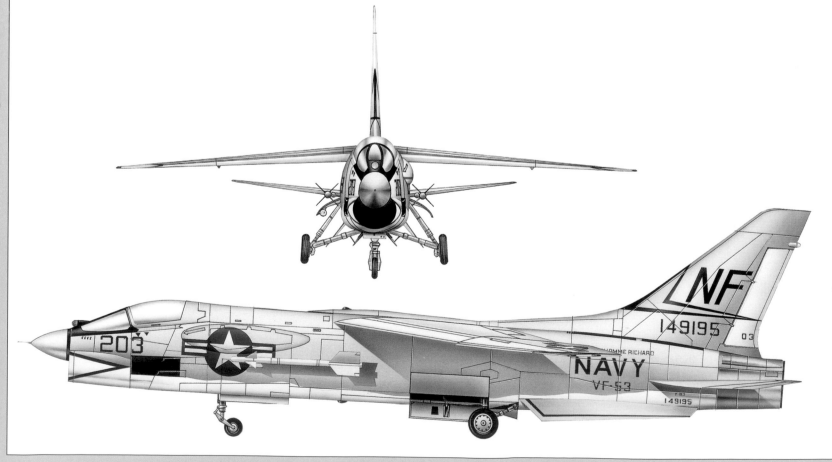

03
USS BON HOMME RICHARD
USS BON HOMME RICHARD
203

NF
149196
NAVY
112

North American F-100 Super Sabre

UNITED STATES

The direct evolution of the F-86 Sabre, the North American F-100 Super Sabre was the first supersonic interceptor in the West. 2294 were built in four basic versions, and it entered service in 1959, remaining in the front line for 18 years until 1972, ending its intense operational career in Vietnam.

North American started work on the project in February 1949, with the aim of perfecting the F-86 to the point of achieving supersonic speeds in horizontal flight. The USAF approved the

program in January 1950. The progress of the Korean War and the urgent need for new and more powerful combat airplanes contributed to accelerating the program, and on November 1 there was a request for two prototypes, the YF-100s. The first of these, completed in great secret, made its maiden flight on May 25,1953. On its first flight, the airplane showed its great potential, easily flying above the speed of sound. These qualities were further demonstrated a few months later, on October 29 when

piloted by the commander of the Edwards Air Force Test Center Colonel Frank K. Everest, the prototype beat the world speed record, flying at 728.5 mph (1214.28 km/h). On the same day, the first of 203 F-100As of the initial series were also tested, and deliveries began in early November.

Operational use, however, was disturbed by a series of serious accidents, which in November 1954 led to the total block of flights pending a technical investigation. The F-100 returned to the skies in November 1954 and production of the initial version ended two months

later. In the meantime, the USAF had authorized the development of a second variant as a fighter-bomber. The first F-100C began tests on January 17, 1955, and deliveries began six months later.

After 476 had been built in 1956, the F-100Cs were replaced on the assembly lines by a new version, which gave the fighter its definitive configuration. The first F-100D appeared on January 24; a total of 1274 were built. In these airplanes (in the drawings) the operational capacities for ground attack were further developed, thanks to a new avionics system for the control of low-level flight and armament management. This, in

addition to tactical nuclear bombs, also included air-to-land and air-to-air missiles. The final variant was the F, an operational two-seater trainer. The first F-100F flew on March 7, 1957, and 339 had been built by October 1959.

In Vietnam, the Super Sabre remained in service until the penultimate year of the war, and was widely used in missions for tactical support and electronic countermeasures. In 1972 the surviving aircraft went to units of the Reserves, where they remained active until 1980.

The F-100s also equipped the air forces of various allied countries. These included Nationalist China, France, Norway, and Turkey.

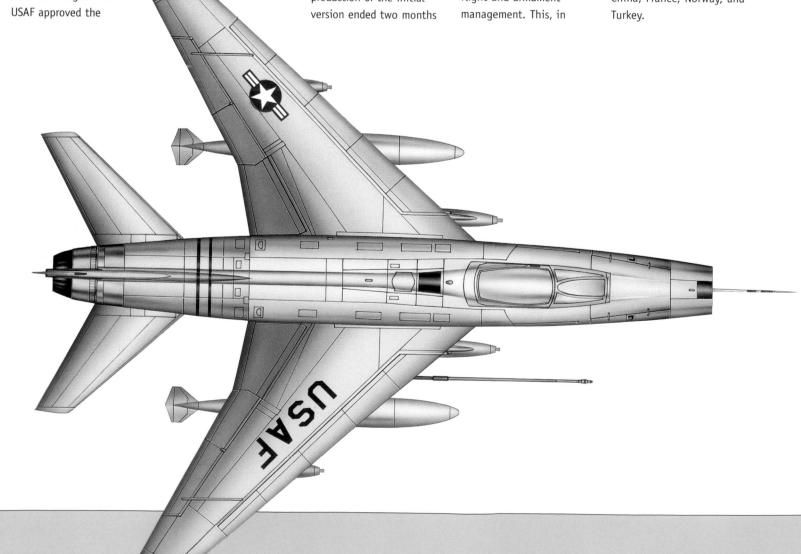

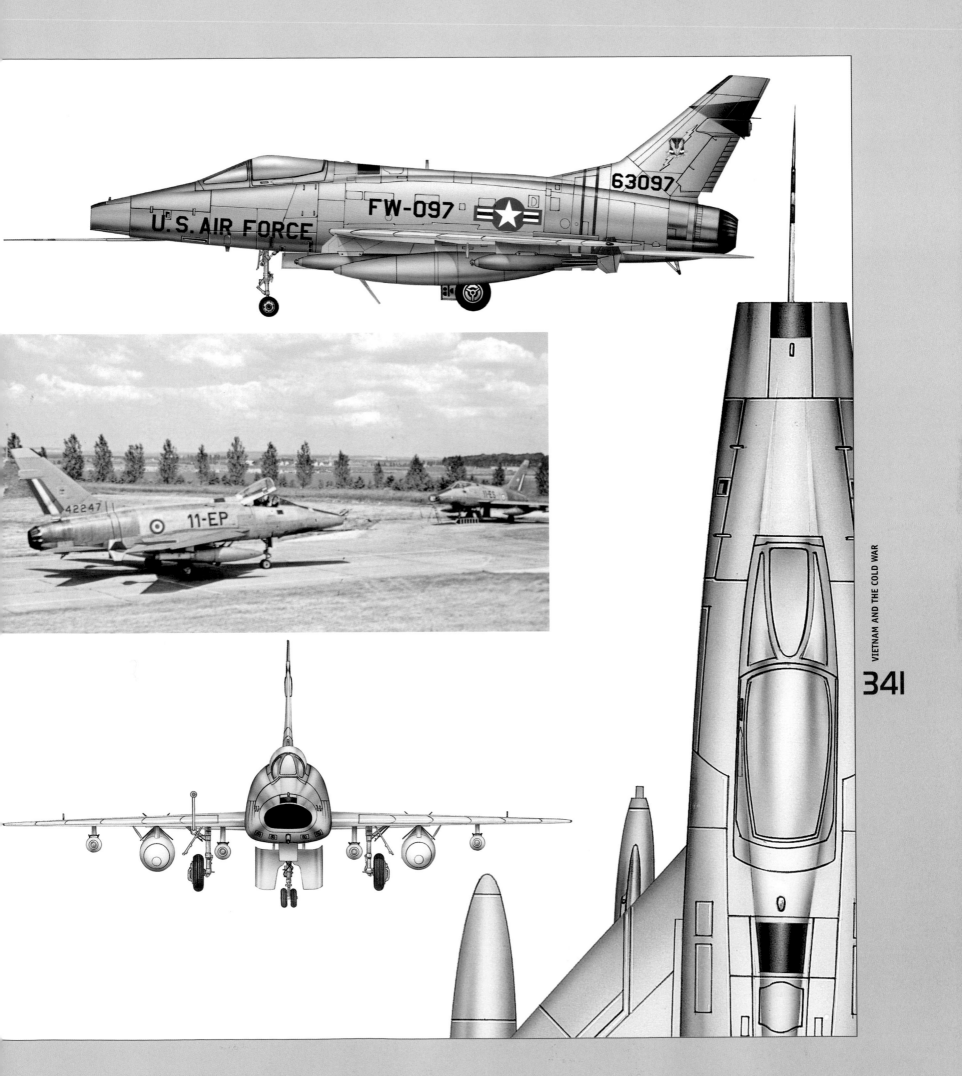

63097
FW-097
U.S. AIR FORCE

42247
11-EP

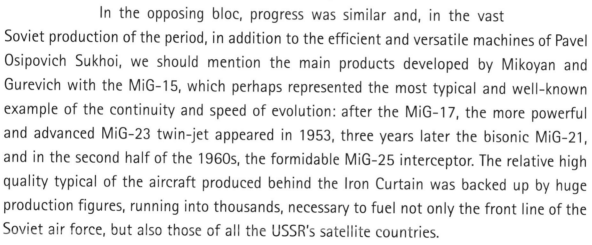

342-343 top The first design studies on the Boeing B-47 date back to the end of the Second World War. The Stratojet, the first swept-wing jet bomber. The airplane remained in service until 1966 and around 1800 were built.

Cases in point are the North American F-100 Super Sabre, the Convair F-102 Delta Dagger, the Lockheed F-104 Starfighter, the Republic F-105 Thunderchief of the USAF, or the LTV F-8 Crusader, the Vought-LTV A-7 Corsair II, the Douglas A-4 Skyhawk, and the McDonnell F-4 Phantom II of the US Navy.

In the opposing bloc, progress was similar and, in the vast Soviet production of the period, in addition to the efficient and versatile machines of Pavel Osipovich Sukhoi, we should mention the main products developed by Mikoyan and Gurevich with the MiG-15, which perhaps represented the most typical and well-known example of the continuity and speed of evolution: after the MiG-17, the more powerful and advanced MiG-23 twin-jet appeared in 1953, three years later the bisonic MiG-21, and in the second half of the 1960s, the formidable MiG-25 interceptor. The relative high quality typical of the aircraft produced behind the Iron Curtain was backed up by huge production figures, running into thousands, necessary to fuel not only the front line of the Soviet air force, but also those of all the USSR's satellite countries.

The new confrontation between these formidable war machines was not long in coming, as the Vietnam War heated up in the mid-1960s. It was another trial of strength, another bloody test of military power, and the release of the tension which had been building up in the first two decades of the Cold War.

342 bottom Successor of the MiG 19 and destined to operate as a short-range interceptor, the MiG-21 was built in large numbers (around 12,000) for the air forces of the Soviet Union and all the countries of the Warsaw Pact.

343 bottom The Boeing B-52 was one of the great protagonists of the war in Vietnam. Equipped with an impressive payload, over 31 tons of bombs, it was used to strike suspected troop concentrations, the track of Ho Chi Minh, and later the capital of North Vietnam, Hanoi.

THE STRATEGIC BOMBER
AND THE BALANCE OF TERROR

The progress of aviation which, with the help of electronics, led to a new generation of fighters, also created a new class of bombers. These were gigantic, fast aircraft, able to fly from one side of the world to the other loaded with deadly weapons, with a strategic potential boosted to the limit by nuclear armaments. These machines in the early decades of the Cold War brought home to the world the nightmare threat of atomic holocaust, as Hiroshima and Nagasaki had experienced back in 1945.

McDonnell F-4 Phantom II

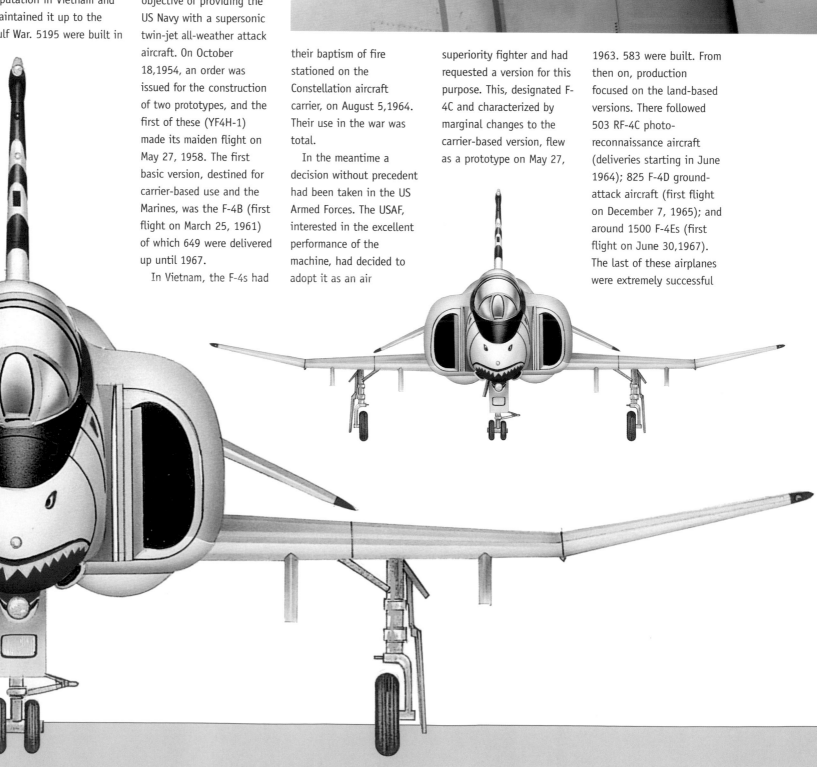

The first real multi-role airplane in the air force, the McDonnell F-4 Phantom II has been unanimously acknowledged as the best fighter-bomber ever built. It earned its reputation in Vietnam and maintained it up to the Gulf War. 5195 were built in dozens of versions (the last left the assembly lines in 1981), and at the beginning of the third millennium, the F-4 was still in front-line service in eight air forces.

Work on the project began in 1953, with the objective of providing the US Navy with a supersonic twin-jet all-weather attack aircraft. On October 18,1954, an order was issued for the construction of two prototypes, and the first of these (YF4H-1) made its maiden flight on May 27, 1958. The first basic version, destined for carrier-based use and the Marines, was the F-4B (first flight on March 25, 1961) of which 649 were delivered up until 1967.

In Vietnam, the F-4s had their baptism of fire stationed on the Constellation aircraft carrier, on August 5,1964. Their use in the war was total.

In the meantime a decision without precedent had been taken in the US Armed Forces. The USAF, interested in the excellent performance of the machine, had decided to adopt it as an air superiority fighter and had requested a version for this purpose. This, designated F-4C and characterized by marginal changes to the carrier-based version, flew as a prototype on May 27, 1963. 583 were built. From then on, production focused on the land-based versions. There followed 503 RF-4C photo-reconnaissance aircraft (deliveries starting in June 1964); 825 F-4D ground-attack aircraft (first flight on December 7, 1965); and around 1500 F-4Es (first flight on June 30,1967). The last of these airplanes were extremely successful

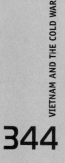

exports and almost a third of those produced went abroad. In particular, Iran ordered 112, Israel another 130, while special variants were prepared for Japan, Great Britain, and Germany. Japan built 140 F-4s of the EJ version under licence, while the German Luftwaffe received 175 F-4Fs, produced from 1973 onwards. Other countries which received the F-4 were Australia, Egypt, Greece, South Korea, Spain, and Turkey. The Phantom II had an important career under the insignia of the RAF and the Royal Navy.

In 1964 Great Britain decided to purchase specific versions of the fighter fitted with Rolls-Royce Spey engines. The first F4-Ks entered service in 1968 with the designation FG.1.

The RAF, which designated them FGR.2, received 118. American air forces, however, remained the main users of the Phantom II, which saw service in Vietnam with the USAF, US Navy, and Marines. In particular, the Navy also equipped its units with a second version after the F-4B, the J (introduced in May 1966; 5220 built), which remained in front-line service until 1975. The USAF, meanwhile, did not withdraw the last of the 2874 Phantom IIs received until 1996.

In the drawings, an F-4B.

Douglas A-4 Skyhawk

UNITED STATES

Almost 3000 were built between 1954 and 1979. These figures alone express the success of the Douglas A-4 Skyhawk and its importance as a combat machine. Versatile, powerful, and reliable, produced in dozens of versions, this light and compact attack airplane took an active part in all the principal conflicts of the 1960s and 70s, and was still being used in combat in 1982 by the Argentinean air force during the Falklands War.

The Skyhawk dates back to the early 1950s, when the US Navy announced a competition for an airplane to replace the ageing Douglas AD Skyraider with a jet aircraft.

The chief designer at Douglas Aircraft, Ed Heinemann, came up with a design in two weeks which not only respected all the requirements, but even

provided for an aircraft whose maximum tak-eoff weight was practically half that laid down under specifications. This characteristic, important for carrier-based use, proved to be the winning card. The prototype made its maiden flight on June 22, 1954 and on August 14 was followed by the first of the pre-production series, designated A4D-1 Skyhawk (165 of these were built, and in 1962 were renamed A-4A). The aircraft entered service on October 26, 1956.

After the second variant, the A4-D2 (A-4B) and the sub-series A-4D2N (A-4C), with a more powerful engine and improved avionics, of which 542 and 638 were built respectively, the first significant updates were seen in the third version, the A-4D5 (A-4E), which appeared on July 12, 1961. Thanks to a lighter engine and lower specific consumption, performance improved significantly.

The A-4E entered service in January 1963, and 499 were built up till April 1966, when the F variant (in the drawings) appeared. These airplanes, in addition to using a different engine, were completely updated in terms of the avionics, which was installed in a characteristic 'hunchback'. 146 were built, plus another 245 two-seater TA-4F trainers. In 1968 the

TA-4J was produced for training, with simplified armament and equipment. In the meantime, on July 10, 1967, production figures had passed the significant milestone of 2000.

In the 1970s, the most important variant was the A-4M (158 built) named Skyhawk II and produced for the Marines, which came out on April 10,1970. These airplanes had even more powerful engines, armaments, and avionics. 117 aircraft of a special version (A-4N) were produced for Israel, which

since 1970 had received a hundred A-4Hs and TA-4Hs (derived from the F series) and another A-4Es from the US Navy. In addition to the US Navy and the Marines, who made intense use of the A-4 in Southeast Asia, the Israeli air force was the largest user of the small Douglas fighter, which was successfully used in the Yom Kippur War in 1973.

Additionally, the Skyhawk was sold to Australia, New Zealand, Singapore, Kuwait, Indonesia, Malaysia, Argentina, and Brazil.

Republic F-105 Thunderchief

UNITED STATES

The Thunderchief was the culmination of a long line of designs produced by Republic and Alexander Kartveli since the Second World War—the great family of "Thunder" fighter planes whose greatest expressions were the P-47 and the F-84. Among the great protagonists of the war in Vietnam, the F-105 became the principal weapon of the USAF Tactical Air Command and in the first five years of service in South-East Asia accounted for over 75 percent of the attack missions performed by the US Air Force. 825 were built, the last of which remained in active service until 1984 in the units of the National Guard.

Republic began work on the program in June 1950 at the beginning of the Korean War, with the intention of producing a successor to the excellent F-84.

The designer Alexander Kartveli used the experience acquired in the creation of the last version of his successful combat airplane, the swept-wing F-84F. The design was not accepted until March 1953 and the prototype was taken on its maiden flight on October 22, 1955; it immediately displayed formidable development potential. It was the largest and heaviest single-engined single-seater aircraft ever built, optimized to penetrate enemy defences at low altitudes, at high speeds, and in all weather conditions, equipped with over six tons of bombs, both conventional and nuclear. It had unprecedented operational capacities and what a 1960s advertising slogan called "an entire air force in the hands of a single man".

The first operational version was the F-105B

(71 built), which started to arrive in the units in May 1958. Production focused on the following variant, the F-105D (in the drawings), which appeared as a prototype on June 9,1959. This version of the Thunderchief entered service in 1961 and in the following three years 610 were completed. The last version produced (143 built) was the F, a two-seater advanced trainer, which started to be delivered in 1963. These airplanes were converted to produce a further variant (the F-105G, 86 built) optimized for electronic warfare.

In Vietnam the Thunderchief (or *Thud,* as the crews nicknamed it) had its baptism of fire on March 1, 1965 from the base of Da Nang. With the continuation of the conflict, however, the lack of full superiority over the Soviet MiGs and the development of the enemy

anti-aircraft missile defences saw the initial successes fade away and marked the beginning of a period of heavy losses.

The situation improved the following year, with the increasingly widespread use of the F

and G versions of the F-105 in the Wild Weasel operations protecting ground attacks. In the entire campaign in South-East Asia, the Thuds completed over 20,000 missions, and 385 were lost.

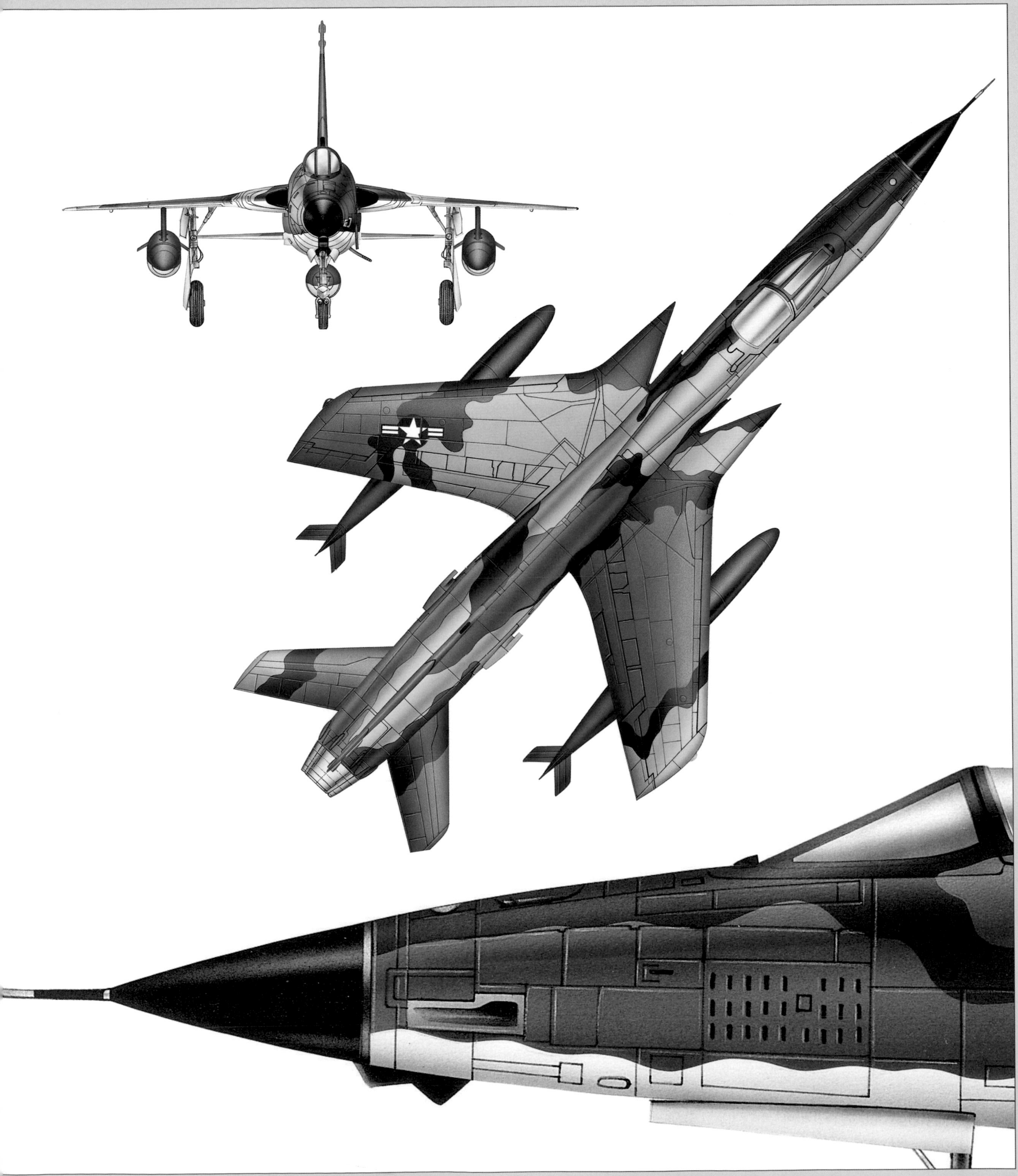

Vought-LTV A-7 Corsair II

UNITED STATES

Conceived in the first half of the 1960s as a replacement for the Douglas A-4 Skyhawk, the Corsair II would reveal itself to be one of the most efficient attack aircraft ever built. The proof of its great worth can be seen in a few figures: in production for 18 years, from 1966 to 1984; 1569 built in a large number of versions; serving in the US Armed Forces until 1991 and still in front-line service in Greece and Portugal in the first years of the new millennium.

The US Navy specifications which led to the design were issued on May 17,1963. They requested the construction of a light, single-seater subsonic attack aircraft, characterized by low production costs and able to carry a maximum bomb load of 14,960 lb (6800 kg). The contract was awarded to LTV (Ling-Temco-Vought, a company into which the Vought Corporation had merged in 1961), and the contract for the realization of seven experimental and 35 pre-series aircraft, designated A-7A and baptized Corsair II in honor of the famous Second World War carrier-based fighter, was drawn up on March 19, 1964. The first prototype flew on September 27, 1965, and on November 15, 1966 qualification tests began on board the aircraft carrier America. The baptism of fire in Vietnam took place on December 4, 1967.

The initial version (193 built) was followed by the A-7B (196 built, first flight on February 6, 1968), with a more powerful engine and operational from January 1967 onwards, and the A-7C (67 built, maiden flight November 25,1968, in service from June 1969 onwards), fitted with a different engine. Much more important was the following variant, the A-7D (in the drawings), developed on the basis of a specific request from the USAF, whose arsenal lacked an aircraft for tactical support and close air support. The prototype, which appeared on September 26, 1968, revealed an even more powerful and better machine, fitted with an Allison TF41-A-1 engine derived from the Rolls-Royce Spey. These Corsair IIs, which entered service in 1969, 459 of which were built, were used widely in the Vietnam War, where they showed their overall worth performing 12,928 combat missions with the loss of only four aircraft. The opportunity to repeat the success of the A-7D was offered to the US Navy with the A-7E, which became the main production model, with 535 built. The prototype made its maiden flight on November 25, 1968, and deliveries started on June 14 the following year. The airplane entered operational service in May 1970 on board the aircraft carrier America.

After the end of the Vietnam War, these Corsair IIs played an active role also in other military operations: in Granada in 1974, in Lebanon in 1983, in Libya in 1986, in 1988 during the Iran-Iraq war, and lastly in 1991 in Operation Desert Storm in the Gulf War.

This conflict also marked the end of the service life of the A-7E: the last one was withdrawn on March 27, 1991.

In addition to being deployed as tactical airplanes, strategic bombers continued to be developed and used as a primary deterrent in the confrontation between East and West for the whole of the 1960s, before giving way to even more devastating and complex weapon systems—intercontinental ballistic missiles, with which the United States and the Soviet Union surrounded themselves as if in some imaginary cocoon that was supposed to protect them from mutual aggression.

This shift in roles, however, took nothing away from the enormous potential of the great bombers, which continued to be used with equal efficiency. The clearest proof of the heights of aeronautical technology level achieved in these machines in the 1950s and 60s is provided by the extremely long career of the Boeing B-52 Stratofortress, perhaps the greatest veteran of military aviation. After over half a century of service covering all the conflicts of the 20th century, it remains one of the irreplaceable components in the USAF arse-

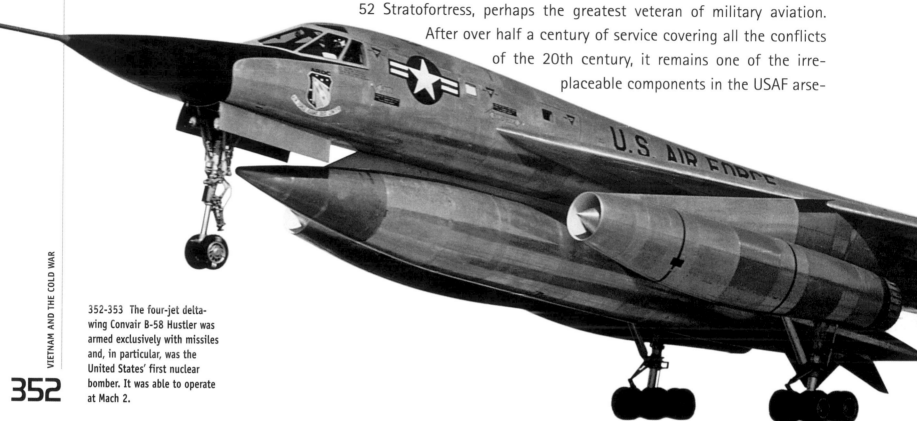

352-353 The four-jet delta-wing Convair B-58 Hustler was armed exclusively with missiles and, in particular, was the United States' first nuclear bomber. It was able to operate at Mach 2.

NATO reporting names for the main Soviet combat aircraft

BOMBERS

Tupolev Tu-16	Badger
Ilyushin Il-28	Beagle
Tupolev Tu-20/Tu-95/Tu-142	Bear
Myasishchev Mya-4	Bison
Tupolev Tu-160	Blackjack
Tupolev Tu-22/Tu-105	Blinder
Tupolev Tu-14	Bosun
Yakovlev Yak-28	Brewer

FIGHTERS

Mikoyan-Gurevich MiG-15	Fagot
Lavochkin La-15	Fantail
Mikoyan-Gurevich MiG-9	Fargo
Mikoyan-Gurevich MiG-19	Farmer
Yakovlev Yak-15	Feather
Sukhoi Su-24	Fencer
Tupolev Tu-28	Fiddler
Yakovlev Yak-28P	Firebar
Mikoyan-Gurevich MiG-21	Fishbed
Sukhoi Su-9	Fishpot
Sukhoi Su-7B/Su-11/Su-17/ Su-20/Su-22	Fitter
Sukhoi Su-15	Flagon
Sukhoi Su-21/Su-27	Flanker
Yakovlev Yak-25/Yak-27	Flashlight

Mikoyan-Gurevich MiG-23/Mig-27	Flogger
Yakovlev Yak-38	Forger
Mikoyan-Gurevich MiG-25	Foxbat
Mikoyan-Gurevich MiG-31	Foxhound
Mikoyan-Gurevich MiG-17	Fresco
Sukhoi Su-25	Frogfoot
Mikoyan-Gurevich MiG-29	Fulcrum

VARIOUS

Ilyushin Il-76	Mainstay
Ilyushin Il-38	May
Tupolev Tu-126	Moss

nal in the third millennium thanks to electronics. Not so much and not only a launch platform for missiles, it is, above all, a sophisticated and highly advanced counter-measures aircraft.

The B-52 was the most successful American jet bomber to emerge from the frenetic race for superiority in the Cold War. Its construction followed a few years after the first aircraft of the new generation, the Boeing B-47 Stratojet, which appeared in 1950. This were followed in 1959 by the Convair B-58 Hustler, a more modern and advanced machine which, despite its exceptional performance (it was able to operate at Mach 2), had a relatively short service life and never managed to match the great operational flexibility of the B-52.

In the opposing bloc, the evolution of great bombers was similar, characterized also by gigantism and by increasing performance, in a cycle which went on uninterrupted until their strategic role was taken over by ballistic missiles. The most significant and well-known exponents of this class of airplanes were the Myasishchev Mya-4 of 1953, the Tupolev Tu-16 1954, the Tupolev Tu-20 of 1957, and the super-

5665

sonic Tupolev Tu-22, which came out in 1960 as a direct response to the B-58 deployed by the USAF. Also in this formidable arsenal was an airplane, while not as modern and advanced as the others, survived longer than any of them This was the Tupolev Tu-20, an enormous four-engined turbo-prop which remained in service for over 30 years, proving itself irreplaceable in an incredible variety of roles extremely different from that of strategic bomber for which it had been designed: reconnaissance, electronic counter-measures, flying radar station, and even deadly platform for launching cruise missiles.

The entire structure of the Soviet air force was rationalized and optimized to efficiently manage this exceptional development of means and to support the prime role it had been assigned in the "balance of power". In the course of a complex reorganization of the Soviet air force in the 1960s, the strategic bombers became part of the ADD (*Aviatsiya Dalnovo Deistviya*, long-range air force).

353 bottom Comparable to the B-47, the Russian Tupolev Tu-16 Badger was deployed from 1954 onwards. This bomber was characterized by engines set into the root of the wing. It was also used in an anti-ship role.

Boeing B-52 Stratofortress

The story of the Boeing B-52 Stratofortress, after 50 years' service in the last century, was far from being over in the early years of the new millennium. Since Vietnam, this immortal giant of the air has played a major role in all the conflicts, proving itself irreplaceable in a large variety of roles, many of which were completely different from that of nuclear deterrent for which was designed at the height of the Cold War. After having celebrated the 50th anniversary of its first flight on April 15, 2002,

the USAF announced its intention to keep the remaining 94 aircraft (out of 744 built) operational until the year 2045.

Work on the project began in far-off 1945, when the USAF asked Boeing to develop a new strategic bomber with nuclear capacity. The initial design was based on turbo-prop engines, but in late 1948, after the decision to adopt jet engines, the entire program was reviewed.

Two prototypes were developed and the maiden flight was taken by the second of these on April 15, 1952. Only three of the initial series, the B-52A, were built, and in August 1954 a long cycle of operational assessment began, ending in November 1957 with their assignment to Strategic Air Command. In the meantime the second variant, the B-52B, had entered service. 50 were built, of which 27 were set up for strategic reconnaissance (RB-52B). The subsequent versions

were characterized by continuous changes to the avionics, engines, and armament. In order they were the C, which appeared on March 9, 1956 (35 built); the D of June 4, 1956 (170 built, destined exclusively for bombing duties (in the drawings); the E, with improved avionics (100 built, maiden flight on October 31, 1957); and the F, with more powerful engines, which came out on May 14, 1958 (89 built). The prototype of the following variant, the B-52G, which first flew on October 26, 1958, introduced important

structural changes to the wing and tail plane. 133 were built of this series, before production moved on to 102 of the last version, the B-52H, which appeared on May 6, 1961. With this version the bomber reached its maximum performance, range, and combat potential, thanks to the adoption of new Pratt & Whitney double flow turbo-jets and the possibility of carrying all types of missiles and conventional arms at the time available. The B-52s made their debut in the Vietnam War, during which they completed 7784 missions by January 1973.

The passing of the years and the evolution of technology did not affect their worth in any way. They played, for example, a crucial rule in the Gulf War in 1991, in the Balkans, and in Afghanistan, operational theaters in which these airplanes, in addition to conventional bombing tasks, also performed those of interdiction with precision weapons and cruise missiles. Low-level attack and marine reconnaissance are the further specializations of the B-52H which still remain in the US arsenal.

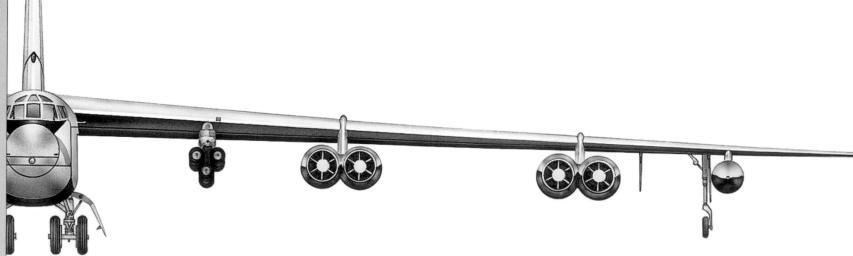

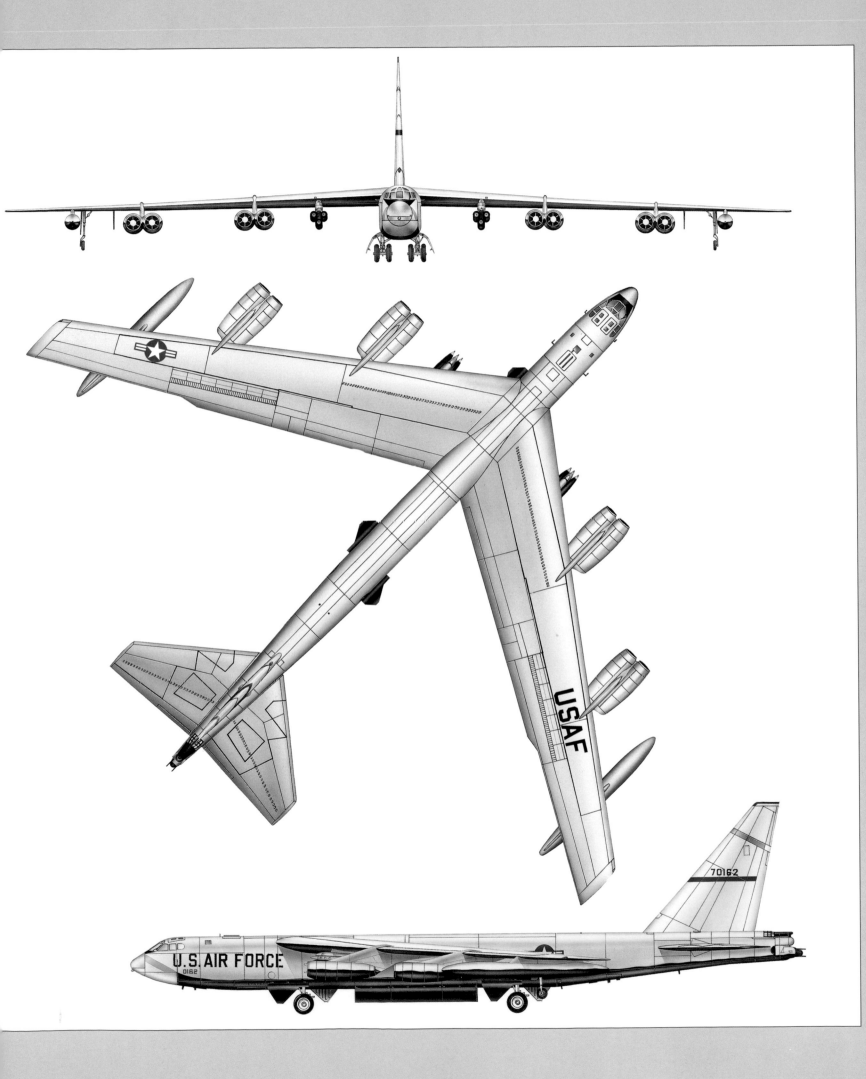

Another three specific structures were created for the rest of the air force, the IAPVO (*Aviatsiya Protivovozdushnoi Oborony Strany*, territorial air defence force); the FA (*Frontovaya Aviatsiya*, tactical air force); and the VVSMF (*Morskaya Aviatsiya*), the land-based navy air corps which performed tasks of marine reconnaissance, coastal patrol, and anti-submarine warfare.

But the United States and the Soviet Union were not the only ones to increase their strategic arsenals. Alongside these two great superpowers leading the race during the 1950s, a third protagonist, Great Britain, brilliantly joined the contest. Boosted by the process of rearmament and aeronautical development triggered off by the Korean War, it developed three large modern bombers, the so-called V series: the Vickers Valiant, which appeared in late 1953; the Avro Vulcan of February 1955; and the Handley Page Victor (February 1956). These airplanes represented the RAF throughout the period of nuclear deterrent. The Vulcan was the best in the world of its class with a delta wing, and the long-lasting, remaining in service until the early 1980s.

356 center and bottom Two of the three British aircraft of the V Bomber force: the Avro Vulcan and Vickers Valiant. All were built in strictly limited numbers, to re-equip the arsenal of Bomber Command in the 1950s.

GREAT BRITAIN
AND EUROPE

356-357 top The twin-jet Hawker Siddeley Buccaneer attack aircraft, an exceptional machine in low-level transonic applications.

357 top right Shortly beforehand, the Royal Navy had also adopted the Supermarine Scimitar which, in addition to two 30-mm cannons, could be fitted with anti-ship missiles.

357 bottom The Avro Shackleton marine reconnaissance aircraft.

In a Europe conditioned by the Cold War, Great Britain still remained for a long time in the small club of the great air powers. Even if during the 1960s the great expansion of the RAF was once more slowed down by budget cuts, the contribution that British industry gave to the strengthening of the West was significant. The development and realisation of the strategic V bombers was only one of the most significant examples of the high level of technology it was able to achieve. And this development was not limited to major aircraft.

During the 1950s the sector of fighters passed rapidly from the first to the second generation, with highly efficient machines which managed to compete on equal terms with American and Soviet aircraft.

Dassault Mirage III

FRANCE

Rarely in the history of modern aviation has an entire family of combat aircraft proved to be as effective as that of the Mirage. This is a name which since the mid-1950s has taken France to the forefront in the aeronautical field. The Mirage III/5 series alone, the best-known and most widely used, accounted for production figures of 1422. Built under licence in four countries, it has equipped the air forces of dozens of nations.

Marcel Dassault started work on the project in 1953. The key to its success was the adoption of the delta wing, whose aerodynamic characteristics made it possible to achieve high cruising speeds while preserving great manouvrability and general performance higher than that of jet aircraft with

conventional wings. The prototype Mirage I, which flew on June 25, 1955, was produced on the basis of a request from the Armée de l'Air, but fell short of specifications, above all in terms of performance in horizontal flight. Dassault then decided to privately develop a new, completely redesigned prototype. Taken on its maiden flight on May 12, 1958, the airplane underwent intensive fine-tuning and finally achieved the target speed of Mach 2 on October 24. There followed an order for 100 of the interceptor version (Mirage IIIC), and the first production aircraft flew on October 9, 1960. Operational use began immediately afterwards in the Armée de l'Air, which used all the variants. The last in the initial generation was the IIIE multi-role aircraft, whose maiden flight was on April 21, 1961 and which

entered service in 1965.

The fighter was extremely successful abroad. Israel was the first customer of Dassault, and it was with the insignia of Heil Ha' Avir that the Mirage had its baptism of fire in June 1967, during the Six-Day War. The final evolution, the Mirage 5 of 1967, was also destined for export. This was a simplified version of the

IIIE designed to meet the particular needs of countries in the Middle East. The last significant variant was the multi-role Mirage 50, which appeared on April 15, 1979. Israel exploited the great added value of the machine more than any other user. The versions produced independently by Israel Aircraft Industries modifying aircraft already purchased from France were extremely important: the Nasher (Eagle) Arthur 1970, basically a Mirage IIIC built without licence, and the Kfir (Lion cub) of 1973, fitted with a General Electric J79 engine. 250 Kfirs were built, and they were still operational in

2001. The success of this hybrid airplane was followed up in South Africa, where in 1987 a variant called the Cheetah entered service, developed by Atlas Aircraft in collaboration with the Israeli industry.

The name Mirage remained in the subsequent designs by Dassault, those which represented the final evolution of the family: the powerful multi-role F.1 of 1973 and Mirage 2000 of 1984. In the same way, as the sign of a strong design identity, in 1963, the name of Mirage IV was given to a series of bombers developed as strategic carriers for French nuclear weapons.

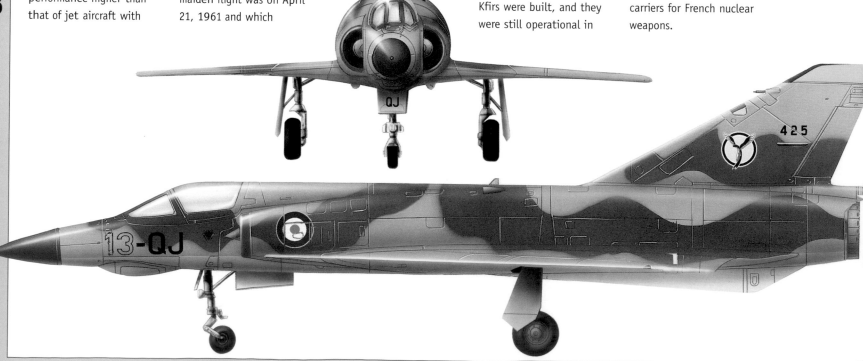

The epitome of this process of growth was represented at the end of the decade by the RAF's powerful bisonic English Electric Lightning interceptor and by the sophisticated Supermarine Scimitar and Hawker Siddeley Sea Vixen of the Fleet Air Arm.

Research also brilliantly explored totally innovative sectors. In that period, the greatest success of British industry was achieved by Hawker Siddeley, who for the first time focused on developing a vertical takeoff and landing fighter. The result was the Harrier, a revolutionary machine which changed a number of long-held tactical concepts of military aircraft. Its appearance after an extremely long period of development represented a new benchmark for air forces, marking the beginning of a period of evolution still fully in course in the 21st century. The first to believe in the enormous potential of the Harrier were the United States, who in 1969 chose the airplane to equip the units of the US Marine Corps, entrusting subsequently to McDonnell-Douglas the development and realisation of particularly advanced and powerful special versions.

In the face of the massive American and Soviet production, in the rest of Europe few other countries found the resources and stimulus necessary to maintain their aircraft industries on a par with the two superpowers. And, while France successfully developed its reborn aircraft industry with the prestigious Mirage series of air-

360 top The anti-submarine aircraft of the French navy, the Breguet Br.1050 Alizé was originally equipped with an unusual turbine/jet mixed propulsion system.

360 bottom The Hawker Siddeley Sea Vixen, a carrier-based fighter which remained in service in the Fleet Air Arm until the early 1970s.

craft by Dassault, the extremely rapid evolution of the Swedish aeronautical industry continued, its growth directly fuelled by the need for national self defence, in light of its western borders with the Soviet Union. Particularly brilliant results were obtained in the sector of fighters, which was developed at a constant rate: in 1955 the Saab 32 Lansen, an effective multirole aircraft, entered service; six years later it was followed by a new powerful combat machine, the Saab 35 Draken, which made a mark as one of the best interceptors of the period; and in 1971 the even more advanced Saab 37 Viggen entered service.

The political, military and economic restrictions resulting from alliances had relegated the other European nations to the inevitable role of minor players in the development of aviation. But the need to keep industrial and research systems competitive was too vital for the most advanced countries to ignore.

361 top Light fighter originally designed for a NATO call for tenders, the Dassault Etendard had a worthy successor in the French Aéronavale with the carrier-based strike fighter Super Etendard equipped with more powerful engines and greater bomb load.

361 bottom The Sepecat Jaguar was the result of the collaboration between France and England in the early 1970s for the production of a supersonic trainer with limited combat capability. 588 were built.

English Electric Canberra

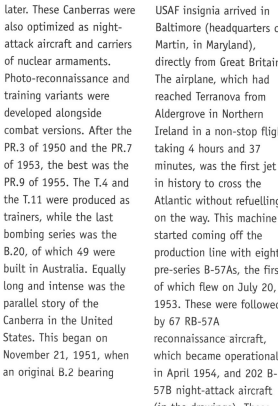

GREAT BRITAIN

The first British jet bomber was the design that brought fame to English Electric in 1949; until then the company had been a minor player in the aircraft industry.

The Canberra, a versatile, reliable, and efficient twin-engined aircraft, was successful in a great variety of roles: day and night bomber, reconnaissance aircraft, trainer, and tactical support aircraft. Its great potential received the most prestigious acknowledgement in 1951 when the USAF chose it to replace the ageing propeller-driven A-26. Martin built over 400 which, designated B-57, were added to the 925 produced in Great Britain. In a long operational career, which went through

the conflict in Korea and Vietnam, the Canberra was still in active service in the RAF in 2005, with five being used as photo-reconnaissance aircraft by 39 Squadron, a unit based in Marham, Norfolk. The prototype flew on May 13, 1949, and production was articulated into a long series of variants for specific roles. The first definitive version (the B.2) was designed for day bombing and became operational in 1951. Three years later the B.6 appeared, with more powerful engines, and was used by Bomber Command until October 1961.

In the meantime the most versatile version of the entire family, the B.8, had already become operational. This was introduced as a prototype on July 23, 1954 and entered service two years

later. These Canberras were also optimized as night-attack aircraft and carriers of nuclear armaments. Photo-reconnaissance and training variants were developed alongside combat versions. After the PR.3 of 1950 and the PR.7 of 1953, the best was the PR.9 of 1955. The T.4 and the T.11 were produced as trainers, while the last bombing series was the B.20, of which 49 were built in Australia. Equally long and intense was the parallel story of the Canberra in the United States. This began on November 21, 1951, when an original B.2 bearing

USAF insignia arrived in Baltimore (headquarters of Martin, in Maryland), directly from Great Britain. The airplane, which had reached Terranova from Aldergrove in Northern Ireland in a non-stop flight taking 4 hours and 37 minutes, was the first jet in history to cross the Atlantic without refuelling on the way. This machine started coming off the production line with eight pre-series B-57As, the first of which flew on July 20, 1953. These were followed by 67 RB-57A reconnaissance aircraft, which became operational in April 1954, and 202 B-57B night-attack aircraft (in the drawings). These airplanes reached the units

in January 1955 and continued to provide front-line service until 1961.

A complete redesign of the basic type took place with the RB-57D reconnaissance and electronic countermeasures version (of which 20 were built), fitted with a longer wing to improve performance at high altitude. The last stratospheric reconnaissance variant was the RB-57F, with further changes to the wing, fuselage, and tail plane, of which 21 were built by General Dynamic. Lastly, for the specific needs of the Vietnam War, 16 B-57Bs were modernized for use as night-attack aircraft and renamed B-57G.

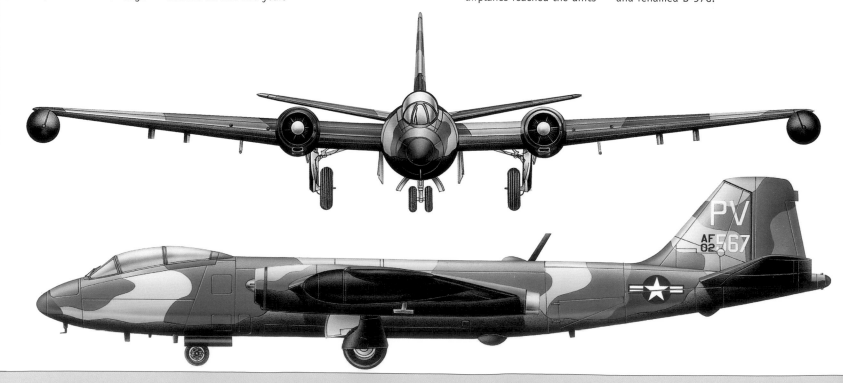

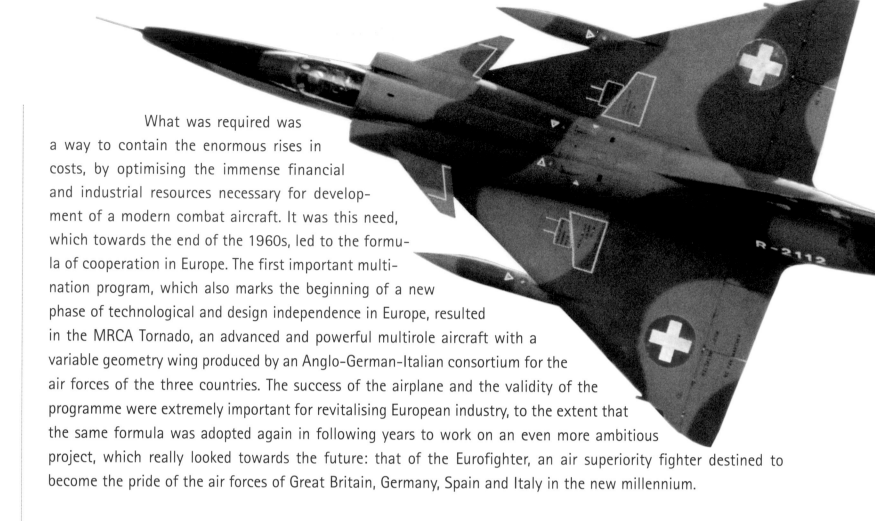

What was required was a way to contain the enormous rises in costs, by optimising the immense financial and industrial resources necessary for development of a modern combat aircraft. It was this need, which towards the end of the 1960s, led to the formula of cooperation in Europe. The first important multination program, which also marks the beginning of a new phase of technological and design independence in Europe, resulted in the MRCA Tornado, an advanced and powerful multirole aircraft with a variable geometry wing produced by an Anglo-German-Italian consortium for the air forces of the three countries. The success of the airplane and the validity of the programme were extremely important for revitalising European industry, to the extent that the same formula was adopted again in following years to work on an even more ambitious project, which really looked towards the future: that of the Eurofighter, an air superiority fighter destined to become the pride of the air forces of Great Britain, Germany, Spain and Italy in the new millennium.

VIETNAM AND THE COLD WAR

THE WAR IN VIETNAM

364

I f the Korean War was the last fought using the means and theories derived from the Second World War, that which followed 15 years later in Vietnam was the first of a new type, with the potential of arsenals multiplied a hundredfold and airplanes transformed into electronically controlled weapons systems and misile platforms.

364 top In the 1960s, Dassault brought out a family of combat aircraft with extremely high performance: the Mirage III of 1960.

364 bottom The Swedish Saab 37 Viggen designed for four primary roles: attack, interception, reconnaissance, and training.

365 top The Douglas A-4 Skyhawk entered service in 1956 and up to 1979, almost 3000 were built in dozens of variants.

365 bottom The most characteristic all-weather subsonic attack aircraft of the US Navy, the versatile and reliable Grumman A-6 Intruder entered service in 1963. It was withdrawn in 1996, while the electronic warfare version, the EA-6 Prowler, is still operational in the third millennium.

Putting aside the specific events of the war and its political repercussions, for the two super-powers, the long and bloody Vietnam War was above all another field test, necessary to gauge each other's military power in a context in which conventional theories of warfare and conventional armaments could be put to the test without triggering off a world war.

There is no doubt the United States directly paid the highest price for the lessons they learned from the conflict. There is also no doubt that the use of their power in Vietnam totally changed the way in which wars had been fought until then. New tactics, new strategic concepts, new victories and new defeats. The clash, which began in August 1964 as a limited campaign, and which ended in January 1973 at the peak of a furious crescendo of bombing, had the effect of exploiting the various weapons electronically as never before, transforming them on a scale that was unprecedented since the Second World War. Air power played a fundamental role, and the USAF and US Navy deployed the most advanced means available. These ranged from the powerful McDonnell F-4 Phantom IIs, the carrier-based A-6 Intruders and the Republic F-105 Thunderchief tactical fighters to the General Dynamics F-111 and Boeing B-52 Stratofortress bombers and the Lockheed F-104 Starfighter interceptors.

General Dynamics F-111

UNITED STATES

When it appeared in the mid-1960s, the General Dynamics F-111 was considered a revolutionary combat machine, with its variable geometry wing and its Mach 2 speed. The career of this large, powerful twin-jet began in the skies over Vietnam and continued until the end of the 1990s, after taking part in all the major conflicts of the second half of the century.

production of 23 pre-series craft: 18 F-118As for the USAF (in the drawings) and 5 F-111Bs for the US Navy. The prototypes took to the air on December 21,1964, and on May 18, 1965 testing began. But after encountering serious problems with the variable geometry wing, the US Navy judged the airplane to be unsuitable for its needs and two years later abandoned the program. The USAF remained the only customer of the F-111 and in 1967 received the

characterized by more powerful engines, a larger wing and more sophisticated avionics. The intention was for these machines to replace the B-58s and B-52s, but increasing costs led to a drastic cut in the requests, which went from the original 210 to 76. It was in this phase that the only variant for export was developed, the F-111C destined for Australia. The RAAF put 24 into service in 1973, with the intention of using them until 2010. Production continued with other tactical support versions for the USAF, with

improvements above all regarding engines and avionics. After the production of 94 F-111Es and 96 F-111Ds (delivered to units in 1970 and 1971), the final variant was the F-111F, which appeared as a prototype in May 1973. These airplanes proved to be the best of the entire family. The last of the 106 built left the assembly lines in November 1976, taking the overall total to 562. The service life of the F-111 was prolonged during the 1980s with a vast modernization program, and the last were withdrawn in 1996, after

having taken part in the Gulf War, alongside EF-111A Raven electronic warfare versions. The development of this series had been started in 1975 with the conversion of 42 F-111As and Fs. The Raven entered service in November 1981 and the last was delivered in 1985. Until April 1998, the remaining aircraft remained stationed in Saudi Arabia.
One month later they were withdrawn from service.

The General Dynamics design was chosen on November 24,1962 to replace both the F-105 of the USAF and the F-4 of the US Navy. The aim was to produce a tactical airplane able to operate at low altitudes in all weather conditions, to allow short take-off from semi-prepared runways, and fly over intercontinental distances at high speed. The initial contract provided for the

first of the 141 ordered. In March 1968, the attack variant, the F-111A, had its baptism of fire in Vietnam, but the experience was not a success, because of the many structural failures which led to its withdrawal from active service. It was only in 1972 that these aircraft re-entered service. In the meantime, a strategic bomber version, the FB-111A, had become operational. This was

Grumman A-6 Intruder

UNITED STATES

Robust, versatile, and reliable, the Grumman A-6 Intruder remained the standard all-weather attack aircraft of the US Navy and the US Marine Corps for over 35 years. Work started on the project during the final phases of the Korean War in 1953, and after a great many adjustments to the specifications, the industrial call for tenders was issued in 1957. The US Navy requested the production of a carrier-based long-range attack aircraft able to operate at extremely low altitudes to avoid being picked up on enemy radar, and to identify and strike targets in any visibility and weather conditions. In December 1957, at the end of a competition which had involved 11 contenders, the design for the G-128 by Grumman was selected. The program reached the operational phase in November 1958, with the order for the construction of four prototypes to be used for assessment.

The first of these made its maiden flight on April 9, 1960, and at the end of testing was put into production in 1962 and given the designation A-6A (in the drawings). This first variant, of which 488 were built, entered front-line service the following year, and in 1965 took part in combat operations in Vietnam.

In 1970, the A-6As made way for a new, more powerful version, the E, in which the airplane reached its optimal configuration. In the course of operational activity, the Intruders were subjected to continuous updates in terms of avionics and engines, and in the late 1980s around 400 were in service, many of which had been obtained by converting the A-6As to the new standards. Another important conversion involved 62 A-6As, which in 1970 were transformed into flying tankers, able to carry over 14,360 lb (9526 kg) of fuel, and renamed KA-6Ds. The A-6Es were withdrawn from active service in December 1996.

The career of the Intruders followed a parallel path to that of its "twin" the EA-6 Prowler destined exclusively for electronic counter-measures.

The first airplanes of this type were developed in 1963, but it was the second version, the B, reaching the units of the US Navy in January 1971, that displayed maximum operational efficiency. Literally stuffed with avionics, and with two crew members dedicated to managing the on-board systems, the EA-6Bs showed themselves to be precious and, thanks to constant updates, were used with great success in all the conflicts toward the end of the century, from the Gulf War to the Balkans in 1999. 120 were built, and their service life is projected to last well into the third millennium.

370 top and 371 top The
Vought-LTV Corsair II of the US
Navy was a robust subsonic
aircraft with excellent range
and a high bomb, missile, and
rocket capacity.

370 bottom The first American
fighter of the 100 series, the
North American F-100 Super
Sabre was the first to exceed
Mach 1 in horizontal flight.

But they soon discovered that their terrible adversaries were not only the jets of Soviet origin which equipped the air force of North Vietnam. The real enemy, much more devious and treacherous, was represented by the impressive anti-aircraft defences which surrounded every target. Batteries of cannons and heavy machineguns, but above all stations of deadly land to air missiles provided in huge quantities by the USSR and China and stationed near the most important military installations. These defences proved to be formidable not only against the incessant low-level attacks that the American fighter-bombers performed against the arms and munitions depots and the tracks which served to provide supplies to the guerrillas, but also in combating high altitude bombing raids. When, in the last years of the war, the raids against North Vietnam were intensified to the maximum, the problem of protecting bomber formations became a priority and every possible resource offered by electronics was used. The increasingly sophisticated countermeasures destined to combat the threat of SA-2 Guideline missiles was soon supplemented by another extremely unusual one: the use of aircraft specialized in the suppression of enemy air defences. Known as "Wild Weasels", these jets (initially the North American F-100 Super Sabre, then the Republic F-105 Thunderchief) were armed with bombs and antiradar missiles and sent to destroy missile stations on land before the arrival of the bombers.

Missions of this type lasted at least three hours and could be performed in two ways. The first consisted in attracting the attention of the defences by flying ahead of an attack force, so that the latter could perform their task undisturbed, and then subsequently escaping. The second tactic involved flying alongside a formation of bombers and going to actively look for the missile posts. The Wild Weasels waited to be picked up by the enemy radar and then launched their weapons. Once the operation had been completed they led the bombers

through the opening towards their targets. Either way, the crews ran huge risks, since they exposed themselves directly to the threat of enemy missiles which almost always targeted the attack aircraft. In such cases the only way of escape was to use electronic countermeasures and violent evasive manoeuvres. Many pilots considered these missions real suicide attacks. But many others became the new aces of aviation, such as Colonel George Acree, who managed to complete an impressive 200 missions in his F-105. Despite the enormous waste of human and material resources, these tactics proved to be particularly effective. The raids of the B-52's, performed at night, were always conducted under the protection of the Wild Weasels and, considering their growing commitment, the USAF had special versions of these airplanes developed which were increasingly specialized and better armed.

371 bottom   With its heavy armament, the Republic F-105 Thunderchief could perform precision strikes at low altitudes. It was an extremely effective strike fighter with nuclear capability.

Douglas AC-47 Gunship

UNITED STATES

After having marked the history of civil aviation in 1953, the incredible career of the Douglas DC-3 found fertile ground under military insignia. On the battlefields of the Second World War and those of Vietnam, the C-47 Dakota proved to be an irreplaceable machine—versatile and reliable, immune to the enormous progress of aeronautical technology. The United States kept it in service until 1975, and in South-East Asia this immortal twin-engined aircraft performed its last missions under the insignia of the USAF. In the Vietnam War, in addition to traditional transport tasks, in which the C-47s performed over 20,000 missions, the aircraft also served in a wide range of other roles: reconnaissance (RC-47), electronic counter-measures (EC-47), training (TC-47,) and rescue (HC-47).

But the most radical transformation of the old Dakota was that which led to the creation of a new type of combat aircraft, the so-called "flying gunships". In November 1965 the 4th Air Command Squadron began to use a modified C-47, called the AC-47 Gunship. The aircraft had a crew of seven men and was armed with five machine guns installed at an angle to fire downward. The armament was then increased with the installation of three 7.62 miniguns with six rotating barrels, able to fire 6000 rounds a minute.

The AC-47s, that the crews renamed *"Spooky"* and *"Puff, the Magic Dragon"*, proved to be deadly weapons in support of ground troops. The airplanes flew for hours surveying the territory, waiting to move into action. Then they began to circle the target, mowing down the targets on the ground with a continuous spray of bullets. At night the effects were impressive.

With the scene lit up by powerful Bengal lights, real columns of fire, and a characteristic terrible thunderous roar announced the arrival of the gunships. From 1965 onward the AC-47s completed over 15,000 missions, proving to be crucial in resolving difficult situations on the ground. Subsequently, similar transformations affected much more modern aircraft such as the Fairchild C-119 Flying Boxcar (AC-119G Shadow and AC-119K Stinger), the Fairchild C-123 Provider (AC-123), and the Lockheed C-130 Hercules (AC-130 Spectre). With these large four-engined aircraft, technology became even more effective and devastating, thanks to sophisticated sensors and sights, and to 20-mm, 40- mm, and even 105-mm caliber weapons.

It should be remembered that of the over 13,000 DC-3s built in a variety of versions, from 1940 onwards Douglas produced 10,123 for military use. To these were added 485 built under licence in Japan with the designation of Showa L2D and around 2000 built in the Soviet Union as Lisunov Li.2s.

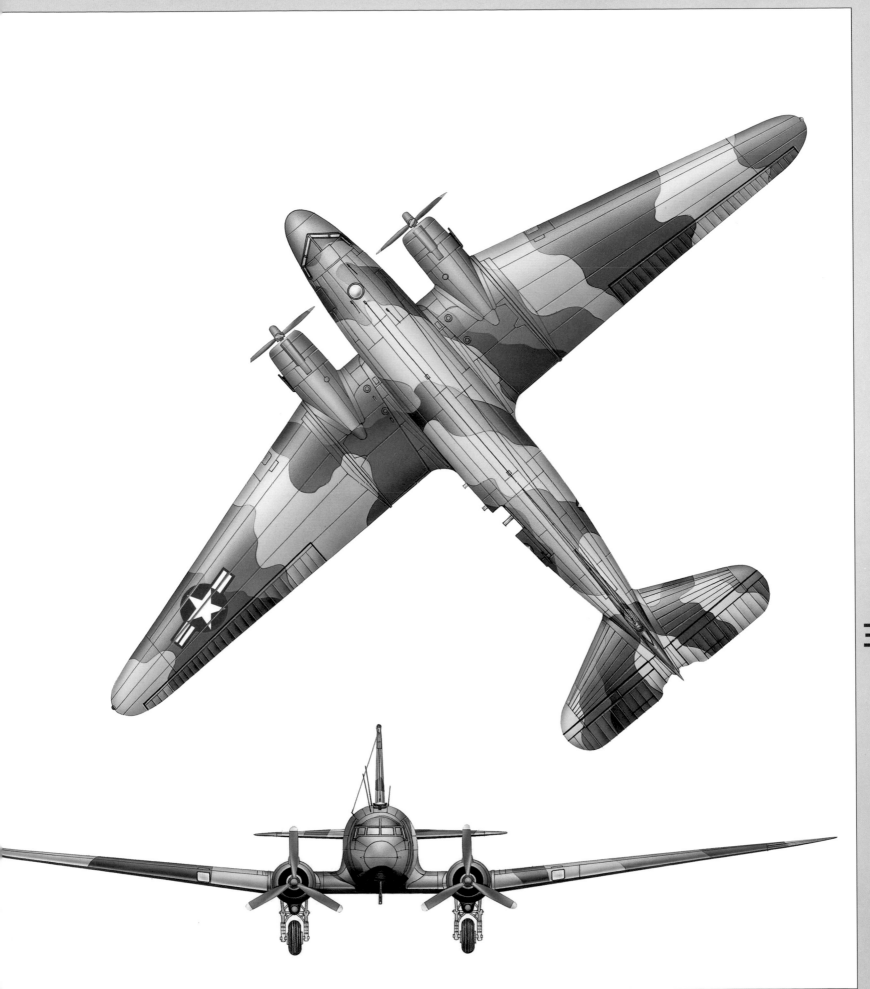

An initial significant improvement was achieved with the introduction in May 1966 of the F-105F to replace the F-100. This fighter-bomber was widely used in the conflict, completing 75% of the USAF's attack missions, and had been converted from a two-seater trainer version. It was armed with deadly AGM-45 Shrike missiles, a passive type of short-range explosive device, able to search for signals emitted by a the radar of a missile post and to lock onto it in order to reach and strike the target. The efficiency of the Wild Weasel units further increased the following year with the appearance of a new version of the Thunderchief, the G, equipped with more advanced avionics together with a variety of types of countermeasures and greater offensive armament capability. In particular, the new AGM-78 Standard missiles were much more precise and had four times higher range than the Shrike.

In the last year of the war, activity became particularly intense, to support the final bombing campaigns. The B-52s released 100,000 tons of bombs on Laos and Cambodia to force Vietnam to start peace negotiations. But this unprecedented effort was unsuccessful. It took 11 days of heavy bombing with 1350 day and night attacks and 36,000 tons of bombs on North Vietnam at the end of December 1972, between the 18th and the 29th, before a truce could be achieved.

374 top The Fairchild A-10 Thunderbolt II, a tactical support aircraft.

374 bottom The Northrop F-5 developed in the mid-1950s as a light fighter; its use was widespread in NATO countries. The USAF used the aircraft in the two-seater T-38 Talon training version.

Never had a war been so pointless. Peace was signed on 27 January 1973 and two years later the United States completely and definitively left the area, abandoning South Vietnam to its fate. For America, the cost of the war in South-East Asia had cost over 58,000 lives. The air forces lost hundreds of pilots and crews, and a total of 8588 airplanes and helicopters, for an estimated value of over $7 bn at the time.

It was a heavy price to pay for an experiment in politics and military doctrine. But, in the brutal logic of warfare, even this terrible experience was considered useful. As had happened in Korea, there were theories and equipment which proved to be effective, others which proved to be inadequate, and still others which opened up new scenarios and provided new resources for the conquest of supremacy. Seen in this light, the American armed forces basically learnt three fundamental lessons in Vietnam. The first and most important was the full awareness of the dominant role played by electronics on the battlefield. The second was the introduction of increasingly sophisticated instruments for missile defence, such as the tactic of the Wild Weasels, which in following years was perfected to the limit with increasingly advanced airplanes, avionics and armaments. The third was that of the tactical use of the combat helicopter, a new generation of machines that were subsequently adopted by all the world's armed forces, proving to be a fundamental means of support for armoured divisions and ground troops.

375 bottom The twin-jet General Dynamics F-111A with a variable geometry wing. Extremely sophisticated navigation apparatus made it possible to fly these aircraft low altitude.

376 top The X-35A.

376 bottom The Lockheed
F-117 Nighthawk.

377 bottom One of the most
fascinating and secret machines
in the history of aviation, the
Lockheed SR. 71 Blackbird, an
extremely high-performance
reconnaissance aircraft.
Designed as a successor to the
U-2, it remained in service in the
USAF from 1966 to 1997.

Towards new technologies

From the 1980s onward, the formidable advances in engines and structures did not manage to significantly change the pure performance of combat aircraft. All the most significant records achieved by military aircraft date back to an earlier period. Examples include an altitude of 120,480 ft (37,650 meters) achieved on August 31,1977 by an experimental version of the MiG-25 fighter (designated E-266M) piloted by Alezander Fedotov; an altitude of 82,972 ft (25,929 meters) in prolonged horizontal flight on July 28,1976 by a Lockheed SR-71A, a strategic reconnaissance craft flown by Captain Robert C. Helt; speed in a straight line of 1955.7 mph (3259.56 km/h), the maximum peak achieved on the same day by a similar aircraft flown by Captain Eldon W. Joersz; a speed of 2020 mph (3367 km/h) in a closed circuit of 600 miles (1000 km) recorded on July 27,1976, again by a

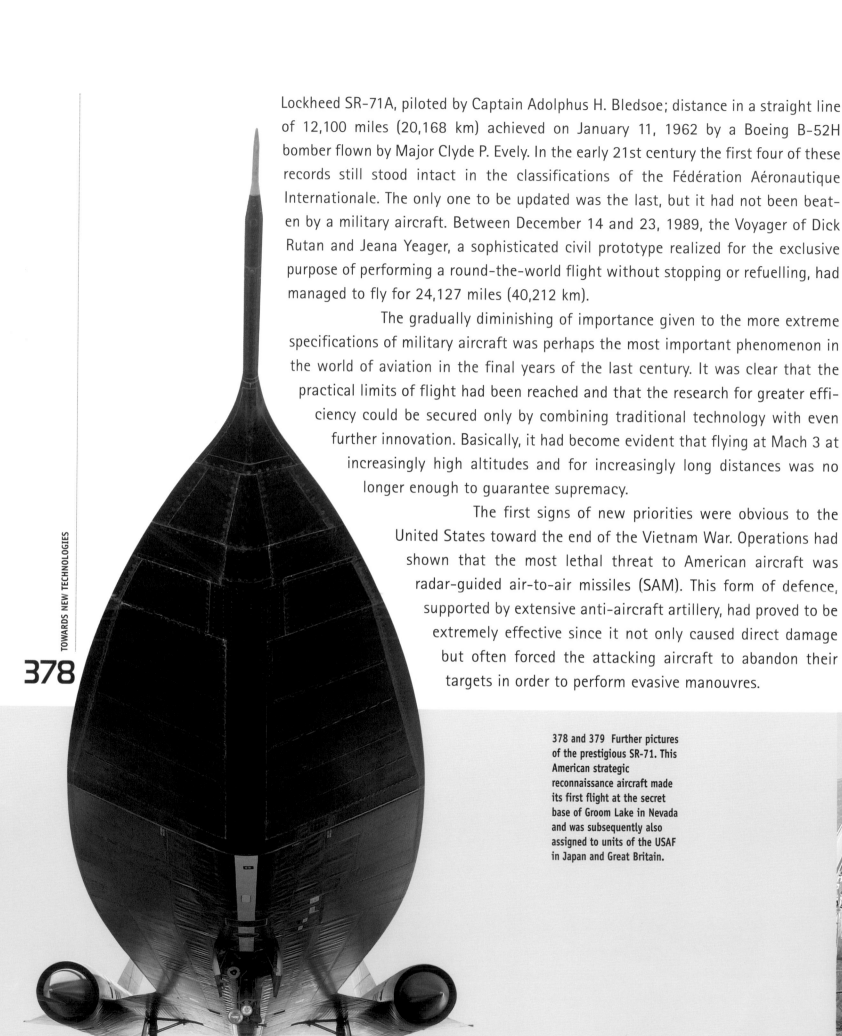

Lockheed SR-71A, piloted by Captain Adolphus H. Bledsoe; distance in a straight line of 12,100 miles (20,168 km) achieved on January 11, 1962 by a Boeing B-52H bomber flown by Major Clyde P. Evely. In the early 21st century the first four of these records still stood intact in the classifications of the Fédération Aéronautique Internationale. The only one to be updated was the last, but it had not been beaten by a military aircraft. Between December 14 and 23, 1989, the Voyager of Dick Rutan and Jeana Yeager, a sophisticated civil prototype realized for the exclusive purpose of performing a round-the-world flight without stopping or refuelling, had managed to fly for 24,127 miles (40,212 km).

The gradually diminishing of importance given to the more extreme specifications of military aircraft was perhaps the most important phenomenon in the world of aviation in the final years of the last century. It was clear that the practical limits of flight had been reached and that the research for greater efficiency could be secured only by combining traditional technology with even further innovation. Basically, it had become evident that flying at Mach 3 at increasingly high altitudes and for increasingly long distances was no longer enough to guarantee supremacy.

The first signs of new priorities were obvious to the United States toward the end of the Vietnam War. Operations had shown that the most lethal threat to American aircraft was radar-guided air-to-air missiles (SAM). This form of defence, supported by extensive anti-aircraft artillery, had proved to be extremely effective since it not only caused direct damage but often forced the attacking aircraft to abandon their targets in order to perform evasive manouvres.

378 and 379 Further pictures of the prestigious SR-71. This American strategic reconnaissance aircraft made its first flight at the secret base of Groom Lake in Nevada and was subsequently also assigned to units of the USAF in Japan and Great Britain.

Further proof came in 1973 during the Yom Kippur War, when, in only 18 days of combat, the Israeli air force lost 109 airplanes, all due to the missile defences of the Egyptian army. This data, extrapolated and projected into the hypothetical scenario of war with the Warsaw Pact, led to extremely worrying conclusions, and Western strategists sounded a new alarm: in the event of war, the sophisticated and integrated missile defence network deployed by the USSR would have decimated NATO's air forces in only two weeks.

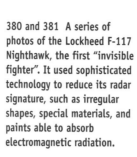

380 and 381 A series of photos of the Lockheed F-117 Nighthawk, the first "invisible fighter". It used sophisticated technology to reduce its radar signature, such as irregular shapes, special materials, and paints able to absorb electromagnetic radiation.

The reaction was rapid and resulted in the launch in 1974 of one of the most secret military programs ever undertaken by the United States. Its objective was particularly ambitious: to develop the technology of radar invisibility ("stealth") and apply it to a revolutionary attack aircraft.

Consequently, advanced research led to a series of extremely innovative prototypes being developed in the California desert. The experiments, tests, and trials continued for seven years and in the end result of these efforts appeared: the Lockheed F-117A Nighthawk, a tactical fighter able to evade radar, infrared, acoustic, and visual detection, a machine that took aviation into a new dimension and marked the beginning of the future.

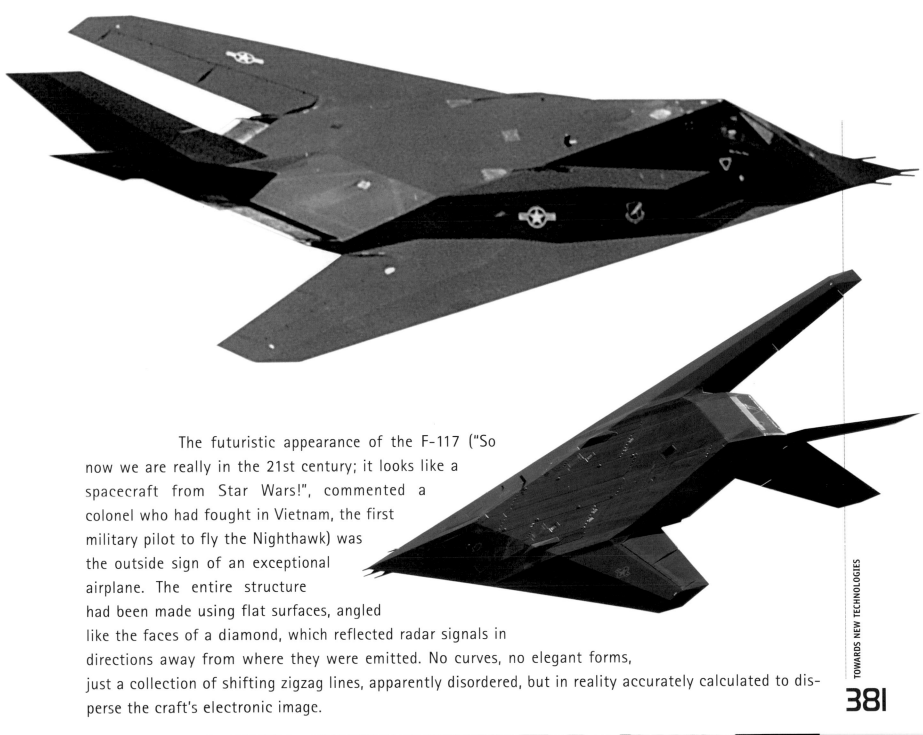

The futuristic appearance of the F-117 ("So now we are really in the 21st century; it looks like a spacecraft from Star Wars!", commented a colonel who had fought in Vietnam, the first military pilot to fly the Nighthawk) was the outside sign of an exceptional airplane. The entire structure had been made using flat surfaces, angled like the faces of a diamond, which reflected radar signals in directions away from where they were emitted. No curves, no elegant forms, just a collection of shifting zigzag lines, apparently disordered, but in reality accurately calculated to disperse the craft's electronic image.

Lockheed F-117 Nighthawk

UNITED STATES

Heralding a new generation of fighting aircraft, the Lockheed F-117 was the result of cutting-edge technology. It appeared on the scene in the late 1980s, and made aviation history as the first fighter plane invisible to electronic observation.

Its great effectiveness, boosted by the enormous potential of its highly sophisticated modern weaponry, came to the fore during the Gulf War and the Balkan conflict.

The program was launched in 1974, when the USAF and the Defense Advanced Research Projects Agency (DARPA) began work on designing a ground-attack aircraft with low electromagnetic observability. The project was entrusted to Lockheed, and the prototype F-117A made its maiden flight on June 18, 1981. Original plans were for a production run of 100, but rising costs saw this figure cut to 59.

The entire program remained shrouded in the deepest secrecy until April 21, 1990, when the "stealth" fighter was officially presented at the Nellis Air Force Base in Nevada to over 100,000 spectators. The aircraft had been in active service for almost seven years and had already experienced a baptism of fire on December 19,1989, during the American intervention in Panama.

The F-117A was given a whole series of names before Nighthawk was settled on. This compact fighter was packed with advanced technology, and to the first American military test pilots seemed like something out of science fiction. In order to ensure low electromagnetic, infra-red, acoustic, and visual observability, various design features were adopted, such as a highly innovative form, an irregular, angular profile designed to disperse radar emissions, and almost maniacal care dedicated to reducing engine noise and heat emissions.

The avionics system was also optimized to manage all phases of flight as well as monitor targets and the weaponry, contained in two small holds, and consisting of a payload of 4994 lb (2270 kg) in laser-guided or electro-optically guided glide bombs.

It was in active service, however, that the stealth fighter revealed its full potential. The F-117As became operational in October 1983, first with the 4450th Tactical Group (a pilot training unit), and then with the 37th Tactical Fighter Wing, formed in October 1989 and based at Tonopah in the Nevada desert.

This unit in over 1300 missions helped demolish Iraqi command posts, communications centers, and military installations during the first Gulf War. And it was the same unit, renamed the 49th Fighter Wing, which on March 24, 1999 commenced operations in the Balkans.

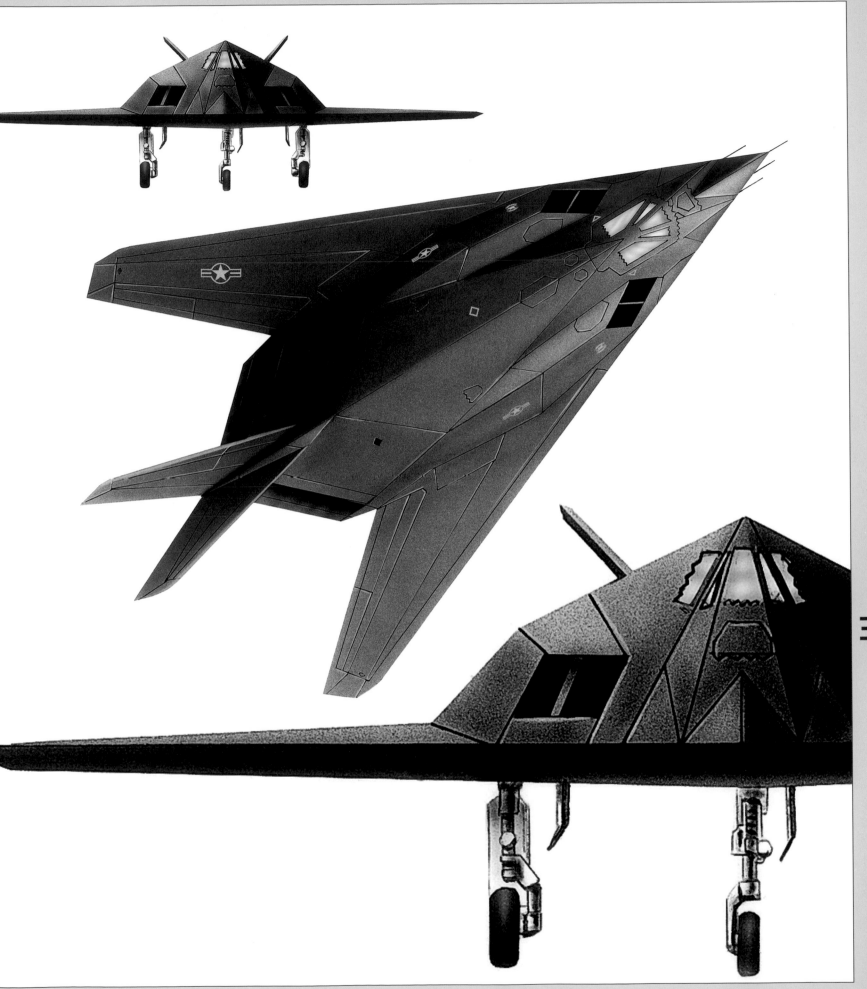

A further contribution to low observability was provided by a covering of special materials able to absorb electromagnetic energy, while particular care had been given to shielding engine emissions and noise in order to reduce vulnerability to infrared missiles and acoustic detection. During tests, it was discovered that the aircraft's signal on the radar was little more than a cloudy spark, indistinguishable from screen disturbance and only identifiable at close range. In practice, it was calculated that the reflective surface was no greater than that of a small bird.

The Nighthawk's trial by fire came in 1991, during the first Gulf War. On January 17 one of these attack aircraft hit the first target of the conflict, the air defence control center in Baghdad. The attack, performed after a night-time approach flight of around 780 miles (1300 km) in enemy territory, was completed by releasing electro-optically guided bombs, the so-called "smart bombs" with their deadly precision. In the 42 days of hostilities, the 36 aircraft serving with the 37th Tactical Fighter Wing of the USAF, completed 1271 missions, and proved to be the most sophisticated and efficient combat jets of the period.

384

384 The multi-role Tornado, in service in the air forces of Great Britain, Germany, Italy, and Saudi Arabia. Almost 1000 have been built in a variety of versions.

THE SCENARIO AT THE END OF THE CENTURY

The first Gulf War, the first conflict after the break-up of the former Soviet empire, was not only a sign of the changed international balance of military forces, but demonstrated above all that air power had definitively shifted to the side of United States. This marked the end of a process which had evolved through the most heated phrases of the confrontation between the two blocs, whose foundations dated back to the final years of the Cold War. It was an indisputable superiority, only partly compensated for by the great modernity of the latest products of the leading Russian designers and by the important technological contribution of those in Europe. Before examining the most advanced programs implemented by the North American aeronautical industry, we should briefly examine the state of military aviation on the eve of the fall of the Berlin Wall, the event which brought to an end an era lasting over 40 years in which the evolution of the airplane had witnessed unprecedented progress.

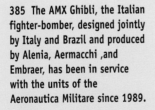

385 The AMX Ghibli, the Italian fighter-bomber, designed jointly by Italy and Brazil and produced by Alenia, Aermacchi ,and Embraer, has been in service with the units of the Aeronautica Militare since 1989.

MRCA Tornado

MULTINATIONAL

The need to regain design and industrial independence from the United States provided the stimulus for Europe to consider the path of cooperation in the late 1960s.

The result of the first important multinational program was the Tornado, an advanced, powerful multi-role aircraft with a variable-geometry wing which made a mark as the most efficient combat machine in its class in the West. The Gulf War provided a baptism of fire for this airplane, which took part in the conflict under British, Italian, and Saudi Arabian insignia.

The program was launched on March 26, 1969, with the setting up of the tri-nation European consortium Panavia, composed of British Aerospace, Messerschmitt-Bölkow-Blohm, and Aeritalia. The objective was to develop the MRCA (Multi-role combat

aircraft) to equip four air forces: the British Royal Air Force, the German Luftwaffe, Marineflieger, and the Aeronautica Militare Italiana. Development of the engine was given to another consortium—Turbo Union—composed of Rolls-Royce, MTU, and Fiat Aviazione. Establishing the design, however, was extremely laborious, considering the many roles the aircraft had to perform: tactical support, interception, air superiority, reconnaissance, counter-measures, long-range interception, and marine attack.

It originally planned to produce 809 aircraft, including 138 trainers: 385 Tornados for Great Britain (220 in the IDS, interdiction and standard attack version and 165 of the ADV, air defence version); 324 aircraft for Germany (212 to the Luftwaffe and 112 to the Navy); and 100 for Italy. The operational program

started in August 1972 with the construction of nine prototypes and six pre-series aircraft. The first Tornado made its maiden flight on August 14, 1974 at Manching, in Germany, and the fine-tuning phase lasted until 1979. The operational use of the IDS variant began in 1982, when it re-equipped the first British, German, and Italian units.

Apart from the ECR electronic warfare version, developed for the Luftwaffe and also used

by the Aeronautica Militare Italiana, the greatest evolution of the Tornado was seen in the second main production variant, the ADV produced for Great Britain. After the first 18 F.2s delivered in 1984, the definitive series was the F.3 (first flight on November 20, 1995), with more powerful engines and improved avionics. 24 of these aircraft were also ordered by Saudi Arabia, who deployed them alongside the 96 IDS

Tornados already in service. Italy also adopted the F.3 in the 1990s, leasing 24 temporarily from the RAF. Production stopped in 1998, but the evolution of the project was ensured by a series of updating programs specifically to do with the avionics, which was destined to prolong the service life of the Tornado well beyond 2015.

388 top The most widely used American carrier-based fighter is the McDonnell-Douglas F/A-18 Hornet, a multi-role aircraft able to perform defence and attack missions without any changes being necessary.

388 bottom The Grumman F-14 Tomcat, the standard air superiority carrier-based fighter on the main aircraft carriers of the American fleet.

THIRD-GENERATION FIGHTERS

From the 1970s onwards, the combat aircraft lined up against each other on the international scene were really the result of a desperate search for superiority. The lessons learned in South-East Asia had been important, and the third generation of fighters saw the development of increasingly fast and sophisticated machines, real weapons systems integrated with avionics, and the latest armaments, which achieved the limit of performance foreseeable for combat aircraft. Once again the two superpowers advanced side by side, in what seemed to be an endless arms race.

While forced to distribute resources along two distinct design lines—land-based aircraft and carrier-based aircraft—American industry nevertheless obtained particularly brilliant results. In 1972 the US Navy brought into service the Grumman F-14 Tomcat, a powerful interceptor with a variable-geometry wing; then, in 1983 the multi-role McDonnell-Douglas A/F-18 Hornet, which definitively replaced the F-4 Phantom II. In 1974 and 1978, the USAF equipped itself with two equally formidable machines: the McDonnell-Douglas F-15 Eagle interceptor and the multi-role General Dynamics F-16 Fighting Falcon, an aircraft which was widely used by NATO forces. Just how high the technological content of these designs was, and how great their development potential is demonstrated by the fact that all these aircraft were still fully operational in the early years of the 21st century, in continuously updated, and more powerful versions.

389 bottom The MiG-29 Fulcrum, an air superiority fighter, is one of Russia's most versatile weapons. It has advanced aerodynamic features, is extremely manouvrable, and can also be used on semi-prepared runways.

Grumman F-14 Tomcat

UNITED STATES

Acclaimed for over 30 years as one of the most formidable multi-role aircraft ever built in the naval sector, the Grumman F-14 Tomcat was the first third-generation fighter in service with the US Navy. Powerful, with Mach 2 performance, and continually updated avionics and engines, it was still in front-line service in the early years of the 21st century, with a service life scheduled up to 2007. Thanks to its variable-geometry wing it was able to perform tasks of interception, escort, reconnaissance, and ground attack with equal efficiency.

The need to find a successor to the F-4 Phantom II was the basis for the program which, in the 1960s, led to the Tomcat. After the failure of the F-111B program in October 1967, Grumman proposed a completely new design to the US Navy which, while keeping the variable-geometry wing, the avionics, and the General Dynamics engines of the prototype, resulted in a much smaller and lighter machine. The feasibility study was accepted and on January 15,1969 a contract was signed for the construction of a prototype and 12 aircraft to be used for research and testing.

The fine-tuning phase proved to be extremely laborious: on December 30, 1970 an accident destroyed the first prototype, the YF-14A, and test flights did not recommence until May 24 the following year. Upon the completion of assessment, production started with an initial order of 26 aircraft.

Deliveries began in June 1972, and the first two units (VF-1 and VF-2 on board the Enterprise) became operational in September 1974. These also had their baptism of fire during the final operations in South-East Asia. The only export order for the Tomcat dates back to that period, when what was then the Imperial Iranian Air Force became the only other air force to use the F-14. This was a source of some controversy, but the supply of 79 aircraft was completed 1976–78. In the meantime, production was running at full rate. In January 1980, 344 14As had been delivered to the US Navy, out of a total of orders which would reach 557. For the whole of the 1980s these airplanes were constantly updated and in 1987 production began to focus on the F-14B version (38 built), which was equipped with more efficient engines (in the drawings). One year later the final variant, the F-14D appeared, with new avionics and more powerful armaments. Deliveries of this aircraft, of which 37 were built, started in 1990. All the airplanes had been converted to this standard by 1998.

The most realistic operational test of the Tomcats was the Gulf War, during which they performed missions of attack, escort, and electronic reconnaissance. In 2001, 125 are still in service.

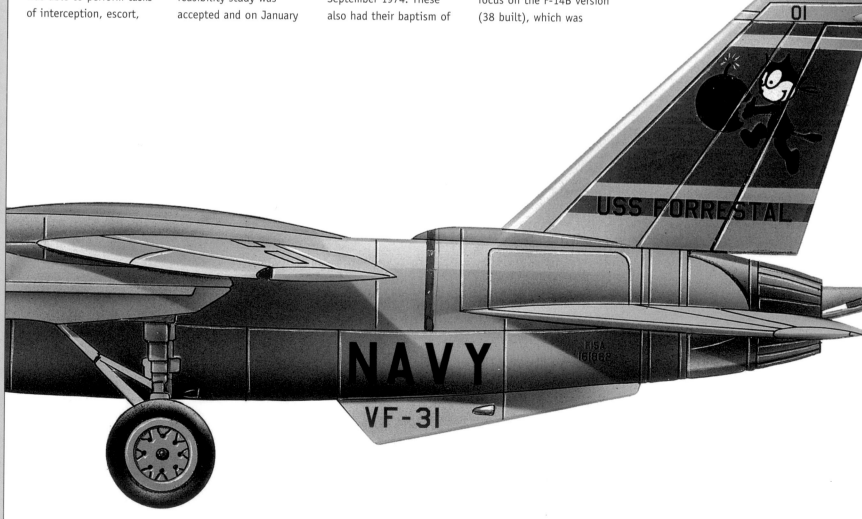

McDonnell-Douglas F-15 Eagle

UNITED STATES

The same need which forced the US Navy to find an advanced replacement for the F-4 Phantom II in the 1970s, led the USAF to develop the McDonnell Douglas F-15 Eagle. Like the F-14 Tomcat of the Navy, for over 30 years this formidable combat airplane represented the best of its generation, and one of the best in the world.

The program, named F-X, was launched in 1965 and the official specifications were presented to the leading US aircraft industries in September 1968. The advanced request was for a single-seater twin-jet able to operate as a pure fighter and in missions of offensive patrol and escort, with performance double that of the Phantom II in terms of climbing speed, acceleration, and manouvrability.

The McDonnell Douglas design won the competition on the basis of an initial contract for the construction of 18 pre-series aircraft in a single-seater configuration (the F-15A) and of 2 two-seater trainers (F-15B). The first prototype left the assembly lines in June 1972 and was taken on its maiden flight on July 27. One year later, on July 7, 1973, the first F-15B appeared.

Deliveries began the following year and the Eagle became operational on January 9, 1976 with the 1st Tactical Fighter Wing based in Langley, Virginia. Overall, 365 F-15As and 59 F-15Bs were built. As from June 1979, production focused on two new versions, the C and D (409 and 61 built respectively), characterized by particularly sophisticated avionics and greater range. These series were the first to exploit the multi-role capabilities of the F-15, which was also designed to perform ground-attack duties with particular efficiency. The following variant, the F-15E, took the potential of the airplane to its

limit. Designated Strike Eagle, it was configured as a two-seater and optimized to perform long-range attack missions in all-weather conditions while conserving intact its air-to-air combat capacities.

The development of this machine was authorised on February 24, 1984 and the first plane made its maiden flight on December 11, 1986. Deliveries began two years later. The Eagle was also supplied to a restricted number of allied countries: Israel deployed around 80 in various versions; Japan from 1980 onwards built 223 under licence; and Saudi Arabia after the 62 aircraft ordered in 1982, at the end of the Gulf War purchased another 72 derived from the F-15Es.

The conflict against Iraq represented the Eagle's crucial test: in particular, during Desert Storm the F-15s accounted for 34 of the 37 air combat victories recorded by the USAF (which in 2005 had an overall force of 522 F-15s, 396 in front-line service. In the same year the production figures of Strike Eagles had reached 217).

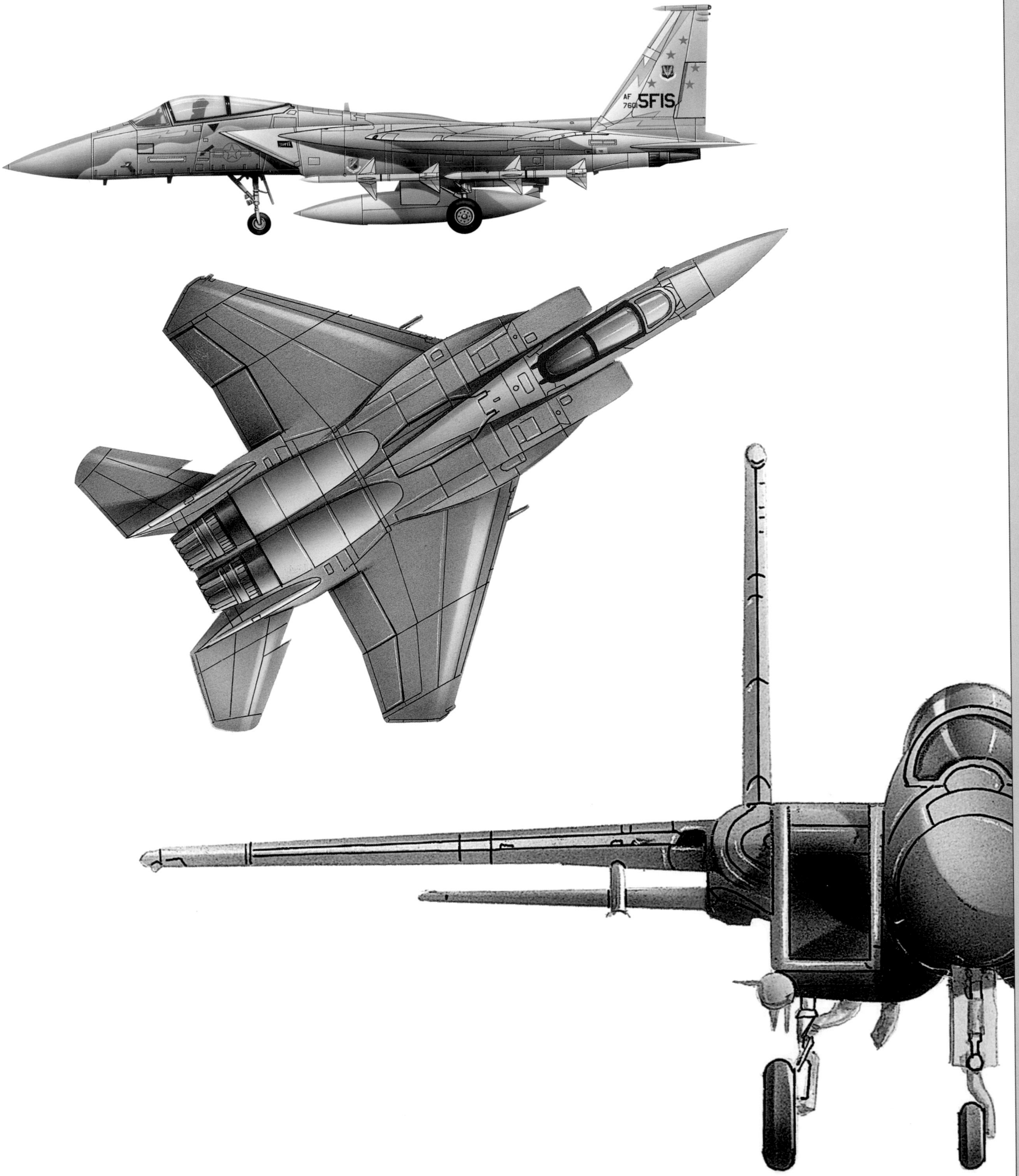
AF
7601
SFIS

General Dynamics F-16 Fighting Falcon

UNITED STATES

More or less a contemporary of the F-15, the General Dynamics F-16 Fighting Falcon offered the same excellent features of the Eagle in a smaller and lighter aircraft. This extremely agile and versatile airplane was the real modern equivalent of the classic fighters of aviation history. Its success was boosted by its enormous diffusion in the West: the almost 4300 built from 1975 onwards equipped the air forces of 23 countries, and the USAF alone deployed 2231, the last of which was delivered on March 24, 2005.

The specifications of the program were made known on February 28, 1972 and the General Dynamics design, whose YF-16 prototype had flown for the first time on January 20, 1974, won the competition. The airplane incorporated for the first time in the world a particularly innovative technology: the control of flight by means of an artificial system of stability entirely managed by the on-board computer and under the control of the pilot by means of fly-by-wire controls. In early 1975 the USAF had already made an initial order for a pre-series run of 11 single-seater F-16As and 4 two-seater F-16Bs. But a few months later there was an unexpected turn of events which definitively launched the program on the international stage: the decision of four NATO countries to adopt the General Dynamics fighter to replace the F-104 Starfighter. Belgium, Denmark, Norway, and Holland chose the F-16 on June 7, 1975 at the end of a competition in which the losers were the Dassault Mirage 2000 and the Swedish Saab Viggen.

The definitive version of the F-16A (in the drawings) first flew on December 8, 1976, followed on August 8, 1977 by the F-16B. Deliveries began the following year and the first operational unit was the 388 Tactical Fighter Wing on January 6, 1979.

Production in the United States soon achieved a high rate and was joined by assembly lines in Belgium and Holland in accordance with the industrial consortium formed by the four nations. The Belgian air force received Europe's first F-16 on January 26, 1979. On June 6, it was Holland's turn, while Denmark and Norway followed in January 1980. From the 1980s onwards, the development of the fighter continued without interruptions. The second major production variant was the F-16C (D in the two-seater version), delivered in July 1984. It incorporated improved avionics, more weaponry, and a more powerful engine, components which underwent further continuous improvements in the course of production.

The Fighting Falcon was a huge success on the international market, with the number of purchasers still rising in the early years of the 21st century.

The major user after the United States was Israel: requests began in August 1977 with an order for 75 aircraft (which then became 260), delivered from January 31, 1980 onward. Italy was added to the list in 2003, with 34 F-16 A/Bs leased from the USA while waiting for the Eurofighter Typhoon to become fully operational. Two units of the Aeronautica Militare, the 18th and 27th Stormo (Flight), became operational in 2004.

McDonnell-Douglas F/A-18 Hornet

UNITED STATES

In the 1980s, the front line of the US Navy was boosted by a new combat aircraft, the F/A-18 Hornet. This sophisticated multi-role craft, which was used in operations alongside the already formidable F-14 Tomcat, proved to be a weapons system with great potential. In the early years of the new millennium, the Hornet represented the jewel of the fleet and of the Marines, with its development clearly projected into the future.

Work started on the program in spring 1974, and the choice fell on a version derived from the Northrop YF-17 prototype, which had been developed by McDonnell-Douglas.

On January 2, 1976, official approval was given and the airplane was designated F-18 Hornet. In the initial phase, two distinct versions were planned, a fighter and an attack aircraft, but in the end they were combined as the F/A-18. The first of the 11 prototypes made its maiden flight on November 18, 1978, gradually followed by the others, two of which were produced in two-seater versions. Sea trials began in May 1980 and the first unit equipped with the Hornets became operational in January 1983. The production program progressed rapidly and was fuelled by a series of orders which took the total to 1150, of which 153 were trainers. The evolution of the airplane continued at the same rate. After the initial variants, the F/A-18 A and B, on September 15, 1986, the first F/A-18C flew, equipped with improved avionics and more powerful weaponry. Deliveries began late the following year. In 1988 there followed the F/A-18D variant, a two-seater night-attack aircraft.

The most advanced versions were put into production in the early 1990s.

In January 1991, the US Navy decided to fund the study of a new, larger, and more powerful series. The prototypes YF-18E (single-seater) and YF-18F (two-seater) were ordered in December the following year and the first flight took place on November 29,1995. The designation Super Hornet was indicative of the characteristics of these airplanes, with better aerodynamic performance, greatly increased range, the possibility to install the latest avionics, maximum weapons load increased to over 8 tons, and the extension of operational roles. The first of these aircraft reached the units in 1999 and production was calculated to be 545 aircraft for the US Navy and Marines. In 2005 over 200 Super Hornets had already been delivered. They had their baptism of fire in November 2002, during the second attack against Iraq.

In addition to the American armed forces, the Hornets entered service with three Allied nations: Canada (188), Australia (75), and Spain (72). After the first Gulf War these countries were joined by Kuwait, with 40 F/A-18s.

398 top left Destined to replace the older MiG-21, the Sukhoi Su-27, with a swing wing, has been in service in the Russian air force since 1970. It has been exported to various allied countries.

398 top right The F-16 Fighting Falcon, over 4000 of which have been built, has been adopted in 23 countries around the world. It is fitted with a fly-by-wire flight control system.

On the other side of the Berlin Wall, the Soviet fighters of the time, while less sophisticated than their American counterparts, were equally powerful and deadly, and were often produced as a direct response to the evolving models of the adversary. Among these emerged the MiG-23 with a variable geometry wing, the Mach 3 MiG-25, the formidable MiG-29, the Sukhoi Su-15 interceptor, the multi-role Su-24 and Su-27. Thesemachines, the last developed behind the Iron Curtain in the Cold War, were the swansong of an aeronautical tradition whose origins dated back to the Second World War.

398 bottom The design of the Gripen dates back to the mid-1980s. Today, the Saab 39, characterized by its delta-canard configuration, is the most advanced fighter of the Swedish air force.

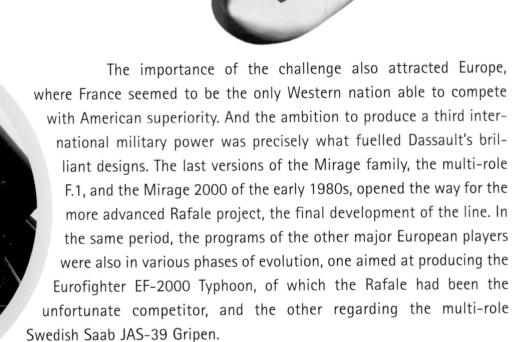

399 The successor of the Mirage (bottom) for the French air force is the Dassault Rafale (top and center), which adopts the delta-canard configuration and makes wide use of electronic systems for flight control. A two-seater version has also been developed.

The importance of the challenge also attracted Europe, where France seemed to be the only Western nation able to compete with American superiority. And the ambition to produce a third international military power was precisely what fuelled Dassault's brilliant designs. The last versions of the Mirage family, the multi-role F.1, and the Mirage 2000 of the early 1980s, opened the way for the more advanced Rafale project, the final development of the line. In the same period, the programs of the other major European players were also in various phases of evolution, one aimed at producing the Eurofighter EF-2000 Typhoon, of which the Rafale had been the unfortunate competitor, and the other regarding the multi-role Swedish Saab JAS-39 Gripen.

Mikoyan-Gurevich MiG-29

SOVIET UNION

The last great exponent of an illustrious old family of combat aircraft, the MiG-29 was also one of the last products of the Cold War. When it was unveiled in 1988 at the Farnborough International Airshow, this multi-role capable of over Mach 2 had already been in service with the Russian air force for five years, and proved fully competitive with its most advanced Western counterparts. Observers called it the best end-of-the-century fighter in the world.

The MiG-29 was designed in the 1970s with the aim of developing a new-generation fighter of equal standard to its American contemporaries, to replace the MiG-21 and MiG-23 in tactical and air defence

roles. The official specifications were issued in 1972 and the program was implemented two years later with the construction of 14 prototypes for initial tests. The first of these flew on October 6, 1977. The design was optimized to give the airplane great performance in terms of manouvrability and acceleration. These results were obtained thanks to a particularly advanced aerodynamic design and to the adoption of two powerful turbofans providing 818,260 lb (300 kg) thrust with an afterburner, ensured an excellent thrust/weight ratio. In developing of the cell the designers were assisted by technicians of TsAGI, the famous Soviet Central Institute of Aerodynamics. Industrial production began in 1982 and around 800 of the new fighters were

delivered to the units in August the following year.

During the massive production run, which accounted for a total of 2000 aircraft, the MiG-29 was developed in a number of versions, continuously updated in terms of avionics, engines, and armament, and optimized for specific roles. In addition to the series destined for export, there was significant

development of a variant destined for carrier-based use. This was the MiG-29K, produced in 1984 and tested between 1989 and 1991 on board the aircraft carrier Admiral Kuznetsov. It was characterized by improved avionics and the adoption of specific anti-ship armament. It was purchased by the Indian navy, in addition to many other countries such as

North Korea, Yugoslavia, Syria, Bulgaria, Croatia, Cuba, Czechoslovakia, Hungary, Iran, Kazakhstan, Malaysia, and Poland. In the early years of the 21st century, the fighter was in service with 21 air forces and was the only Russian aircraft deployed by NATO, due to the fact that the German Luftwaffe had received the aircraft in service with the German Democratic Republic.

Dassault-Breguet Rafale

FRANCE

The successful design series by Dassault witnessed its latest evolution in the 1990s with a formidable new multi-role aircraft, the Rafale. This powerful and sophisticated Mach 2 twinjet, however, did not manage to make a mark on the international market, thanks to its great rival, the Eurofighter Typhoon.

Work started on the project in 1983, and was conducted by the ACX (Avions de Combat Expérimental) division of Dassault. The study was entirely alternative to that being conducted by Great Britain, Germany, and Italy in their work on the European fighter, and was continued even after France left the Eurofighter program in July 1985. The first technological demonstrator, designated Rafale A, appeared six months later and was taken on its maiden flight on July 4,1986.

Despite the failure in Europe, the aims of the project remained extremely ambitious. The intention was to produce a technologically advanced latest-generation airplane, which could substitute no fewer than five types of machines in service with the Armée de l'Air and the Aéronavale: the Crusader, the Super Etendard, the Jaguar, the Mirage III/5, the Mirage IV, and the Mirage 2000. To this end, another four prototypes in three different configurations were built: the single-seater Rafale C for the Armée de l'Air (first flight on May 19, 1991), the single-seater carrier-based Rafale M for the Aéronavale (December 12, 1991), and the two-seater Rafale B for the Armée de l'Air (April 30, 1993). These airplanes underwent a long and intense period of testing and fine-tuning, necessary to optimize the production variants offered to the French Armed Forces, and eventually provided excellent performance and formidable development potential.

The production program, however, was slowed down greatly by the combined effect of rising costs and cuts to the defence budget. After the 13 pre-series aircraft requested in 1993, it was not until January 1997 that a first contract for 48 airplanes was signed (21 Rafale Bs, 12 Rafale Cs, and 15 Rafale Ms), joined four years later by a second order for another 61 aircraft of the various versions, to be delivered by the end of 2007.

The first production Rafales were those of the Aéronavale, who received the aircraft of the initial production lot in December 2001. These entered service six months later on board the aircraft carrier Charles De Gaulle. Deliveries to the Armée de l'Air began with the two-seater version in December 2000 and in late 2004 the units had 61 of the aircraft in service overall.

The two armed forces are scheduled to receive 60 and 212 airplanes respectively by 2020.

404

In particular, this small but powerful and sophisticated light multi-role is considered the best in the world in its category and its development is projected into the first two decades of the 21st-century, in an international market which appears extremely interested. Together with the Dassault Rafale and the Eurofighter Typhoon, the Saab fighter is the most advanced European product in the sector of latest-generation military jets.

404 Four European countries—Great Britain, Germany, Italy, and Spain— have adopted the Eurofighter EF-2000 Typhoon, the multi-role fighter produced today in multinational collaboration as part of a program set to build 620. Like the other most advanced machines, it is a canard with particularly advanced avionics.

THE LAST STRATEGIC BOMBERS

D espite the deadly network of intercontinental ballistic missiles, the final developments of the strategic bomber conceived as a nuclear deterrent were seen precisely during the 1980s: in the United States, boosted by the Reagan administration's recommencement of the arms race; in the Soviet bloc, as an expected response to this. The last aircraft of this generation were from many points of view extremely similar, directly competing rivals resulting from the same operational requirements: the Rockwell International B-1 and the Tupolev 160. These two giants both had variable-geometry wings, with engine nacelles grouped in pairs at the center of the fuselage; they provided supersonic performance; and the avionics were particularly sophisticated, optimized for the automatic control of flight even at low altitudes and weaponry management. The armament was composed entirely of cruise missiles, the most advanced weapon systems available at the time.

405 Only 100 Rockwell B-1 Lancers were built.
The aircraft was supposed to replace the older B-52s in the USAF bombing units from 1985. It is armed with cruise missiles and electronic defence systems.

Eurofighter EF-2000 Typhoon

MULTINATIONAL

After the success of the Tornado, the major European aeronautical industries once more proposed the formula of cooperation for developing an even more advanced combat machine, the Typhoon, a powerful and sophisticated Mach 2 interceptor destined for the air forces of Great Britain, Germany, Italy, and Spain.

The Eurofighter program was formally launched on October 21, 1986, with the setting up by the four countries of industrial consortiums for the development of the airplane and the engines. This marked the end of an extremely long phase of preparation which had begun in the 1970s, characterized by continuous disputes and rivalries and hindered by the enormous economic and industrial interests at stake, above all due to the attitude of French industry, determined to achieve technological superiority over its European partners. The situation was unblocked on August 2, 1985, when France definitively abandoned the common fighter program.

The industrial collaboration of the Eurofighter consortium divided the production of the cell between British Aerospace, the German MBB and Dornier, Italy's Aeritalia (later Alenia), and CASA in Spain. The Eurojet consortium entrusted the construction of the engines to Rolls-Royce, the German Mtu, Fiat Aviazione, and the Spanish ITP.

The definitive program, named Eurofighter 2000, started in December 1992, with the development of seven prototypes. The first to fly was the German DA1, on March 27, 1994.

Ten days later, on April 6, this was joined by the English prototype, the DA2, and on June 4, 1995, the Italian DA3 made its maiden flight. The others followed between August 1996 and March 1997.

In the month of December the move to the production phase was authorized on the basis of a program in which 620 aircraft would be built by the year 2018, and divided between the four partners as follows:

232 aircraft (of which 37 two-seaters) to Great Britain; 180 (33) to Germany; 121 (5) to Italy, and 87 (15) to Spain.

These quantities were subsequently increased with the issue of 90 options (65 by Great Britain, 16 by Spain, and 9 by Italy) and an order for 18 aircraft from Austria. Deliveries to the four partners of the production models started in 2003 with the two-seater variant, while the first single-seaters followed in early 2005.

The B-1 was the first to be developed toward the end of the 1960s. The original intention was for fleets of these bombers to complement the North American defence system, working alongside land-based ballistic missiles and those deployed by nuclear submarines. But the program underwent serious delays and in 1977, after the construction of three prototypes, it was blocked by US President Jimmy Carter because of the enormous rise in costs. Four years later the entire project was recommenced by the new administration and completed, albeit with extremely reduced quantities compared to those originally planned. The B-1, which entered service in 1985, was able to transport 22 cruise missiles and to strike targets all over the world. Its Soviet rival, with greater weight and size and better performance, made its maiden flight as a prototype in 1982 and entered service five years later. However, despite its enormous potential, the Tupolev Tu-160 never managed to replace in a strategic role its more famous predecessor, the Tu-26 of 1975, perhaps the most widespread Soviet bomber of the period.

THE AIRCRAFT OF THE FUTURE

The leap in quality which characterizes the most advanced military aircraft is provided by the increasingly extreme application of stealth technology, introduced in the United States with the Lockheed F-117. The logical step forward, after the great success of this tactical fighter, was to use the enormous fund of experience acquired in the phases of research and development to produce an even more important

408 The Northrop-Grumman B-2 Spirit bomber with stealth capabilities was not any luckier than its predecessor. Only 21 were built due to increased production costs and the many fine-tuning problems.

409 The Lockheed Martin-Boeing F-22 Raptor originates from the ATF (Advanced Tactical Fighter) specifications issued by the USAF. The American super fighter has exceptional speed performance and carries its armaments in compartments inside the fuselage.

machine: a new-generation strategic bomber, basically immune to the most sophisticated enemy counter-measures and defences, armed with cruise missiles with nuclear warheads, able to penetrate deep into enemy airspace, complete the mission, and return to base.

Also in this case, the development of the program, designated ATB (Advanced Technology Bomber), remained shrouded in the deepest secrecy for many years. The Northrop B-2, baptized Spirit, was presented to the world only in November 1988 and did not fail to amaze observers even more than its predecessor had done. The B-2 had the configuration of a flying wing, a design originating in similar work performed by Northrop immediately after the Second World War in the construction of the B-35 and B-49 bombers. Moreover, unlike the angular lines of the F-117, the forms of the fuselage blended softly into the wing, which also housed the four engines. The only external irregularities were in the trailing edge of the wing, with its zigzag "beaver tail" profile. The avionics system was particularly advanced, and in addition to managing armament and counter-measures, was also responsible for control of the airplane, which was fundamentally unstable.

Northrop B-2 Spirit

UNITED STATES

The technology applied for the first time in the development of the F-117 was the starting point for the work on an even more ambitious project: the construction of a new-generation strategic bomber equipped with advanced stealth characteristics.

During the 1980s this led to the Northrop B-2 Spirit, the result of research at the highest level, whose potential was tested for the first time in the Balkans.

The program was launched with the objective of complementing and replacing the Rockwell B-1, and the development of the new bomber was entrusted to Northrop, assisted by Boeing Aerospace and the LTV Vought Aero Product Division.

The entire phase of research, design, and testing, which involved an investment of around $23 billion at the time, was covered by the strictest military secrecy and only on April 20, 1988 did the USAF issue an artist's drawing of the airplane.

On November 22 there was the official presentation ceremony and the first flight of the prototype was performed on July 17,1989.

By that date, a contract had already been signed for the production of 135 B-2s, 120 with nuclear armament capability. This figure, however, was not respected. In the early 1990s, changes in the international climate imposed drastic cuts to military expenditure and, as had happened with the B-1 program, the B-2 also fell victim to the steep growth in development and production costs, estimated at $2.2 billion per aircraft.

In the end, only 21 were completed, entering service in a single unit, the 509th Bomb Wing based in Whiteman, Missouri.

Apart from the advanced applications of stealth technology, the Spirit's great efficiency was due to its sophisticated aerodynamic design which, translated into the original flying wing configuration,made this airplane unique in the history of aviation.

Lockheed Martin-Boeing F/A-22 Raptor

UNITED STATES

The first combat aircraft of the fourth generation and the first air superiority fighter 'invisible' to radar, the Lockheed Martin-Boeing F/A-22 Raptor developed and perfected the already high technological content experimented in the F-117 and the B-2.

In the 1970s a group of technicians from Lockheed Martin and General Dynamics launched a series of studies on the possibilities of developing a combat airplane to succeed the McDonnell-Douglas F-15.

This research work proved to be extremely useful when in September 1985, the USAF asked industries for feasibility proposals for an advanced tactical fighter. Various projects were presented, and on October 31,1986, the selection was made: the Lockheed Martin YF-22 and the Northrop YF-23.

The two companies headed their respective industrial groups, formed respectively with Boeing-General Dynamics and McDonnell-Douglas. Comparative assessment, however, turned out to be extremely long, and it was only on April 23, 1991, that the YF-22 was declared the winner and given the designation of

Lightning II. The subsequent phase, dedicated to the development of the definitive configuration of the fighter and the debugging of the systems, avionics, and armament lasted another four years, and it was not until February 1995 that the final design was approved. The first pre-series aircraft, definitively designated A/F-22 Raptor, flew in September 1997. These delays were a serious blow to the entire program which, already weighed down by extremely heavy costs, was severely criticized and considered as possibly useless in the

new post-Cold War scenario. After a long and heated debate, an initial compromise on production levels arrived on August 16, 2001: the USAF, which hoped to receive 750 airplanes, saw its requests cut to 295. Subsequently, this

quantity was further reduced to 180. In 2005 around 40 airplanes were delivered, while the first unit equipped with the Raptor, the 27th Fighter Squadron based in Langley, planned to begin operations in December.

Despite these strong

limitations to the original program, since its debut the F/A-22 has made a mark as the most advanced combat airplane in the world. Among its most important characteristics are its very low observability, extreme manouvrability, and the possibility, thanks to its sophisticated avionics, to anticipate any threat, perfectly embodying the logic which had guided its development: "first look/first kill".

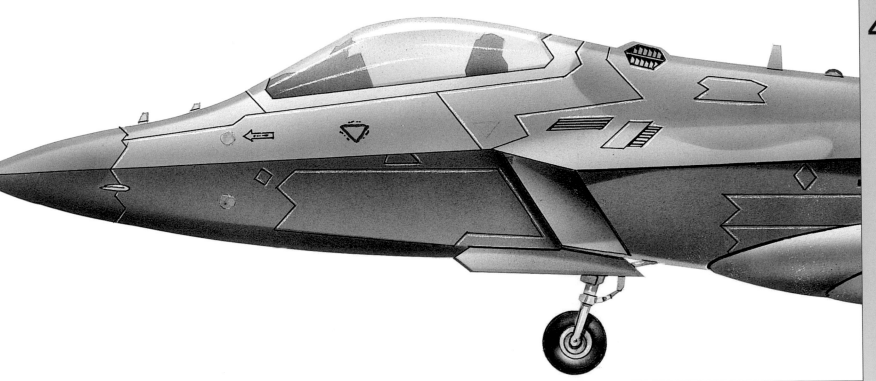

The B-2 was declared fully operational in December 2003 after being tested in combat during the Kosovo conflict. The key to its success was in the revolutionary combination of the most advanced stealth technologies with extremely high aerodynamic efficiency, and a high weapons load. During the first eight weeks of Operation Allied Force in 1999, the Northrop bombers destroyed 33 percent of all the Serbian targets by flying without stopping from their base at Whiteman, Missouri and then flying back. Subsequently, the Spirit was also used in Afghanistan and Iraq.

All that was needed to complete the triad of aircraft of the future was a new air superiority fighter, and US industry subsequently began research in the most advanced field. In this case, however, the task was more complex. While in the first stealth aircraft it had been possible to optimize engine emissions by voluntarily opting for subsonic performance, the new ATF (Advanced Tactical Fighter) program launched in 1985 required the development of a Mach 2 aircraft, driven by two engines with afterburners and over 30,800 lb (14,000 kg) of thrust. The technicians and the designers found themselves facing problems never encountered before, which were apparently unsolvable. It took them five years to find an effective compromise between the many needs, and the winner of the competition, the Lockheed Martin-Boeing F/A-22 Raptor, did not receive its final configuration until 1995. By that time, however, in a changed geopolitical scenario, the program had accumulated serious delays. Moreover, development costs had risen sharply, and the project risked being abandoned. After a series of compromises, which drastically reduced the quantities earmarked for the USAF, the airplane entered production in 2001, with the beginning of the operational phase forecast for December 2005.

The Raptor is the most advanced "super-fighter" in existence, a new international benchmark. Its concentration of avant-garde technology ranges from the innovative materials present in almost 30 percent of the structure and the turbo-fans with rotating nozzles, to the totally integrated avionics which manage all the aircraft's functions. This is a real system of artificial intelligence, able

414 top and 414-415 In-flight refuelling has now become common practice in all the main air forces of the world to ensure global range. In the photo, the refuelling probe of a Boeing KC-135 attached to a Raptor fighter.

415 top The General Dynamics F-16.

415 bottom right The only vertical take-off fighter today in service is the Harrier. The aircraft, with adjustable nozzles, was designed in England by Hawker and the most recent version, the AV-8, is in service with various air forces (Royal Navy, US Navy, Marines, Spain) and was also chosen by the Marina Militare italiana for carrier-based use on aircraft carrier Garibaldi.

amongst other things to "perceive" any kind of threat in advance and react with deadly efficiency. Moreover, the combination of design solutions adopted to ensure low observability has achieved almost incredible results: while 15 years previously the radar signature of the F-117 was equivalent to that of a small bird, American technicians claim that the F/A-22 appears on the screens as if it was a bumblebee instead of being an airplane weighing 27 tons.

THE NEW MILLENNIUM

The Advanced Tactical Fighter opened a new era of development for the military airplane, fuelled by the changing needs of defence in the 21st century and characterized by even greater innovation. It was no coincidence that on October 26, 2001, six weeks after the attack on the Twin Towers in New York, the United States launched the development phase of the JSF (Joint Strike Fighter) project, aimed at producing the "most lethal, secure, and reliable weapons system of the new generation", a combat machine "difficult to find, hit, and down", optimized for the battlefields of the future.

BAe/McDonnell-Douglas AV-8 Harrier II

GREAT BRITAIN

In the world of military aviation few revolutions have been as important as that triggered off by the Harrier, the first vertical take-off combat aircraft. However, this avant-garde machine had to wait almost a decade before its design was finalized.

The idea of producing a vertical take-off and landing fighter (V/STOL) came in 1957 to Sydney Camm, the great English designer who was technical director at Hawker Aircraft.

The program had a long and labored gestation period, due to the difficulty in finalizing the engine design, which had to provide vertical thrust by means of adjustable side exhaust jets. On October 21, 1960 tests began on the P.1127 prototype and this airplane was followed by another five experimental machines. The first aircraft

of this pre-series flew on August 31, 1966. Named the Harrier, it was put into production as the GR.1 tactical support and reconnaissance aircraft. Some 78 were built and entered service with the RAF in April 1969.

The second main series was the GR.3 (36 built), with a more powerful engine and ordered in 1976. In the meantime, the United States had become extremely interested in the machine's potential. In 1969 they had ordered 12 Harriers, designating them AV-8A, to equip units of the Marines, and between 1971 and 1977 they received another 100. The static phase which had previously prevented the airplane from making a mark in the naval field was unblocked when the Harrier entered service under American insignia. In May 1975 the British Royal Navy decided to adopt the vertical take-off and landing fighter, ordering 36 in a special version, the Sea Harrier FRS.1 (first flight on August 20, 1978), which it put into service in April 1980. The Royal Navy were

joined in 1980 by the Indian navy, which ordered 27 Harriers for its two aircraft carriers. It was McDonnell-Douglas, after purchasing the production licence, who produced the subsequent variant, the AV-8B Harrier II, and gave a significant boost to development of the machine. This version (in the drawings) developed especially for the Marines, was completely redesigned and became even more efficient.

The first of the two prototypes flew on November 9, 1978, and the airplane entered service on January 12, 1984 on the basis of a request for 295 single-seater AV-8Bs and 28 two-seater trainers (TAV-8B). The final version was the

AV-8B Plus of 1993, equipped with new avionics and armament, which entered service in 1994. The Harrier IIs were purchased by Spain, which had already bought 11 AV-8As in 1976, and by Italy (16 single-seaters and 2 two-seaters), for use on board the aircraft carrier Garibaldi. Subsequent English series were all derived from the American variants: the final versions in the RAF were the GR.5, GR.7, and GR.9, with further improvements to avionics and the engine. The last naval variant was the FA.2, in service since 1993.

The Harriers of the Royal Navy had their baptism of fire in the Falklands War of 1982, the Marines' AV-8Bs in the first Gulf War.

418 and 419 The prototypes of the three versions of the F-35: the B (418 top), equipped with STOVL (short take off and vertical landing) capability; the C for the US Navy (419); and the A for the USAF (418 bottom).

The product of the JSF program is the F-35, an "intelligent" polyvalent attack aircraft, with supersonic performance and advanced stealth characteristics, able to operate with deadly efficiency in any environmental conditions. This is a truly global weapon, which will enter service with the American and British armed forces and those of the allied countries "to deal with any kind of aggression".

New instruments for achieving new equilibriums, then. The endless race for supremacy continues, amidst the unknowns of a world deeply changed by the chain of events set in motion by international terrorism, adding to the tensions of the many unstable areas of the planet.

This is the F-35's operational frame of reference. With the three basic fighter versions, the US Navy intends to complement the potential of the F/A-18E-F Hornet; the USAF to replace the F-16 Fighting Falcon and complement the F/A-22 Raptor; the US Marine Corps to replace its AV-8B Harrier II and F/A-18. The RAF and the Royal Navy will use it to replace all the Harriers in service. With the aim of cutting costs, the program has also been opened to other partners. The development phase, lasting a decade, and already funded with $25 billion, is headed by Lockheed Martin, assisted by Northrop Grumman, and British Aerospace Systems. The partners, in addition to the United States and Great Britain, include Italy, Holland, Turkey, Canada, Denmark, Norway, and Australia. The total requirements are estimated to be around 3000 aircraft. The first F-35 is scheduled to fly in late 2006, and full operational status is scheduled for 2010, with a service life of a further 20 years.

TECHNICAL DETAILS

YEAR	NAME	TYPE	NATION	ENGINE	SIZE m	WEIGHT kg	SPEED km/h	RANGE h/km	CEILING m
1906	Santos-Dumont 14 bis	-	F	1 x Antoinette 8 cyl.	11.2x9.7x3.4	300	40	-	-
1908	Wright A	-	USA	1 x Wright 4 cyl.	11.1x8.8X2.4	544	71	-	-
1909	Blériot XI	-	F	1 x Anzani 3 cyl.	7.8x8x2.5	300	58	-	-
1909	Antoinette IV	-	F	1 x Antoinette 8 cyl.	12.8x11.4x2.9	590	70	-	-
1910	Etrich Taube	-	A	1 x Mercedes 6 cyl.	14.3x9.8x3.1	870	115	-	-
1911	Curtiss Hydro A.1	-	USA	1 x Curtiss 8 cyl.	11.2x8.4x2.8	714	105 c.	-	-
1912	Breguet III	-	F	1 x Canton-Unné 7 cyl.	13.6x8.8x2.9	949	100	7,00'	-
1914	Maurice Farman M.F.11	R	F	1 x Renault 8 cyl.	16.1x9.4x3.1	928	106	3,45'	3,800
1914	Macchi Parasol	R	I	1 x Gnome	13x7.2 –		125	-	2,700
1914	Morane-Saulnier N	C	F	1 x Le Rhône	8.3x6.7x2.5	510	165	1,30'	4,000
1914	Caproni Ca.18	B	I	1 x Gnome	10.9x7.6 –	-	130	-	-
1914	R.A.F. B.E.2c	B	GB	1 x R.A.F. 8 cyl.	11.2x8.3x3.3	972	116	3,15'	3,048
1914	Vickers F.B.5	C	GB	1 x Gnome	11.1x8.2x3.5	930	113	4,00'	2,743
1914	Avro 504 A	B	GB	1 x Gnome	10.9x8.9x3.1	713	132	3,00'	3,950
1914	Voisin 3	B	F	1 x Canton-Unné	14.7x9.5x3.8	1,370	120	500	3,500
1915	Nieuport 11	C	F	1 x Le Rhône	7.5x5.8x2.4	480	156	2,30'	4,600
1915	Sikorsky Ilya Mourometz V	B	RUS	Rus4 x Sunbeam 6 cyl.	29.8x17.1x4.7	4,589	121	5,00'	3,000
1915	Caudron G.4	B	F	2 x Le Rhône	17.2x7.1x2.6	1,330	132	3,30'	4,300
1915	Siemens-Schuckert R.I	B	D	3 x Benz	28.0x17.4 –	-	130	-	-
1915	R.A.F. F.E.2b	C-R	GB	1 x Beardmore 6 cyl.	14.5x9.8x3.8	1,378	146	2,30'	3,350
1915	Short 184	R-B	GB	1 x Sunbeam 12 cyl.	19.4x13.4x4.1	2,269	140	-	2,743
1915	L.V.G. C.II	R	D	1 x Mercedes 6 cyl.	12.8x8.1x2.9	1,402	130	4,00'	5,030
1915	Rumpler C.I	R	D	1 x Mercedes 6 cyl.	12.1x7.8x3.0	1,330	152	4,00'	5,030
1915	Aviatik C.I	R	D	1 x Mercedes 6 cyl.	12.5x8x3.2	1,286	120	3,30'	4,000
1915	Fokker E.III	C	D	1 x Oberursel	9.4x7.2x2.7	608	141	1,30'	3,660
1915	Lloyd C.II	R	A	1 x Hiero 6 cyl.	14x9x3.4	1,350	128	2,30'	3,000
1915	Farman F.40	R-B	F	1 x Renault	17.6x9.2x3.8	1,120	135	2,20'	4,900
1915	Caudron G.4	B	F	2 x Le Rhône	17.2x7.1x2.6	1,330	132	3,30'	4,300
1916	Hansa-Brandenburg D.I	C	A	1 x Austro-Daimler 6 cyl.	8.5x6.3x2.7	917	187	2,30'	5,000
1916	Nieuport 17	C	F	1 x Le Rhône	8.1x5.7x2.4	565	177	2,00'	5,300
1916	Spad S.VII	C	F	1 x Hispano-Suiza	7.7x6.1x2.3	703	191.5	2,15'	5,334
1916	R.A.F. R.E.8	R-B	GB	1 x R.A.F. 12 cyl.	12.9x8.4x3.4	1,215	164	4,15'	4,115
1916	Handley-Page 0/100	B	GB	2 x Rolls-Royce	30.4x19.1x6.7	6,352	153	6,00'	2,134
1916	Sopwith Pup	C	GB	1 x Le Rhône	8.0x5.8x2.8	556	179.4	3,00'	5,334
1916	Airco D.H.2	C	GB	1 x Gnome	8.6x7.6x2.8	654	150	2,45'	4,420
1916	Albatros D.II	C	D	1 x Mercedes 6 cyl.	8.5x7.4x2.7	886	175	1,30'	5,180
1916	Hansa-Brandenburg C.I	A	G	A1 x Austro-Daimler 6 cyl.	12.2x8.4x3.3	1,310	140	3,00'	5,800
1917	Bristol F.2B	C	GB	1 x Rolls-Royce 2 cyl.	11.9x7.8x2.9	1,261	196	3,00'	6,096
1917	Sopwith Triplane	C	GB	1 x Clerget	8.0x5.8x3.2	699	181	2,45'	6,248
1917	Bristol M.1C	C	GB	1 x Le Rhône	9.3x6.2x2.3	611	209.2	1,45'	6,096
1917	R.A.F. S.E.5	C	GB	1 x Hispano-Suiza 8 cyl.	8.1x6.3x2.8	877	196.3	2,30'	5,791
1917	R.A.F. S.E.5a	C	GB	1 x Wolseley 8 cyl.	8.1x6.3x2.8	902	222	3,00'	5,944
1917	Sopwith F.1 Camel	C	GB	1 x Clerget	8.5x5.7x2.5	659	185	2,30'	5,791
1917	Gotha G.V	B	D	2 x Mercedes 6 cyl.	23.7x12.3x4.3	3,967	140	840	6,500
1917	Albatros D.III	C	D	1 x Mercedes 6 cyl.	9.0x7.3x2.9	884	176	2,00'	5,500
1917	Fokker Dr.I	C	D	1 x Le Rhône	7.1x5.7x2.9	585	165	1,30'	6,100
1917	SAML S.2	R	I	1 x Fiat 6 cyl.	12.1x8.5x2.9	1,395	162	3,30'	5,000
1917	SIA 7B.1	R	I	1 x Fiat 6 cyl.	13.3x9.0x3	1,567	186.6	4,00'	7,000
1917	Spad S.XIII	C	F	1 x Hispano-Suiza 8 cyl.	8.2x6.3x2.4	820	222	2,00'	6,650
1917	Hanriot HD.1	C	F	1 x Le Rhône	8.6x5.8x2.5	605	183	2,30'	6,300
1917	Thomas-Morse S.4	A	USA	1 x Le Rhône	8.0x5.6x2.4	622	152.9	2,30'	4,572
1917	Morane-Saulnier AI	C	F	1 x Gnome	8.5x5.6x2.4	650	207.6	2,30'	7,000
1919	Martin MB.2	B	USA	2x Liberty 12 cyl.	22.6x13.0x4.4	5,465	160	900	2,590
1924	Fiat C.R.1	C	I	1 x Isotta-Fraschini 8 cyl.	8.9x6.2x2.4	1,155	270	650	7,450
1925	Army Curtiss R3C-2	Compet.	USA	1 x Curtiss 12 cyl.	6.7x6.1 –	1,242	426	402	8,047
1926	Vickers Victoria V	T	GB	2 x Napier Lion 12 cyl.	26.6x18.1x5.4 –	8,045	177	1,240	4,900

YEAR	NAME	TYPE	NATION	ENGINE	SIZE m	WEIGHT kg	SPEED km/h	RANGE km	CEILING m
1926	Fiat C.R.20	C	I	1 x Fiat 12 cyl.	9.8x6.7x2.7	1,360	275	750	7,500
1927	Ryan Spirit of St. Louis	–	USA	1 x Wright Whirlwind	14.0x8.3x2.4	2,379	180	6,600	5,000
1929	Bristol Bulldog Mk.IIA	C	GB	1 x Bristol 9 cyl.	10.3x7.6x2.9	1,587	280	–	8,230
1929	Hawker Hart	B	GB	1 x Rolls-Royce 12 cyl.	11.3x8.9x3.1	2,063	296	756	6,500
1931	Supermarine S.6B	Compet.	GB	1 x Rolls-Royce 12 cyl.	9.1x8.7x3.7	2,761	656	–	–
1931	Tupolev TB-3	B	URSS	4 x M.17F (BMW) 12 cyl.	39.5x24.5x8.4	17,400	215	2,200	3,800
1932	Avro Tutor	A	GB	1 x Armstrong	10.3x8.0	–	196	–	–
1932	Junkers Ju.52/3m	T	D	3 x BMW Hornet 9 cyl.	29.2x18.9x5.5	9,200	245	914	5,200
1933	Macchi-Castoldi M.C.72	Compet.	I	1 x Fiat 24 cyl.	9.4x8.3x3.3	2,907	711.462	–	–
1934	Curtiss A.12 Shrike	A	USA	1x Wright Cyclone 9 cyl.	13.4x9.8x2.8	2,672	282	724	4,618
1934	Boeing P.26-A	C	USA	1 x Pratt & Whitney 9 cyl.	8.5x7.2x3.1	1,365	377	1,022	8,352
1934	Dewoitine D.510	C	F	1 x Hispano-Suiza	12.0x7.9	–	393	–	–
1934	Heinkel He.51	C	D	1 x BMW 12 cyl.	10.9x8.3x3.2	1,900	330	570	7,700
1934	Junkers Ju.86	T	D	2 x Rolls-Royce 12 cyl.	22.5x17.4x4.8	7,700	255	1,100	6,100
1934	Polikarpov I-15	C	URSS	1 x M.25 9 cyl.	9.1x6.3x2.9	1,420	360	725	10,000
1935	Martin B.10B	B	USA	2 x Wright Cyclone 9 cyl.	21.4x13.6x4.7	7,429	343	965	7,376
1935	Imam Ro.37	R	I	1 x Fiat 12 cyl.	11.0x8.6x2.9	2,390	325	1,650	6,700
1935	SIAI Marchetti S.M.81	B	I	3 x Alfa Romeo 9 cyl.	24.0x17.8x4.3	10,505	340	1,800	7,000
1935	Fiat C.R.32	C	I	1 x Fiat 12 cyl.	9.5x7.4x2.6	1,850	375	750	8,800
1935	Avia B.534	C	CS	1 x Avia-Hispano Suiza 12 cyl.	9.4x8.2x2.7	1,980	394	600	10,600
1935	Caproni Ca.133	T	I	3 x Piaggio 7 cyl.	21.4x15.4x4.0	6,700	230	1,350	5,500
1936	Tupolev SB-2	B	URSS	2 x Klimov 12 cyl.	20.3x12.2x3.2	5,725	424	1,200	9,500
1936	Fairey Swordfish Mk.I	S	GB	1 x Bristol Pegasus 9 cyl.	13.8x11.0x3.9	4,190	224	879	3,260
1936	Henschel Hs.123 A-1	C	D	1 x BMW 9 cyl.	10.5x8.3x3.2	2,200	317	860	9,000
1937	Polikarpov I-16/10	C	URSS	1 x M.25B 9 cyl.	9.0x6.0x2.4	1,678	464	800	9,000
1937	Hawker Hurricane Mk.I	C	GB	1 x Rolls-Royce 12 cyl.	12.1x9.5x3.9	2,816	518	845	10,180
1937	CANT Z.506B	B	I	3 x Alfa Romeo 9 cyl.	26.5x19.2x7.4	12,400	364	2,745	7,500
1937	SIAI Marchetti S.M.79	B-S	I	3 x Alfa Romeo 9 cyl.	21.2x15.6x4.6	10,500	430	1,900	7,000
1937	Fiat B.R.20	B	I	2 x Fiat 18 cyl.	21.5x16.1x4.3	9,900	432	3,000	9,000
1937	Fairey Battle Mk.I	B	GB	1 x Rolls-Royce 12 cyl.	16.4x15.8x4.7	4,895	388	1,690	7,160
1937	Gloster Gladiator Mk.I	C	GB	1 x Bristol Mercury 9 cyl.	9.8x8.3x3.1	2,155	407	690	10,000
1937	Douglas TBD-1 Devastator	S	USA	1 x Pratt & Whitney 14 cyl.	15.2x10.6x4.6	4,624	332	1,150	6,000
1937	PZL P.23 B	A	PL	1 x PZL-Bristol Pegasus 9 cyl.	13.9x9.6x3.3	3,526	319	1,260	7,300
1937	Hawker Hurricane Mk.I	C	GB	1 x Rolls-Royce 12 cyl.	12.1x9.5x3.9	2,816	518	845	10,180
1938	Morane-Saulnier M.S.406	C	F	1 x Hispano-Suiza 12 cyl.	10.6x8.1x2.8	2,720	486	800	9,400
1938	Mitsubishi A5M4	C	J	1 x Nakajima Kotubuki 9 cyl.	11.0x7.5x3.2	1,671	434	1,200	9,800
1938	Westland Lysander Mk.I	Coll.	GB	1 x Bristol Mercury 9 cyl.	15.2x9.2x3.5	2,685	369	965	7,900
1938	Short Sunderland Mk.I	R	GB	4 x Bristol Pegasus 9 cyl.	34.3x26.1x10.0	20,200	338	4,800	5,500
1938	Heinkel He.100	C	D	1 x Daimler Benz	9.4x8.1	–	670	–	–
1938	Fokker G.1A	C	NL	2 x Bristol Mercury 9 cyl.	17.1x11.5x3.4	4,790	475	1,520	9,300
1938	Fokker D.XXI	C	NL	1 x Bristol Mercury 9 cyl.	11.0x8.2x2.9	2,050	460	950	11,000
1938	Potez 630	C	F	2 x Hispano-Suiza 14 cyl.	16.0x11.0x3.6	3,845	370	1,225	10,000
1938	Supermarine Spitfire Mk.I	C	GB	1 x Rolls-Royce 12 cyl.	11.2x9.1x3.4	2,415	571	805	10,360
1938	CANT Z.1007bis	B	I	3 x Piaggio 14 cyl.	24.8x18.4x5.2	13,621	456	2,000	8,400
1938	Handley Page Hampden Mk.I	B	GB	2 x Bristol Pegasus 9 cyl.	21.0x16.3x4.5	8,508	409	3,034	6,920
1938	Vickers Wellington Mk.I	B	GB	2 x Bristol Pegasus 9 cyl.	26.2x19.6x5.3	12,910	378	1,930	5,500
1939	Heinkel He.111 H-2	B	D	2 x Junkers Jumo 12 cyl.	22.6x16.3x4.0	14,000	405	2,060	8,500
1939	Fiat C.R.42	C	I	1 x Fiat 14 cyl.	9.7x8.2x3.3	2,295	440	785	10,500
1939	Caproni Ca.311	R	I	2 x Piaggio 7 cyl.	16.2x11.7x3.6	4,822	365	1,600	7,400
1939	Macchi M.C.200	C	I	1 x Fiat 14 cyl.	10.6x8.1x3.5	2,208	512	870	8,750
1939	Fiat G.50	C	I	1 x Fiat 14 cyl.	10.9x7.8x2.9	2,395	473	675	10,730
1939	Fieseler Fi.156 C-2	R	D	1 x Argus 8 cyl.	14.2x9.9x3.0	1,320	175	390	5,200
1939	Curtiss P-36C	C	USA	1 x Pratt & Whitney 14 cyl.	11.3x8.6x3.7	2,790	500	1,320	10,300
1939	Messerschmitt Bf.109 E-1	C	D	1 x Daimler Benz 12 cyl.	9.8x8.6x2.5	2,010	550	660	10,500
1939	Lioré et Olivier LeO 451	B	F	2 x Gnome-Rhône 14 cyl.	22.5x17.1x5.2	11,385	494	2,300	9,000

YEAR	NAME	TYPE	NATION	ENGINE	SIZE m	WEIGHT kg	SPEED km/h	RANGE km	CEILING m
1939	Messerschmitt Bf.110 C-1	C	D	2 x Daimler Benz 12 cyl.	16.2x12.0x4.1	6,028	540	1,125	10,000
1939	Dornier Do.17 Z-2	B	D	2 x BMW 9 cyl.	18.0x15.7x4.5	8,590	410	1,160	8,200
1940	Bloch 174	R	F	2 x Gnome-Rhône 14 cyl.	17.9x12.2x3.5	7,150	530	1,650	11,000
1940	Dewoitine D.520	C	F	1 x Hispano-Suiza 12 cyl.	10.1x8.7x2.5	2,780	529	998	11,000
1940	Blohm und Voss Bv.141 A	R	D	1 x BMW 9 cyl.	15.4x12.1x4.1	3,895	399	1,140	9,000
1940	Curtiss C-46A Commando	T	USA	2 x Pratt & Whitney 18 cyl.	32.9x23.2x6.6	21,772	314	2,896	7,470
1940	Dornier Do.217 E-1	B	D	2 x BMW 14 cyl.	19.0x18.1x5.0	14,980	515	2,300	7,500
1940	Focke Wulf Fw.200 C-1	B-R	D	4 x BMW 9 cyl.	30.8x23.4x6.3	22,700	360	3,550	5,800
1940	Kawanishi H6K4	R	J	4 x Mitsubishi Kinsei 14 cyl.	40.0x25.6x6.2	17,000	340	6,080	9,610
1940	Nakajima Ki-43-Ia Hayabusa	C	J	1 x Nakajima 14 cyl.	11.4x8.8x3.2	2,048	495	1,200	11,750
1940	Mitsubishi A6M2 Reisen	C	J	1 x Nakajima 14 cyl.	12.0x9.0x3.0	2,410	534	3,105	10,000
1940	Bristol Beaufighter Mk.IF	C	GB	2 x Bristol Hercules 14 cyl.	17.6x12.5x4.8	9,500	516	1,890	8,000
1940	Fairey Fulmar Mk.I	C	GB	1 x Rolls-Royce 12 cyl.	14.1x12.2x4.2	4,440	426	1,290	7,900
1940	Petlyakov Pe-8	B	URSS	4 x Mikulin 12 cyl.	39.9x22.4x6.1	33,325	438	5,445	9,750
1940	Vought OS2U-1 Kingfisher	R	USA	1 x Pratt & Whitney 9 cyl.	10.9x10.3x4.5	1,815	264	1,300	5,950
1940	Rogozarski IK-3	C	YU	1 x Avia-Hispano-Suiza 12 cyl.	10.2x8.3x3.2	2,400	526	500	8,000
1940	Grumman F4F-3 Wildcat	C	USA	1 x Pratt & Whitney 14 cyl.	11.5x8.7x3.6	3,176	531	1,360	11,430
1940	Westland Whirlwind Mk.I	C-B	GB	2 x Rolls-Royce 12 cyl.	13.7x9.9x3.5	4,652	579	-	9,150
1940	Short Stirling Mk.I	B	GB	4 x Bristol Hercules 14 cyl.	30.2x26.6x6.9	31,752	418	3,100	5,180
1940	Handley Page Halifax Mk.I	B	GB	4 x Rolls-Royce 12 cyl.	30.1x21.3x6.3	26,274	426	3,000	6,950
1940	Bristol Beaufighter Mk.IF	C	GB	2 x Bristol Hercules 14 cyl.	17.6x12.5x4.8	9,500	516	1,890	8,000
1941	Blohm und Voss Bv.138 B-1	R	D	3 x Junkers Jumo 6 cyl.	26.9x19.8x5.9	14,390	290	3,880	4,200
1941	Focke Wulf Fw.190 A-1	C	D	1 x BMW 14 cyl.	10.5x8.8x3.9	3,973	626	800	10,600
1941	Macchi M.C.202	C	I	1 x Daimler Benz 12 cyl.	10.5x8.8x3.0	2,937	600	765	11,500
1941	Reggiane Re.2001	C	I	1 x Daimler Benz 12 cyl.	11.0x8.3x3.1	3,170	563	1,100	11,000
1941	Mitsubishi G4M1	B	J	2 x Mitsubishi 14 cyl.	25.0x20.0x6.0	9,500	428	6,030	8,840
1941	Mitsubishi Ki-21-IIb	B	J	2 x Mitsubishi 14 cyl.	22.5x16.0x4.8	9,710	486	2,700	10,000
1941	Mitsubishi Ki-46-II	R	J	2 x Mitsubishi 14 cyl.	14.7x11.0x3.8	5,050	604	2,474	10,720
1941	Hawker Typhoon Mk.IB	C-B	GB	1 x Napier Sabre 24 cyl.	12.6x9.7x4.6	5,170	663	1,500	10,700
1941	Supermarine Spitfire Mk.VB	C	GB	1 x Rolls-Royce 12 cyl.	11.2x9.1x3.4	2,911	602	750	11,280
1941	Petlyakov Pe-2	B	URSS	2 x Klimov 12 cyl.	17.1x12.6x4.0	7,680	540	1,500	8,800
1941	Curtiss P-40B Warhawk	C	USA	1 x Allison 12 cyl.	11.3x9.6x3.2	3,450	566	1,500	9,875
1941	Bell P-39D Airacobra	C	USA	1 x Allison 12 cyl.	10.3x9.1x3.6	3,720	592	1,290	9,785
1941	North American B-25A Mitchell	B	USA	2 x Wright 14 cyl.	20.6x16.4x4.8	12,292	507	2,170	8,230
1941	Consolidated PBY-5A Catalina	R	USA	2 x Pratt & Whitney 14 cyl.	31.7x19.4x6.1	16,066	281	3,780	5,520
1941	Brewster F2A-3 Buffalo	C	USA	1 x Wright 9 cyl.	10.6x8.0x3.6	3,247	517	1,553	10,120
1941	Republic P-43A Lancer	C	USA	1 x Pratt & Whitney 14 cyl.	10.9x8.6x4.2	3,600	562	1,290	11,580
1941	Grumman J2F-5 Duck	Coll.	USA	1 x Wright 9 cyl.	11.8x10.3x4.6	3,044	302	1,255	8,230
1941	Hawker Hurricane Mk.IIC	C-B	GB	1 x Rolls-Royce 12 cyl.	12.1x9.8x3.9	3,533	545	740	10,850
1941	Douglas AC-47 Gunship	A	USA	2 x Pratt & Whitney 9 cyl.	28.9x19.6x5.2	11,805	368	2,400	7,075
1942	Blohm und Voss Bv.222 A	R	D	6 x BMW 9 cyl.	46.0x36.5x10.9	45,540	310	7,000	6,500
1942	Kawasaki Ki-45 KAIa	C	J	2 x Nakajima 14 cyl.	15.0x10.6x3.7	5,276	547	2,260	10,730
1942	Kawasaki Ki-48-II	B	J	2 x Nakajima 14 cyl.	17.4x12.7x3.8	6,500	505	2,400	10,100
1942	Douglas Boston Mk.III	B	GB	2 x Wright Cyclone 14 cyl.	18.6x14.3x4.8	11,325	490	1,650	7,400
1942	de Havilland Mosquito Mk.IV	B	GB	2 x Rolls-Royce Merlin 12 cyl.	16.5x12.4x4.6	9,720	611	2,200	8,800
1942	Ilyushin Il-2M3	A	URSS	1 x Mikulin 12 cyl.	14.6x11.6x3.4	5,510	404	600	6,000
1942	Lockheed P-38F Lightning	C	USA	2 x Allison 12 cyl.	15.8x11.5x2.9	8,165	636	724	11,890
1942	Boeing B-17E Flying Fortress	B	USA	4 x Wright 9 cyl.	31.6x22.5x5.8	24,040	510	3,220	11,150
1942	Martin B-26B Marauder	B	USA	2 x Pratt & Whitney 18 cyl.	19.8x17.7x6.0	15,422	510	1,850	7,200
1942	Avro Lancaster Mk.I	B	GB	2 x Rolls-Royce Merlin 12 cyl.	31.0x21.1x6.1	31,752	462	2,670	7,500
1942	Grumman TBF-1 Avenger	S	USA	1 x Wright Cyclone 14 cyl.	16.5x12.1x5.0	7,215	436	1,950	6,800
1942	I.A.R. 80	C	R	1 x I.A.R.-Gnome-Rhône 14 cyl.	10.0x8.1x3.6	2,485	510	950	10,500
1943	Junkers Ju.188 E-1	B	D	2 x BMW 801 14 cyl.	22.0x14.9x4.4	14,491	499	1,950	9,350
1943	Fiat G.55	C	I	1 x Daimler Benz 12 cyl.	11.8x9.3x3.7	3,720	620	1,650	12,700
1943	Reggiane Re.2005	C	I	1 x Daimler Benz 12 cyl.	11.0x8.7x3.1	3,610	678	1,250	12,000
1943	Macchi M.C.205	C	I	1 x Daimler Benz 12 cyl.	10.5x8.8x3.0	3,224	650	1,040	11,350
1943	Nakajima Ki-84-Ia Hayate	C	J	1 x Nakajima 18 cyl.	11.2x9.9x3.3	3,613	631	1,695	10,500
1943	Kawasaki Ki-61-I Hien	C	J	1 x Kawasaki 12 cyl.	12.0x8.7x3.7	2,950	592	1,100	11,600
1943	Kawanishi H8K2	R	J	4 x Mitsubishi 14 cyl.	38.0x28.1x9.1	24,500	466	7,150	8,850
1943	Mitsubishi J2M3 Raiden	C	J	1 x Mitsubishi 14 cyl.	10.8x9.9x3.9	3,435	587	1,900	11,700
1943	Fairey Firefly Mk.I	C	GB	1 x Rolls-Royce 12 cyl.	13.5x11.4x4.1	6,350	508	2,100	8,500

YEAR	NAME	TYPE	NATION	ENGINE	SIZE m	WEIGHT kg	SPEED km/h	RANGE h/km	CEILING m
1943	Yakovlev Yak-9D	C	URSS	1 x Klimov 12 cyl.	10.0x8.5x2.4	3,115	600	1,300	10,000
1943	Lavochkin La-5FN	C	URSS	1 x Shvetsov 14 cyl.	9.8x8.5x2.8	3,360	647	700	10,000
1943	Bell P-63A	C	USA	1 x Allison 12 cyl.	11.6x9.9x3.8	4,763	656	725	13,100
1943	Consolidated B-24J	B	USA	4 x Pratt & Whitney 14 cyl.	33.5x20.4x5.4	29,484	467	3,380	8,500
1943	Heinkel He.219 A-2/R1	C	D	2 x Daimler Benz 12 cyl.	18.5x15.5x4.1	11,200	670	2,000	12,700
1943	North American P-51A	C	USA	1 x Allison 12 cyl.	11.2x9.8x3.7	3,992	628	1,200	9,550
1943	Republic P-47C Thunderbolt	C	USA	1 x Pratt & Whitney 18 cyl.	12.4x11.0x4.3	6,770	697	885	12,800
1943	Curtiss SB2C-1 Helldiver	B	USA	1 x Wright 14 cyl.	15.1x11.1x4.0	7,537	452	1,785	7,650
1943	Commonwealth CA-12	C	AUS	1 x Pratt & Whitney 14 cyl.	11.0x7.7x3.5	3,492	486	1,500	8,840
1943	F.F.V.S. J 22	C	S	1 x Pratt & Whitney 14 cyl.	10.0x7.8x2.7	2,850	576	1,250	9,150
1944	Hawker Tempest Mk.V	B-C	GB	1 x Napier Sabre 24 cyl.	12.5x10.2x5.1	5,210	702	2,500	11,100
1944	Ilyushin Il-10	A	URSS	1 x Mikulin 12 cyl.	13.9x12.2x3.5	6,335	500	650	-
1944	Douglas A-26B Invader	B	USA	2 x Pratt & Whitney 18 cyl.	21.3x15.2x5.6	15,876	571	2,250	6,750
1944	Bell P-59A Airacomet	C	USA	2 x General Electric	13.8x11.8x3.7	6,214	665	845	14,100
1944	Yakovlev Yak-3	A-C	URSS	1 x Klimov 12 cyl.	9.2x8.5x2.3	2,660	648	900	10,900
1944	Northrop P-61B Black Widow	C	USA	2 x Pratt & Whitney 18 cyl.	20.1x15.1x4.4	13,472	589	4,830	10,100
1944	Junkers Ju.88 G-7	C	D	2 x Junkers Jumo 12 cyl.	20.8x15.5x4.8	13,100	626	2,250	10,000
1944	Arado Ar.234 B-2	B	D	2 x Junkers Jumo	14.1x12.6x4.3	8,410	742	1,630	10,000
1944	Dornier Do.335 A-1	C	D	2 x Daimler Benz 12 cyl.	13.8x13.8x5.0	9,585	763	2,060	11,400
1944	Junkers Ju.88 G-7	C	D	2 x Junkers Jumo 12 cyl.	20.8x15.5x4.8	13,100	626	2,250	10,000
1944	Messerschmitt Me.262A-1a	C	D	2 x Junkers Jumo	12.4x10.6x3.8	6,396	869	1,050	11,450
1944	Grumman F6F-5 Hellcat	C	USA	1 x Pratt & Whitney 18 cyl.	13.0x10.2x3.9	5,670	621	1,670	11,370
1944	Vought F4U-1D Corsair	C	USA	1 x Pratt & Whitney 18 cyl.	12.4x10.1x4.6	5,950	684	1,635	11,280
1944	Myrsky II	C	SF	1 x SFA-Pratt & Whitney 14 cyl.	11.0x8.3x3.0	2,950	530	500	9,000
1944	Messerschmitt Me.163B-1a	C	D	1 x Walter HWK	9.3x5.7x2.5	3,950	900	7.5 min.	12,000
1944	Boeing B-29A Superfortress	B	USA	1 x Wright 18 cyl.	43.0x30.1x9.0	63,958	576	6,600	9,700
1945	Bachem Ba.349 B-1	I	D	1 x Walter HWK	3.9x6.0x2.2	2,230	997	58	9,800
1945	Nakajima Kikka	B	J	2 x Ne-20	10.0x8.1x2.9	3,500	712	950	12,000
1945	Yokosuka MXY7	-	J	3 razzi tipo 4MK.1	5.1x6.0x1.1	2,140	648	37	-
1945	Mitsubishi J8M1	C	J	1 x Toko Ro.2	9.5x6.0x2.7	3,885	900	5.37'	12,000
1945	Heinkel He.162 A-2	C	D	1 x BMW	7.2x9.0x2.5	2,690	838	975	12,000
1945	Gloster Meteor Mk.III	C	GB	2 x Rolls-Royce Derwent	13.1x12.5x3.9	6,260	793	2,156	13,400
1946	Bell X-1	S	USA	1 x Reaction Motor	8.5x9.4x3.3	5,443	1,545	-	21,340
1947	Mikoyan-Gurevich MiG-15	C	URSS	1 x Rolls-Royce Nene	10.0x11.0x3.4	5,700	1,070	1,960	15,200
1947	Hawker Sea Fury F.B.11	C-B	GB	1 x Bristol Centaurus 18 cyl.	11.7x10.5x4.8	5,670	740	1,130	10,970
1947	Grumman F9F-2 Panther	C	USA	1 x Pratt & Whitney	11.5x11.3x3.4	8,842	846	2,180	13,600
1948	de Havilland Vampire F.B.5	C-B	GB	1 x de Havilland Goblin	11.5x9.3x2.6	5,620	882	1,960	13,410
1948	Lockheed F-80C Shooting Star	C-B	USA	1 x General Electric	11.8x10.5x3.4	7,646	933	2,220	13,030
1948	Ilyushin Il-28	B	URSS	2 x Klimov VK-1	21.4x17.6x6.7	21,000	900	1,135	12,300
1949	Dessault M.D.450 Ouragan	C	F	1 x Hispano-Suiza	13.1x10.7x4.1	7,900	940	920	13,000
1950	English Electric Canberra B.2	B	GB	2 x Rolls-Royce	19.4x19.9x4.7	20,185	917	4,274	14,630
1950	Cessna L-19A Bird Dog	Coll.	USA	1 x Continental 4 cyl.	10.9x7.8x2.2	1,088	243	850	5,640
1950	North American F-86E	C	USA	1 x General Electric	11.3x11.4x4.4	7,419	1,086	1,260	14,720
1950	Mikoyan-Gurevich MiG-17F	C	URSS	1 x Klimov VK-1F	9.6x11.0x3.3	6,069	1,145	2,250	16,600
1950	Gloster Meteor N.F.11	C	GB	3 x Rolls-Royce Derwent	13.1x14.7x4.2	9,088	960	1,480	12,192
1951	Northrop F-89D Scorpion	C	USA	2 x Allison	18.1x16.4x5.3	19,160	1,023	2,200	14,995
1951	Vought F7U-3M Cutlass	C	USA	2 x Westinghouse	11.7x13.4x4.4	14,353	1,094	1,060	12,190
1951	Douglas AD-5W Skyraider	R	USA	1 x Wright 18 cyl.	15.2x12.2x4.8	11,340	501	2,080	3,230
1952	Douglas AD-6 Skyraider	A	USA	1 x Wright 18 cyl.	15.2x11.8x4.7	11,340	518	1,840	3,690
1952	Convair B-36H	B	USA	6 x Pratt & Whitney 28 cyl.	70.1x49.4x14.2	185,976	661	10,940	12,160
1952	Dassault Mystère IV-A	C-B	F	1 x Hispano-Suiza	11.1x12.8x4.4	7,500	1,120	917	13,715
1952	Douglas X-3	S	USA	2 x Westinghouse	6.9x20.3x3.8	-	1,045	-	10,670
1953	Boeing B-47E Stratojet	B	USA	6 x General Electric	35.3x33.4x8.5	93,759	975	6,435	12,345
1953	Mikoyan-Gurevich MiG-19	C	URSS	2 x Mikulin	9.0x13.0x4.0	8,700	1,480	2,200	17,900
1953	Vickers Valiant B.1	B	GB	4 x Rolls-Royce	34.8x32.9x9.8	63,504	912	5,550	16,460
1953	Republic RF-84F Thunderflash	R	USA	1 x Wright	10.2x14.5x4.5	12,700	1,092	3,540	14,020
1953	Grumman F9F-8 Cougar	C	USA	1 x Pratt & Whitney	11.0x12.9x4.5	9,072	1,110	1,610	15,250
1954	Sud-Ouest SO-4050	B	F	2 x SNECMA Atar	15.1x5.8x4.9	20,700	1,102	2,575	15,000
1954	English Electric Canberra B.8	B	GB	2 x Rolls-Royce	19.4x19.9x4.7	23,130	933	1,287	14,630
1954	Hawker Hunter F.6	C	GB	1 x Rolls-Royce	10.2x13.9x4.0	8,051	1,142	3,085	15,700

ILLUSTRATIONS CREDITS